A BRIEF HISTORY OF
THAILAND

A BRIEF HISTORY OF
THAILAND

MONARCHY, WAR AND RESILIENCE: THE FASCINATING STORY
OF THE GILDED KINGDOM AT THE HEART OF ASIA

RICHARD A. RUTH

TUTTLE Publishing
Tokyo | Rutland, Vermont | Singapore

"Books to Span the East and West"

Tuttle Publishing was founded in 1832 in the small New England town of Rutland, Vermont [USA]. Our core values remain as strong today as they were then—to publish best-in-class books which bring people together one page at a time. In 1948, we established a publishing office in Japan—and Tuttle is now a leader in publishing English-language books about the arts, languages and cultures of Asia. The world has become a much smaller place today and Asia's economic and cultural influence has grown. Yet the need for meaningful dialogue and information about this diverse region has never been greater. Over the past seven decades, Tuttle has published thousands of books on subjects ranging from martial arts and paper crafts to language learning and literature—and our talented authors, illustrators, designers and photographers have won many prestigious awards. We welcome you to explore the wealth of information available on Asia at **www.tuttlepublishing.com**.

Published by Tuttle Publishing, an imprint of Periplus Editions (HK) Ltd.

www.tuttlepublishing.com

Copyright © 2021 by Richard A. Ruth

Library of Congress Control Number:
2021944142

ISBN 978-0-8048-5121-3

26 25 24 23 22 21
10 9 8 7 6 5 4 3 2 1
2109TP
Printed in Singapore

TUTTLE PUBLISHING® is a registered trademark of Tuttle Publishing, a division of Periplus Editions (HK) Ltd.

Distributed by:

North America, Latin America & Europe
Tuttle Publishing
364 Innovation Drive
North Clarendon VT 05759 9436, USA
Tel: 1(802) 773 8930
Fax: 1(802) 773 6993
info@tuttlepublishing.com
www.tuttlepublishing.com

Asia Pacific
Berkeley Books Pte Ltd
3 Kallang Sector #04-01
Singapore 349278
Tel: (65) 6741 2178
Fax: (65) 6741 2179
inquiries@periplus.com.sg
www.tuttlepublishing.com

Japan
Tuttle Publishing
Yaekari Building 3rd Floor
5-4-12 Osaki Shinagawa-ku
Tokyo 141 0032 Japan
Tel: 81 (3) 5437 0171
Fax: 81 (3) 5437 0755
sales@tuttle.co.jp
www.tuttle.co.jp

CONTENTS

INTRODUCTION

The Cultural Foundations of Modern Thailand

Thailand, or Prathet Thai in the Thai language, means "the land of the Thai people." To many Westerners, Thailand is most immediately associated with a set of spicy-sweet dishes served in the many thousands of Thai restaurants that now enrich the collective palate of our cities and towns. It is difficult to find a sizable town in North America, the United Kingdom, or Australia that does not have at least one Thai restaurant. But the predictable menu options – green curry (*kaeng khiao wan*), *pad thai* noodles, *massaman* curry, and *som tham* papaya salad – are misleading in their seeming authenticity and uniformity. In reality, the *pad thai* noodle dish is a Thai variation of a Chinese noodle dish; the *massaman* curry is a contribution of ethnic Malays from the Muslim areas of Thailand's south; and the *som tham* salad, which many consider to be the quintessential Thai dish, is a contribution of the ethnic Lao from Thailand's northeast. Even the desserts, the wonderfully eggy coconut custards that you find in better Thai restaurants, can be traced to Portuguese residents of Siam in the sixteenth and seventeenth centuries. The green curry might be the most authentically Thai dish, but was developed from the spices and vegetables that entered Thailand from other places. Perhaps only the wonderfully aromatic *khao hom malit*, or jasmine rice, is authentically Thai. But it, too, owes its development to strains of rice drawn from neighboring Cambodia, Laos, and other areas of mainland Southeast Asia. Thailand itself, like the familiar restaurant menu, is an amalgamation of many cultures, ethnicities, belief systems, and traditions from all over Asia and, indeed, from all over the world. Many of the things that we identify now as Thai are only "Thai" in the modern sense of national culture. Thailand was, and is, more than the land of the Thais. It is an enormously diverse and multifaceted country whose people and culture have been drawn from throughout Southeast Asia, as well as from East and South Asia. The Chinese, Lao, Muslim, and even *farang* (Caucasian or white) cultural elements that we see in those restaurant menus all play an important part in Thailand's history, including the political and cultural changes examined in this book. This is especially true for Thailand's capital, known to the world as Bangkok. The culture of the capital and its historical actors and agents that we identify simply as Thai are really much more than that. Like Bangkok, they are diverse, complex, cosmopolitan, and dynamic.

Outside Influences on Thailand's History and Culture

Thailand is a tropical country in mainland Southeast Asia. It abuts Myanmar (Burma) for much of its western border. To the north and northeast, Thailand is separated from Laos mostly by the Mekong (Mae Kong) River. To the east, Thailand borders Cambodia. The deep south of Thailand shares a border with Malaysia. All these Southeast Asian nations, in both their premodern and colonial configurations, played important roles in Thailand's history. The people of these surrounding countries, the ethnicities and cultures with which they are identified, have also contributed to what we now accept as Thai culture. Missing from this list is China, which, except for a brief period during World War II, has not shared a land border with the nation of Thailand or its premodern predecessors. However, China has contributed much to Thailand. Chinese people of various ethnicities came to Thailand in large numbers over the last three hundred years to trade and work. Many returned to China if they could, but others chose to settle in Siam, later Thailand, and to make their lives as contributors to the evolving culture. A significant proportion of Thailand's population, especially in urban areas, have Chinese ancestors. The Chinese are an important part of Thailand's history and culture, and it is important to keep in mind that they are not an alien "other" who can be held in contrast to an indigenous and legitimate Thai citizen. Thailand's ethnic Chinese assimilated more successfully than they did almost anywhere else in Southeast Asia. To be Thai today, one must acknowledge that you could be part Chinese, just as you could be part Khmer or Lao or Burmese or Malay, or any of the upland peoples who make up Thailand's multiethnic, multicultural human tableau. Today, there are also many Thais who are part *farang*, hailing from the countries of Europe, North America, or Australia. Thus, to be Thai means you could claim heritage with many different cultures.

The Thai People

The Thai people belong to a larger ethnolinguistic category called the Tai, who live in an area stretching from China's far southern tip to deep inside mainland Southeast Asia. Among the peoples in this Tai category are the Thai of central Thailand, the Lao of Laos, the Shan of eastern Burma, the Black Tai of northwestern Vietnam, and the Zhuang of China. Within Thailand itself, there are the Lanna-Thai of the north, the Isan-Thai of the northeast, and others. All Tai people share common elements of their language and culture, but that does not necessarily mean that they can communicate easily with one other. A Thai person born in Ayutthaya, for example, might only understand roughly half or less of what a Lao from Vientiane is telling her. That same Thai person, if she were to travel to the southern parts of Yunnan Province in China and meet some of the Tai people living in Sipsongpanna (Xishuangbanna), would understand even less of the local Dai language, which sounds more like northern Thai or Lao. There are great variances in Tai cultures even as we recognize that there are important similarities. For now, it is good enough to know that scholars recognize Tai as a broad cultural category of peoples across mainland Southeast Asia, and Thai is a subset of that category.

The label "Thai" in the political sense refers to a citizen of Thailand, a nation with a significant population of non-Tai peoples, including Chinese, Khmer, Vietnamese, Malays, and all the so-called "hill tribes," or upland peoples, such as the Hmong, Lisu, Lahu, Ahka, and others. Care must be taken when talking about Thai as a nationality, as a cultural identity, and as a language. Nearly all Thailand's citizens speak Thai, or central Thai (*phasa klang*) as the national language, but many do not speak it as their first language. They may have grown up speaking Lao, Khmer, Malay, Teochew, Hmong, or another language at home. But since the Thai government's implementation of a national school system in the early twentieth century, a process that intensified after World War II, all non-Thais in Thailand have learned central Thai at school and use it to communicate in official correspondence, even if they do not speak it at home.

Thailand is a monsoon-influenced country. Its agricultural cycles and related traditions are guided by the massive amount of rain that falls from about the middle of April to early November. Thailand is thus well suited for growing what has become its principal export: rice. Today, Thailand is the world's leading exporter of rice, and its varieties of rice, especially the earlier mentioned *khao hom malit*, are prized everywhere for their aromatic qualities and delicious taste. Likewise, the sheer amount of water that falls on Thailand and flows down its many rivers has necessitated the development of a sophisticated hydrological culture. In the past, Siam, as Thailand was known before 1939, was famous for the number of its irrigation, drainage, and communication canals crisscrossing the country. People traveled on canals and rivers far more than they did on roads. Bangkok, which was not connected to the rest of the country by an all-weather road until the twentieth century, was known to Westerners as "the Venice of the East" because of its reliance on canals. Some Thai longtail boats (*ruahangyao*) still zip up and down Bangkok's remaining canals and riverways as public transportation and delivery vessels. And while most of the old transportation canals have been filled in and the reliance on canals largely diminished, you need only visit Bangkok during the rainy season to see that the old water routes have not forgotten their former abodes. When it rains heavily, the water lays itself over the cityscape, and many of the old canal patterns will reappear over the roads as swelling water finds its way back to its old locations.

Arrival of the Thai People

Rice has always been Thailand's most important crop. The people of the valleys, especially in the Chao Phraya valley in central Thailand, grew wet rice. These rice farmers built their houses on stilts to keep them above flood stage and to provide protection against noxious pests, such as scorpions and snakes, as well as dangerous predators like tigers and bears. To assist them in their rice cultivation, these farmers used domesticated water buffalo to plow their fields. Rice remains an economic, culinary, and cultural staple of Thailand. Thais call white rice *khao suai*, literally "beautiful rice," because of the pearly white polish now possible through modern milling (the method for doing this was, incidentally, developed in Thailand). The people of Thailand's northeast grow and consume *khao niao*, or sticky rice, as their staple crop. Also called glutinous rice, it is the wonderfully gummy rice that you can easily press into a ball and dip into the food you are eating. Although all of Thailand eats *khao niao* in greater and lesser amounts, it is associated chiefly with Lao-speaking peoples.

In the past, the upland peoples, the *chao khao*, often pursued slash-and-burn rice cultivation. They would burn off the forest layer to create a swidden and let the rain showers provide the water for their rice cultivation. Today, the Thai government has largely ended this rice-growing strategy, although it is a reminder of the fundamentally different cultures between lowland people who settled in the river valleys and the mobile upland peoples who lived in the hills and mountains. This important division is often obscured by the distorting and deceptive flatness of most political maps. More so than north and south, upland and valley have determined cultural and social patterns in Thailand just as they have in most areas of mainland Southeast Asia.

There have always been people in Thailand. Thai paleontologists have found evidence of human ancestors in the mountains that separate Burma from Thailand that could date back hundreds of thousands of years to the period of prehistory that paleontologists associate with the hominid remains known as Java Man and Peking Man. In terms of the far more recent homo sapiens, there is evidence of a Bronze Age culture dating from about 4000 BC. The most famous is found at Ban Chiang in the northeastern province of Udon Thani.

It is not clear when Thai people arrived on the scene. The Tai people of Thailand trace their origins to what is now southern China, to Yunnan Province, and then made their way down from the Yunnanese hills from probably around the seventh century AD. They settled into an area already inhabited by people in the Mon-Khmer language group and were absorbed into those Mon-Khmer civilizations. One common explanation of why the Tai people moved into Southeast Asia is that expanding Han Chinese populations pushed these Tai people further south. The Mongol invasions of the fourteenth century may have accelerated the process. These southward-moving Tai groups who chose to seek out new territory were probably guided by a charismatic leader, a "man of prowess," to use historian Oliver Wolters' memorable phrase. It is likely that capable and charismatic women also helped hold the groups together and solve the problems that arose. They were not refugees or explorers. They were more akin to pioneers who sought less-contested river valleys where they could grow rice and raise vegetables. They were not fleeing their Tai homelands as much as expanding the Tai universe. These Tai people did not have a written language. They are relatively late adopters of written languages in Asia. They relied instead on an oral tradition to convey their ideas.

These early Thais had their own spiritual beliefs, adherents to what is often (and imprecisely) called animism, the belief that spirits inhabit all-natural objects. They believed in *phi* (pronounced "pee"), ghosts or spirits, both beneficial and malevolent, and *khwan*, which might be translated as a spirit, psyche, or "soul stuff." The *phi* were natural spirits that reside in trees and rocks and plants, as well as the spirits of their deceased ancestors. Tai people of old believed that all actions in the visible world could be influenced by the conduct of these invisible spirits interacting around them.

Thais today still embrace *phi* and *khwan* as important elements in their daily life, and acknowledge the presence of an individual soul called a *winyan* that endures after death. Many farmers stop to acknowledge the *phi* in the rice and the water before harvesting their crops, pressing their hands together, bowing their heads, and asking for permission to cut the plants. Nearly every home in both rural and urban areas has a *san phra phum*, a shrine shaped like a house or palace, dedicated to the guardian spirit of the land. These shrines, called "spirit houses" in English, are the dwelling sites of earth spirits and other *phi*. Located outside human homes, the shrines, sitting atop brightly colored pillars or multiposted platforms, are placed carefully according to the recommendation of a Brahmin priest. The human owners fill them with quaint statuettes to represent the earth spirits and their departed ancestors. They also provide figures of musicians, dancers, and animal companions to keep them amused. There will almost always be a statuette of Phra Chai Mongkol, the guardian of the land, holding a dagger and a bag of silver. People offer food, soft drinks, and incense to the shrines each day. The care paid to these shrines is evidence of the enduring importance of *phi* in everyday life.

As the ancient Tai peoples came south, they entered into territory inhabited mainly by those of the Mon-Khmer ethnolinguistic group. The Mon still live in southern Myanmar, while the Khmer are the main ethnic group of Cambodia. These two groups occupied what is now the marshy floodplains of the southern part of central Thailand. As the Tai people came south over hundreds of years, they mixed with the Mon-Khmer inhabitants, absorbing language and cultural elements from them even as they nudged some communities ever slowly east and west, and eventually off the Chao Phraya valley into Burma and Cambodia.

The Adoption of Buddhism

Among the most important things the Tai picked up from these groups were more universal, less esoteric belief systems, best described as a Hindu-Buddhist cosmology or worldview. They would have come across representations of Brahmanism, commonly referred to as "Hinduism," and other systems from South Asia. The Thais learned how these groups practiced Buddhism. Multiple forms of Buddhism, specifically Mahayana Buddhism such as that practiced in China and other parts of East Asia, had been in Burma and Cambodia for hundreds of years before the Thais arrived. Buddhism was one of the many belief systems embraced, sponsored, or presided over by the kings of Bagan (Pagan) in Burma. Later, they adopted the principles and practices of Theravada Buddhism, "the wisdom of the elders," first from a small group of Mon practitioners in southern Burma and then later from monks who practiced it in Sri Lanka. Theravada is often described as a purer or less-adorned practice of Buddhism. Adherents to Theravada Buddhism try hard to follow what they believe are the Buddha's original teachings. They stress good conduct and merit-making that will advance one's chances of salvation and rebirth into a better life. Thais harbor a notion of karma that offers explanations for the difficulties and rewards in life. They tend to believe that present suffering is the result of bad behavior in a previous life, while correspondingly good behavior in this life will lead to a better life in future incarnations. Theravada Buddhists do not emphasize the role of Bodhisattvas, the magical Buddhas-in-waiting revered in Mahayana Buddhism, and generally reject the richly mystical Buddhist schools that flourished in China, Japan, Korea, and Vietnam. Theravada Buddhism is practiced by nearly all Thailand's Buddhists today.

Buddhism has always been the center of Thai society. Until recently, all Buddhist temple complexes (*wat*) were the heart of village life. Even the simple structures of old were the principal gathering places for important events of every community. The monks, who came from the households and families that surrounded the *wat*, were the teachers of that village. In addition to explaining the precepts of Buddhism and teaching newly ordained monks how to behave, they also provided nearly all of what we would now regard as secular education. They taught all males how to read and write, sometimes in several languages, as well as logic, rhetoric, and public speaking. They also taught medicine and its related discipline of massage, and boxing and other forms of self-defense. Some taught *sayasat*, the esoteric practices sometimes called "black magic," that includes love potions, invulnerability spells, and protective amulets.

All males usually spent some time as monks. Beyond the normal schooling that boys received from monks, they were expected to don robes twice in their youth, many spending time as novices (*nen*) at around age seven, and as they approached the age for marriage at around twenty, returning to the *wat* as monks. Young men who did not spend time in a Buddhist *wat* were regarded as not being fully tempered or fully civilized and therefore not fully trustworthy to take up leadership roles in the community. It could be a period of a year or more. More commonly, especially in recent times, it lasted the length of one rainy season. Or it could be for as short as a week or even a night if the young man could not afford the time away from his job or family responsibilities. Women played less codified roles in a temple's activities, but they contributed vital services as devotees and organizers of the ceremonies and activities that occurred within the grounds of a temple.

Buddhism was, and still is, enormously important to Thailand. This cannot be overstated. Conversely, the Thais wholeheartedly embrace a dynamic belief system that combines a broad spectrum of notions that go far beyond Buddhism. Many Thais are amazingly pragmatic when it comes to adopting spiritual principles that support or complement their own. A visitor to a Thai market, such as the famed Chatuchak Weekend Market in Bangkok, will find scores of devotional objects, icons, and texts from numerous religious traditions from all over the world. All of them play a role in the rich syncretic tradition that endures in Thai people's lives today.

Not Indo-China

It is tempting to call this corner of the world "Indo-China," and believe that Thai culture is indebted to India and China because the Tai people came out of southern China and came in contact with belief systems and cultures from India. But Thailand's traditional culture is not the product of borrowings from India and China. The Tai people adopted those elements that matched or harmonized with elements of their indigenous belief systems. That they worshiped, and still revere, the Hindu gods Shiva, Vishnu, Indra, Brahma, Rama, and others means that they most likely matched these Indic forms to deities or expressions of cosmological power that already existed long before they encountered the Indic borrowings in the Mon-Khmer cultures. The import of Indic Buddhism into Southeast Asia strengthened the connection between existing spiritual beliefs and their manifestation as Indic divinities. The appearance of the elephant god Ganesh in a Bangkok shopping mall is probably more from Thais projecting existing beliefs onto a familiar global icon than it is from any outright appropriation of a foreign god.

The Thais did not absorb Indic culture uncritically. They took what was useful, what was comfortable, and what helped amplify or refine what they already believed. They adopted Brahmanic court rituals, the Indian epic *Ramayana* (which Thais call *Ramakien*), and celebrations of natural cycles like the *loi krathong* festival in which they cast out small floats made of banana leaves with candles and coins on them to express gratitude for the monsoon rains that have fed their crops through the growing season. These expressions they adapted from Indian practices. But they did not take everything. Importantly, they did not take the caste system. Thailand's society was a hierarchical structure throughout most of its modern history, and it largely remains that way today. But it is not a caste-based system with all of the prohibitions regarding occupations and spiritual pollution that are part of India's caste system. Thais rejected these ideas. They also did not take purdah (the practice of sequestering women) from India. To the contrary, women were more visible and engaged in public enterprises, such as conducting business, handling money, and doing hard manual labor, than they were in nearly any other country in Asia or the West throughout the premodern era and into modern times. It can also be argued that women were valued in Thai culture more so than their counterparts in India or the West. Unmarried women in many Tai cultures had the latitude to initiate romantic and sexual relationships before settling down to start a family, and it was common for the groom's family to pay a bride price to the bride's family ahead of a marriage in which the groom was expected to leave his family and move in with his wife's family. Many of these matrilocal practices survive.

It is important not to overstate the rights that women have had in Thailand's society. Women have generally been blocked from playing prominent roles in Thailand's national political arena in the modern era. With the exception of a few queens and princesses whose influence was largely funneled through their husbands or who operated beyond the public view, Thailand's male-dominated political culture has not allowed women leaders to emerge. Some Thai women rose to prominence as writers and activists in the modern period, but there have been no Thai equivalents of the female queens and prime ministers in other countries. It was not until the twenty-first century, in August 2011, that Thailand had its first female prime minister. Even then it can be argued that Yingluck Shinawatra rose as a proxy for her deposed older brother rather than a power in her own right. Gender equality in politics is an area where Thailand has lagged behind many countries in the modern era.

Emergence of Powerful Thai Kingdoms

The earliest Thai kingdoms to exert power over large sections of mainland Southeast Asia did not emerge until the twelfth and thirteenth centuries. The first was Sukhothai, located in what is now the northern section of central Thailand. It dominated the affairs of the surrounding Tai city-states until the beginning of the fifteenth century. The other important Thai state to emerge was Ayutthaya, located farther south than Sukhothai and about forty miles north of Bangkok. It became the dominant power in large sections of mainland Southeast Asia in a four hundred-year period that stretched from the fourteenth to the eighteenth century. Since the early twentieth century, students in Thai schools have been taught that Thailand's history can be traced as a neat linear descent from Sukhothai to Ayutthaya to Bangkok in a kind of southerly advance, with each state being the logical historical successor of the previous one. This is overly simplified and misleading because it ignores the complex and multilayered relationships between dozens, if not hundreds, of kingdoms, principalities, city-states, chiefdoms, and smaller political units that existed in the premodern era, all of which had an influence on the development of the state that would become Thailand.

Recounting Thailand's Modern History

There is no standard narrative for Thailand's modern history. Some scholars have looked at kingship and civilian and military governance, with all the actors coming from the ruling classes of Bangkok. Others have focused on economic history to tell the story of the lives of the common people who make their living in agricultural pursuits in the rural areas of Thailand's provinces. Yet others have favored foreign relations, or focused on culture. There is no single approach that will satisfy all opinions. In this volume, I will present the main episodes of Thailand's history with a concentration on political change and the enduring tension among systems of authoritarianism, power sharing, and democracy. I will provide examples of how these tensions have affected non-elites by including experiences from memoirs and other accounts of the everyday lives of Thai people during this period.

A Brief History of Thailand is a general introduction to Thailand's history in the modern era for readers who have no background in Thai studies. It is ideal for students, travelers, and people who want an accessible narrative of the major events in the Bangkok era. Its principal focus is on Thai leaders and other important figures who have shaped the course of the kingdom over the last 250 years. It concentrates on

Bangkok while addressing how the center's policies affected the people of the provinces. It also considers Thailand's cultures, social systems, and religions, and their effect on different historical episodes, especially Buddhism in various popular forms, how Buddhist culture has shaped Thailand's society generally throughout its modern history, and how it affected the development of crucial episodes in this period.

In writing this book, I have drawn upon a wealth of published research, including books, articles, and conference papers by leading scholars working in Thai studies, who have been responsible for creating the dominant and counter narratives of Thailand's history. As the book is aimed at a general audience, it does not include the academic convention of footnotes or endnotes. Instead, I have acknowledged scholars and their principal works in the text and provided full publication details in the Bibliography. I have also drawn upon my own experiences and observations while living in Thailand, as well as my original research in archives in Thailand, Britain, and the United States.

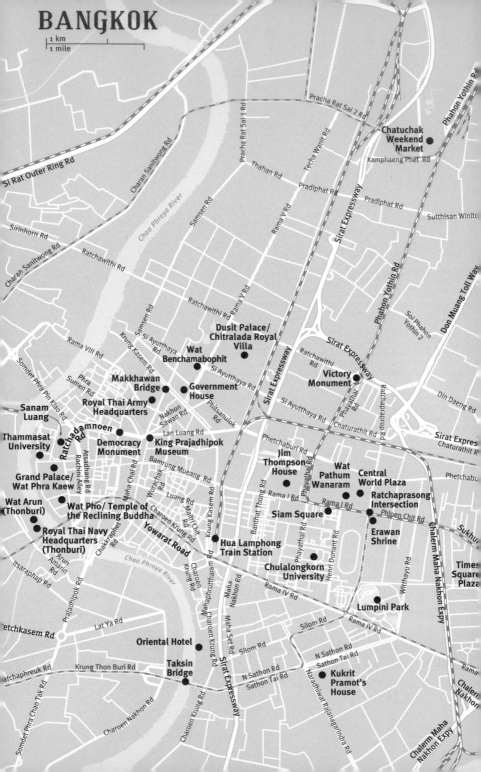

CHAPTER 1

OF COUPS AND KINGS: THE MAKING OF MODERN THAILAND

At 9:30 pm on September 19, 2006, people across Thailand who were watching television on the army-owned station Channel 5 were alarmed when their regular program suddenly vanished. In its place, the station broadcast still images of Thai patriotic symbols – flags, monuments, and natural landscapes – against a background of music composed by Thailand's king. Many people watching guessed immediately what this abrupt change in programming and sudden acknowledgement of the king's creative powers signaled. They had seen it happen before. Many had lived through similar disruptions in their lives, while younger viewers would have been able to guess based on their knowledge of Thai history. Still, there were those who had their doubts. They checked other televisions stations and turned on their radios to discover that other stations had ceased regular programming or gone off the air. It was clear what this interruption signified. One more Thai government had fallen victim to a military takeover. The kingdom had suffered its latest coup d'état.

If those citizens watching Channel 5 in Bangkok needed confirmation of their suspicions, they only had to look outside. Throughout the city, tanks, trucks, and armored personnel carriers of the Royal Thai Army took up key positions in spots associated historically with the seizure of power by the military. Tanks were positioned at Government House, police stations, telecommunications outlets, and the main traffic arteries into the city. Soon commandos swooped in on the prime minister's residence and surrounded it. The building's occupant, Prime Minister Thaksin Shinawatra, was not at home. He had gone abroad, to New York, for a meeting of the United Nations General Assembly. He knew, as many elected and unelected prime ministers had before him, that by leaving Bangkok he had increased the likelihood of a coup attempt against him. Thaksin had gone anyway, reassured perhaps by the growing consensus that the days of coups d'état in Thailand were finally over. But he was wrong.

Thaksin's Rise to Power

Thaksin had been elected under a newly created constitution that was hailed at the time as the most democratic composition of national principles that Thailand had ever possessed. So expansive were the rights guaranteed in this document that it was optimistically dubbed by political observers as "the People's constitution." Thaksin had come to power in 2001 in an election that gave his Thai Rak Thai ("Thais Who Love Thais") Party, which he had founded, the largest number of seats in parliament and a strong mandate to rule. Moreover, he had real support throughout the nation. His populist schemes that gave more affordable health care and resources to combat drug dealers had won the approval of millions in Thailand's rural areas. He had vested a lot of money in those rural areas for local leaders to use as they saw fit to improve their constituents' economic circumstances. He had won over many who had felt neglected by Bangkok's leaders in previous periods. A few years later, Thaksin had earned a second term when his Thai Rak Thai Party won the general elections by a landslide.

But Thaksin was not popular with everyone. There were people, especially in Bangkok, who viewed the former telecommunications tycoon as an authoritarian wolf dressed in democratic sheep's clothing. They objected to his bullying of the press when they questioned him or tried to investigate accusations of corruption, nepotism, vote buying, questionable business arrangements, and extrajudicial executions. Some in the Royal Thai Army did not like him. They blamed him for exacerbating tensions in the southern parts of Thailand that had reignited a separatist insurgency in Thailand's Muslim majority provinces in 2004. They did not like the way he had rearranged the military leadership to give positions of power to those with family connections and other cronies. They accused him of disrespecting King Bhumibol Adulyadej, a dire offense in a country where patriotism involves a stated devotion to the monarchy.

When television transmissions resumed later that night, a pretty TV host, a former Miss Thailand who worked for the station, announced that the Royal Thai Army was now in charge of the capital and that all was well in the kingdom. She thanked viewers for their cooperation and apologized for any inconvenience the night's events might have caused. Thaksin, meanwhile, watched his downfall explained on a television set on the other side of the world.

As depressingly regular as coup d'états have been in the last seventy years, it had been more than fifteen years since the last one. Bangkokians took advantage of the day off after the declaration of martial law to go out and see how their city had been transformed by the latest military power grab. What they saw was both timeless and new. The stern-faced soldiers who participated in the early phases of the coup had tied yellow ribbons to their weapons and uniforms as symbols of their loyalty to their king. These and the open boulevards created by the placement of tanks at city choke points gave Bangkok a festive air. People took photos with the troops. They gave garlands, especially yellow ones, to the soldiers, who draped them over their M-16 rifles and on their armored vehicles. Foreign tourists adjusted their itineraries to come out and see the coup makers. Foreigners photographed themselves in front of the tanks and amidst the soldiers who were warily watching the urban horizon for signs of a countercoup or some kind of resistance. Thai families spread out blankets in the now empty streets and picnicked among the beflowered and beribboned tanks. People played music and laughed and joked and socialized. They shared their food with the soldiers who waited out the day under the hot tropical sun. The formerly tense districts started to look as if a holiday fair or an urban carnival had been set up amidst the military hardware.

The group of army officers who had staged the coup put an end to the frivolity. They ordered the picnickers and photographers off the streets. Having announced the reasons for the coup, a mixture of anticorruption and national salvation, in the early hours of the morning of September 20, they wanted the roads to remain clear for when they could order the troops back to their barracks. Coups were serious business. They were also ugly, the generals suggested in their announcement, as if Thailand's citizens needed a reminder of this grim truth. Thailand's modern history has been a struggle between authoritarianism and liberty, between military power and civilian governance, between dire propaganda about the threats to national integrity and the popular Thai pursuit of *sanuk* (fun) in all matters great and small.

King Taksin the Great

The Taksin Bridge in Thailand's capital stretches across the Chao Phraya River, linking the municipalities of Thonburi and Bangkok. It is named after King Taksin the Great (r. 1767–82), a brilliant and energetic warrior-turned-king and first ruler of the newly created Thai kingdom that followed Ayutthaya. The span joins Thonburi, Taksin's aborted city-state, with Bangkok, capital of the Chakri dynasty monarchs who succeeded him. The reign of King Taksin was itself a kind of historical bridge linking premodern Thailand with the modern nation. This book thus begins with the adventures of a resourceful Sino-Thai warrior named Taksin and concludes with the downfall of a popular Sino-Thai premier named Thaksin. Beyond the superficial similarity of having a name whose English transliteration differs only by the letter "H," the two figures have much in common. They both began as commoners who relied on Southeast Asian Chinese business networks for their ascent to power. Both understood the importance of popular support in a kingdom whose rulers have often ignored the aspirations of the masses. And both were brought down by conservative elites who resented being led by a commoner who dared to wield power like a king. The leadership struggles that unfolded in the two centuries separating these two men are the stories we will explore.

Birth of the Chakri Dynasty

Thailand was born out of the ashes of a mighty empire. Ayutthaya was the wealthy and powerful center of a political entity that dominated the inland trade routes and foreign coastal commerce of mainland Southeast Asia for four centuries. From 1351 to 1767, Ayutthaya, the "invincible city" or "city of war," a name appropriated from an

Indian kingdom and mythical birthplace of the god Rama, sewed together the various vassal states (*mueang*) of the Tai peoples under its loose authority. It exploited the natural and human resources of these weaker inland states in a network of reciprocal power relationships. Its rulers rightly claimed that it was the successor to the powerful Khmer empire centered on what is now called Angkor in Cambodia. Ayutthaya exchanged finished products and natural resources with the kingdoms and empires of East, South, and Southwestern Asia, as well as with China, Korea, Japan, India, Persia, and Arabia.

It was also a city-state tempered by internal bloodshed and external warfare. Lacking clear mechanisms for royal succession, nearly every king's death brought on a period of bloody fighting as members of various royal factions fought, stabbed, poisoned, and shot their rivals, all struggling to put their family's candidate on the throne of this powerful polity. But as strong as it was, Ayutthaya was not, as its name claimed, invincible. It was often at war with other Tai kingdoms resisting Ayutthaya's claims of suzerainty. Twice it was destroyed, utterly sacked, by massive armies from different kingdoms in Burma. Its four hundred-year history is neatly bisected by these traumatic Burmese-led campaigns. In 1564, the Burmese kingdom of Pegu defeated Ayutthaya, leveled the city, and dragged the Thai royal family off to Burma. Ayutthaya managed to wrest its independence back from Pegu, and enjoyed two hundred more years of power and prosperity. The first European travelers to mainland Southeast Asia, the Portuguese, Dutch, and French, marveled at the wealth and the cosmopolitan mix of peoples found within this city-state.

The Destruction of Ayutthaya

Ayutthaya came to an end in 1767. Cut into the banks of the Chao Phraya River and surrounded by walls and moats, it was ostensibly a well-protected site. But its defenses were not absolute. A Burmese force of more than 40,000 besieged the city starting in 1765. Ayutthaya's defenders held out for more than a year but were slowly weakened and starved by the Burmese troops that encircled it. When Ayutthaya surrendered in April 1767, the Burmese rushed in and looted its treasures, burned its buildings, and carried off the material wealth and the human captives that were prized over territory in eighteenth-century Southeast Asian warfare. Rampaging Burmese soldiers hacked off the heads of many of the large Buddha images that adorned the city's grand temple complexes, the beautiful *wat* of brick, stucco, and wood that were adorned with gold, silver, and colored glass. The heads, hands, legs, feet, and torsos of these Buddhist images can be seen in the ruins of Ayutthaya today. Visitors to Ayutthaya's historical parks step over piles of these stone body parts abandoned in the fields around what has become a major tourist attraction in Thailand. They serve as a haunting visual reminder of the carnage that befell the human population there.

The present focal point of this centuries-old destruction is a single stone Buddha head that someone put into the base of a Bodhi tree at Wat Mahathat. In subsequent decades, the tree has grown around the head to form a protective cradle. Thais gather around this joint creation of human and arboreal energy to ask for blessings. It is a beautiful example of Thailand's syncretic religious tradition, an enduring mix of Buddhism and animism – the reverence for spirits within all-natural objects, which thrives in the country. Mother Nature offers her love and protection to the Buddha and his followers in this splendid amalgamation. The Buddha head wears the tree like a splendid crown.

The former grandeur of Ayutthaya weighed heavily on the memories of Thai leaders as they worked to restore their position in regional affairs in the decades after a new Thai kingdom was established in Thonburi and, later, Bangkok. This memory of Ayutthaya would continue to impose itself on the imaginations of Thais as they composed a premodern history, a historical preamble, to the nation that would emerge in its place.

Thailand's birth was painful. It came into being amidst the hellish suffering that accompanies prolonged warfare. While Ayutthaya remained smoldering in the aftermath of its destruction, the rural areas surrounding it were thrown into chaos. The destruction of Ayutthaya caused enormous suffering in the rice-growing areas and orchards of the Chao Phraya River valley. The sacking of the great Thai city and the marauding armies disrupted the planting cycles and commercial systems that had fed and provided for hundreds of thousands of people. It also disrupted the trade in forest products, crops, and finished goods upon which many relied for their livelihood. Law and order succumbed to waves of violence carried out by bandits, many of whom were starving former soldiers and farmers. Refugees fleeing the ruined city and failing farms fell victim to desperate gangs. The last ruler of Ayutthaya, King Ekkathat, starved to death while hiding in a nearby forest.

The Rise of Taksin

The rise of a new Thai kingdom came about because of the ambitions of a young man by the name of Sin. His mother was Thai, his father a Teochew Chinese who worked as a tax collector and gambling den operator. Marked by an omen in infancy when a snake wrapped itself around his body, Sin came to the attention of a prominent noble family who took him in and raised him to serve the court. During his childhood, he studied at a Buddhist monastery for his primary education. Later, while serving as a court page, he continued his education in governmental administration, commercial affairs, and foreign relations. At age twenty, he went back into the monastery for further Buddhist study and training. Unusual for young men of his time, he stayed at the *wat* for three years rather than the more typical one season. He seemed to be serious about Buddhist ideals and the practice of meditation. It is easy to imagine that his strong foundation in Buddhism would serve him well as a warrior, especially his focus on mindfulness and discipline. It is just as easy to imagine that his Buddhist obsessions would lead to his ruin in the political realm.

When Sin reached adulthood, King Ekkathat assigned him to the province of Tak on the Siamese-Burmese border. There he rose to the position of governor and bore the administrative title *phraya*. He came to be known by a melding of his area of responsibility, Tak, with his given name, Sin, to form Taksin. Tak province was a rustic backwater compared to the glorious Ayutthaya metropole. But it was near the mountain pass that Burma's armies normally used when attacking the Thai kingdoms of the lower Chao Phraya River valley. That proximity gave Taksin another useful component to his education. He had an army under his direct command, and with it he gained experience pushing back various Burmese incursions into Thai territory in the early 1760s. When Burma attacked Siam in 1764, Taksin brought his army to Ayutthaya to contribute to its defense. As Ayutthaya's defense grew more precarious, he took his forces outside the wall to harass and divert the main force besieging the town. Taksin and his army were outside the city walls when fire spread through Ayutthaya, and Burmese troops finally breached the city's walls and sacked the city. With Ayutthaya lost to the attackers, Taksin led his army east, to Rayong and Chanthaburi, where they rested and regrouped. He acquired rice and other goods to feed his troops and their supporters. With King Ekkathat and most of the royal family dead, and most of Ayutthaya's soldiers killed, captured, or scattered, Taksin took it upon himself to drive out the Burmese and reestablish the Thai in the Chao Phraya valley.

Taksin was not the only one vying to become the new human center of the Thai universe. Other challengers from the former tribute states of Ayutthaya attempted to assert themselves as the dominant ruler of the Southeast Asian mainland. Taksin, however, despite his unusual circumstances as a half-Chinese governor, had certain advantages over the rulers of the surrounding city-states. As the product of mixed Chinese and Thai heritage, he had entry into both worlds. There is evidence that Taksin had spent his youth traveling throughout Asia amongst Chinese merchants and mariners as they plied the watery lines of the Chinese junk trade. While still a youngster, he had probably visited China, India, Vietnam, and many of the kingdoms of maritime Southeast Asia. Both his birth father and the noble family that raised him would have had commercial dealings with foreign traders from throughout the region. Taksin had inherited contacts with powerful and wealthy Chinese trading families that operated there. Significantly, he would have spoken the various dialects of Chinese that facilitated trade in these ports. He also spoke Vietnamese and some Indian languages. It is these commercial and cultural contacts that Taksin turned to when he needed the money and material resources necessary to establish his new Thai kingdom and to support the army that would have to protect it in its infancy.

Taksin also possessed the traits necessary to attract followers. He had audacity and drive, and probably something akin to genius. He had an excellent military mind, charisma, and courage. Even his reckless attitude in battle served him well in these desperate circumstances. On the battlefield, he won far more times than he lost. He led from the front, and suffered injuries fighting alongside his troops. Amidst the chaos that followed the fall of Ayutthaya, Taksin was able to defeat several local governors (*chao*), who sought to wipe him and his army out. He successfully drove out the Burmese-appointed governors and small military units in the towns of the Chao Phraya River valley. And he masterminded a plan to rebuild a successor to Ayutthaya that could withstand the Burmese and other regional powers.

A New Kingdom at Thonburi

In late 1767, Taksin brought his 5,000 men by boat from eastern Siam back into Burmese-occupied territory where they attacked and captured the town of Thonburi. Now properly alarmed by the brilliant Thai general's campaigns, Burma sent available troops from areas around Ayutthaya against Taksin. Rather than wait for the Burmese to arrive, Taksin led his forces to hit the enemy troops as they moved, defeating them in a series of scattered battles. With room to breathe, Taksin had himself crowned king in December 1767.

Taksin used the lull that followed to build up Thonburi. The site was a good one. It was closer to the Gulf of Siam, which gave him access to ocean-going vessels carrying goods between India and China as part of what is called the junk trade. It was far enough above the Gulf of Siam and beyond the sandbar obstacle near the mouth of the Chao Phraya River to make seaborne raids by enemy ships difficult. Its location promised security and access to money. Thonburi already possessed a well-armed fortress that had been used to protect Ayutthaya. Taksin reinforced the fortification and added more buildings, including *wat*, to make it more like an imperial capital. He had only a short period in which to put together his new kingdom. The Burmese were not going to stand by and allow him to set up a new state that would defend itself and threaten their security. It is easy to imagine his satisfaction when he discovered that the Burmese were suddenly occupied with fending off a Chinese invasion on its northeastern border. The Qing rulers had sent a military force against the northern areas of Burma in the mid-1760s as part of a longer border dispute. Having underestimated the Burmese defenders, China failed to advance into Burma and suffered a high number of casualties from the fighting and from tropical disease. In 1767, they sent a much larger and better-trained Qing force deep into Burma's territory and nearly captured the Burmese capital at Ava before being pushed back. Taksin used this brief but precious respite to cobble together a new state that he hoped would prove as resilient as the once powerful Ayutthaya.

After military defense, the most urgent task facing Taksin was to feed the starving refugees that wandered about the landscape in search of food. He needed the uprooted people to return to their farming areas and to plant the next harvest that would carry his nascent city into its next year. He also needed those who gathered forest products to resume their trade with Thonburi. In the meantime, he used his borrowed resources to buy food to give out. Taksin's distribution of food saved many lives and restored order to the shattered farming communities of the Chao Phraya valley. Compounding the war-related disruption of the planting cycles, drought and a plague of rats further devastated the farming communities. Accounts of the time describe some riverways choked with the bodies of the dead.

Monetary support alone would not have been enough to establish Taksin as a king. He needed more than that if he was going to convince others that he was an acceptable successor to the powerful kings of Ayutthaya. He needed legitimacy. That abstract entity, however, turned out to be trickier to secure. Taksin understood the splendid variances of Thai power in the late eighteenth century. He knew how it worked and how to work it. Growing up in a noble family gave him relationships with the aristocracy that were almost familial. It also gave him an insider's education into the arcane and often treacherous world of royal politics. His tenure as the governor of Tak had given him the fundamentals and experience of political and military leadership. His later military service for a besieged Ayutthaya gave him a close-up view of the consequences of poor diplomacy, careless statecraft, and inadequate military strategy. He was more than a half-Chinese interloper, and more than a ragtag survivor, he was a cosmopolitan and charismatic figure who knew how power, money, and politics worked. In this phase, he used diplomacy, patronage, and warfare to make his case to the surrounding polities that he had the right qualities to be recognized as a legitimate king. For a short span, he seemed like the ideal figure to summon the Thai phoenix out of the hellfire that had consumed it.

Securing the Thonburi Reign

No sooner had Taksin established his Thonburi kingdom on the west bank of the Chao Phraya River than Burma launched campaigns against the kingdoms across northern Siam. The main Burmese army came from the north where it had occupied the Tai kingdom of Chiang Mai. The objective was to punish the kingdoms that had pledged support to Taksin. The Burmese and Thai armies clashed repeatedly throughout the mid-1770s, with battle lines going back and forth around the northern city of Phichai. Taksin, in the tradition of Ayutthaya's early warrior kings, led some of the forces against the Burmese, but he led them on horseback, in contrast to the elephants that his Ayutthaya predecessors had taken into battle. Using smart cavalry tactics, Taksin guided his troops to a series of improbable victories against a larger and better-equipped Burmese force. He was an inspiring campaigner, visible and active to rouse morale. He was also a cruel commander. He punished disobedience with summary execution, often by decapitation. In at least one case, he carried out the gory task himself. By 1779, Taksin had pushed the Burmese out of Siamese territory, bringing Chiang Mai, Tak, Ratchaburi, and other occupied cities under his control. Taksin's resounding victories ensured that the Burmese, decimated and demoralized in defeat, would be unable to threaten his kingdom for at least a few years.

Taksin did not rest his armies, however. In the years that followed, he moved against enemies and potential enemies to the north, northeast, and east. He was aided in these campaigns by a pair of brothers who were his scrappy and talented equals: Thong Duang and Bunma (sometimes called by their noble titles Chakri and Surasi). Their father was a Thai nobleman, their mother, his fourth wife, was part Chinese. Taksin had been friends with Bunma in his youth, and through him came to know and trust Thong Duang. In 1779, Taksin sent Thong Duang and Bunma against the Lao kingdom of Vientiane to punish it for supporting the Burmese. Vientiane had aided Burma's armies against Ayutthaya's ally Chiang Mai on their way south toward Ayutthaya. The brothers' attack on the "disloyal" Lao kingdom was thorough and unmerciful. Their troops bore spears, lances, swords, bows and arrows, small arms, and cannon as they clashed with similarly armed Lao forces. Thong Duang's Thai forces sacked Vientiane and hauled away its most precious possessions: sacred Buddhist statues and all of its people. The two statues were the Phra Bang and the Phra Kaeo Morakot images. The latter image, whose full title is Phra Phutha Maha Mani Rattana Patimakon, is the green jade Buddha figure known as the Emerald Buddha. Both of these Buddha images have murky histories that seem to indicate they originated in the Theravada kingdoms of Sri Lanka long ago. Both had also been the war prizes of the various Tai kingdoms throughout the premodern era. Possession of these celebrated icons gave Taksin a measure of sacral power while he was establishing his legitimacy among his followers. It would have also added further reassurance to those rulers from the surrounding Tai kingdoms as they debated whether to throw their lot in with the upstart kingdom of Thonburi.

The other prize, the human population, was even more important. Thong Duang ordered the defeated population surrounding Vientiane to be moved forcibly to the other side of the Mekong River. This action was both symbolic and practical. It is important to remember that most mainland Southeast Asian kingdoms did not fight to capture territory but to capture people for labor. In a region of the world where populations were relatively scant, these conquering armies prized people who could do skilled and unskilled work in areas closer to their own kingdoms. Victorious armies would capture the defeated and put them to work clearing forests, digging canals, and planting rice to feed the center. Perhaps more importantly, they sought skilled labor from scribes, artisans, and musicians who could enhance the luster of their courts. In moving the entire population of Vientiane to areas closer to Thonburi, Thong Duang achieved two important goals. He ensured that his Lao rival could not bounce back quickly and launch a counterattack against Thonburi. He also fed the population of the central Chao Phraya valley by adding more rice-growing labor to the southern realms.

While Thong Duang was scoring victory upon victory for the new Thonburi regime, Taksin set about stabilizing society. He worked tirelessly to establish a functioning bureaucracy that could administer Thonburi beyond the expedient systems of wartime. He sought to bring order to the chaotic ranks of the *sangha*, the monastic community of monks (*bhikkhu*). He had a profound devotion to Buddhist ideals, and targeted what he identified as corrupt or heretical Buddhist monks. The punishments he meted out ranged from expulsion to trial by fire to execution. He also donated food, new robes, and supplies to the monks whom he found to be devout and learned. He restored damaged temples and built new ones. He persuaded the small Roman Catholic community to pledge its loyalty to his state, and punished those who refused with imprisonment or banishment. Throughout this state-building and social reform process, Taksin joined Thong Duang and Bunma on military expeditions throughout the region. There is strong evidence to suggest that Taksin enjoyed the support of the people, nobles and commoners alike, for returning stability, success, and pride to the Thai. And then he seemed to come undone.

Taksin's Downfall

According to the oft-repeated story of this period, Taksin went insane. He is reported to have developed delusions of grandeur that intensified exponentially. The truth is probably more complex than that. It seems unlikely that such a successful manager of people and circumstances would go so quickly and so profoundly insane. According to the story, his downfall began with his obsessive interest in Buddhism. Once installed as king, Taksin devoted himself to studying Buddhist meditation. Under the guidance of scholarly monks, he came to believe he was a *sodaban* (*sotapanna*, or "stream-winner"), a kind of Buddhist holy figure who can overcome the obstacles that block nearly everyone else from becoming a Bodhisattva. He aimed to acquire the powers of levitation. Allegedly, his delusions brought out his cruelty. He apparently tested his rarefied spiritual status by demanding that the monks in Thonburi bow before him in a gesture of deep prostration. Monks are not obliged to bow to kings in any manner as they hold, theoretically, higher status than even a monarch. Taksin believed his religious achievements and royal title trumped the status of the *bhikkhu*. He reportedly whipped those who refused to bow to him, and even punished the supreme patriarch for his noncompliance. His harsh actions stirred unease among the surviving Ayutthaya nobles, many of whom had never accepted the upstart Taksin as their king. Their fear set in motion what would become a full-scale rebellion.

In March 1782, a faction opposed to Taksin launched a rebellion from their base in Ayutthaya. Taksin sent a military force to quash the uprising. The official leading the punitive force turned on Taksin and joined the rebels. Their combined forces then marched on Thonburi and easily captured the city. The rebels arrested Taksin and took him prisoner. Taksin was able to forestall his doom by voluntarily stepping down as king, offering to don robes and to live out his life as a monk in a monastery. Asian rulers in many historical circumstances have used this method of exchanging the crown for robes in religious exile. Sometimes, they stay away without interfering in the new regime. But some use the respite to rally their forces ahead of trying to regain power. For the time being, Taksin was allowed to live while the turncoat official and other court figures sought a new king. Thong Duang, Taksin's trusted general, was away on campaign when news of the rebellion reached him. He returned to Thonburi to put himself forward as Taksin's successor. Having descended from Ayutthaya high nobility and in command of what appeared to be the strongest military force in the region, Thong Duang won the support necessary to become king.

The problem was Taksin. How do you contend with a former ruler whose energies, ideas, and contacts rebuilt the Thai empire after its near annihilation? What do you do to an insane ex-king who now threatens to undo all of the good that many have been striving for? The new court sentenced Taksin to death. According to the old story, he was tied into a velvet bag and beaten to death with sandalwood paddles. The custom of the velvet bag ensured that royal blood would not suffer the insult of touching the ground ahead of cremation. In this version, Taksin, the commoner who became a savior and a ruler, died like a true king.

Despite the popularity of this sentimentally gruesome tale, it might not be true. There is only one source for it, and it is flimsy. It is more likely that he was beheaded. The more reliable version of events suggests that his remains were thrown outside the city walls without a proper burial or cremation. In this telling, he is dispatched to eternity with insult and ignobility. It is easy to imagine that Taksin's alleged insanity may have been little more than a cover story for a group of surviving Ayutthaya royals and nobility who objected to the presence of a half-Chinese parvenu who acted like a king and claimed supernatural powers. They may have gotten rid of him to restore their influence and prestige in a court that did not recognize fully their former status. The story of Taksin's downfall is one of the most memorable tales of Thai history. But because it is based on thin sources, we have to be cautious in accepting it at face value.

One would imagine that an "insane king" who allegedly savaged Buddhist monks would be regarded with disgust by Thais. But the opposite is true. Taksin is remembered fondly throughout Thailand today. His handsome, mustached face, with its stern gaze beneath a broad-brimmed hat or archaic helmet, can be found in fanciful portraits that adorn the many public and private shrines dedicated to his memory, the greatest of which can be found in the grand devotional hall at Wat Arun in Thonburi. Statues of Taksin upon a rearing horse in battle are also common. His image is worn on magic amulets that are especially popular with soldiers. This warm historical embrace, even belatedly, testifies to the appreciation that many Thais have for the audacious official who rescued the scattered and starving Thai people of the lower Chao Phraya valley from ruin and put them, in a sense, back on the map. He is a people's hero. And his veneration adds another element of doubt, at least from a popular Thai perspective, about the story of Taksin's alleged insanity.

A New Kingdom at Bangkok

Thong Duang stayed in Thonburi and maneuvered to make himself Taksin's successor. He killed members of Taksin's family and other loyalists. He secured support from the rebel factions that had risen up against Taksin. History would show that their endorsement was a wise move. In backing this savvy and hard-hearted general, these nobles had elevated a figure of great administrative talent and vision. In April 1782, Thong Duang crowned himself and took the throne as King Ramathibodi. Later, he would be called Phra Phutthayotfa Chulalok, but is more commonly remembered as Rama I (r. 1782–1809). His previous title, Chakri, is the name of Thailand's royal dynasty in the modern era.

Rama I moved fast to build his own kingdom that would be free of the taint of cabals and regicide that ended Taksin's short reign. Instead of occupying Takskin's ill-fated throne in Thonburi, Rama I set up a new capital on the west side of the Chao Phraya River. This location had advantages over Thonburi, the first being that any Burmese army intent on attacking it would first have to cross the river. The second is that the eastern side had more open areas for the construction of new buildings. Rama I constructed the city as a fortified palace city with supporting buildings set beside the river and ringed with canals to create a moat-ringed island that could be better defended by its occupants. Towers along the walls aided defense against potential besiegers.

In a physical and symbolic sense, Rama I's new kingdom was meant to stand as the successor to Ayutthaya. Some of the bricks for its buildings, walls, and courtyards were recycled from the ruins of Ayutthaya, brought downriver on barges to build the new capital, the grandeur of the lost city thus spliced into the architectural DNA of its successor. The human labor that built it largely comprised war captives and other slaves taken from some Khmer, Lao, and Malay polities, areas over which Ayutthaya had claimed suzerainty. The captive workforce built palaces and temples, traditionally the only forms of lasting monumental architecture in Southeast Asia, like those that dotted the landscape of the former Thai kingdom. As with Ayutthaya before it, Rama I's new kingdom became a cosmopolitan society of Asian traders, merchants, craftsmen, soldiers, and religious figures from across the region, continent, and globe. Rama I called his kingdom Rattanakosin and his capital city came to be known as Krung Thep Maha Nakhon, "the Great City of Angels." Foreign merchants, sailors, and diplomats, however, used the term Bangkok for the city and Siam for the polity.

Rama I's decision to create a better fortified capital was far-sighted. Shortly after beginning work on the new city, Rama I found himself the target of a huge Burmese invasion force in 1785. Its size and composition were similar to the one that had decisively crushed the more powerful Thai kingdom of Ayutthaya a few years earlier. Rama I was ready. His spies among the Mon had warned him of Burma's battle plans. He received similar intelligence from some of the Thai states on the Burmese-Siamese border. Burma's King Bodawpaya sent more than 100,000 soldiers toward Bangkok. Unlike in previous Burmese invasions of Siam, Bodawpaya divided his force into five armies, including both land and seaborne troops. This strategy meant that Siam would have to fight on different fronts to the north, west, and south. His first attack was against the island of Phuket in April 1785, a move designed to deny the Thais military supplies from foreign sources. Burma's attack on Phuket failed, but its main force remained ready to move against Bangkok on land. Rama I did not wait for the five-pronged Burmese force to get into position so as not to risk being encircled and starved in a siege as had the last rulers of Ayutthaya. Instead, he rode out with his forces and met the main Burmese force coming from the west. This largest of the five invading armies was under the leadership of Bodawpaya himself. The two kings, both revolutionary in their own spheres, came to fight it out on ancient battlefields like so many Burmese and Thai warrior kings of old, only this time the outcome would determine the balance of power on the Southeast Asian mainland in the modern era.

Rama I had learned a lot from his campaigns against the Lao, Tai, and Khmer kingdoms. As the German historian Klaus Wenk illustrates in his study *The Restoration of Thailand Under Rama I*, the new monarch used his accumulated military knowledge to keep the Burmese out of the Tai realms. He moved some 70,000 Thai troops to Lat Ya, just outside the modern city of Kanchanaburi, in October 1785. There, they hurriedly constructed fortified camps with ramparts and trenches that stretched across the opening passageway of the strategically vital Three Pagoda Pass. If the Thais could deny the Burmese the use of the pass, the invaders would have to make a slow and arduous journey over densely jungled mountains. The Burmese easily pushed aside a small Mon force loyal to Siam before coming upon the Thai's main force at Lat Ya. Initially, the Thais fared badly against Bodawpaya's army. They were under the command of Rama I's brother, Bunma (Surasi), who held the position of *uparat*, a title sometimes translated as viceroy, vice king, or front palace king. The two sides pounded each other with cannons and mortars before sending out troops to fight in the open fields. The Thais dispatched commandos to harass the Burmese supply lines. Bunma made his expectations for bravery clear when he beheaded timid commanders and displayed their heads on pikes. As the weeks of fighting wore on, the Burmese troops suffered hunger and demoralization from a lack of food and supplies. Soon, the advantage began to turn to the Thai side. The Thais also used psychological warfare techniques by sending away some of their armies under cover of darkness only to have them return the following morning bearing new banners. The Burmese believed the "new" Thai troops were reinforcements. Stressed and weak, the Burmese fell victim to wild rumors of an impending arrival of a giant Thai force. King Bodawpaya is reported to have fled in panic, and his armies fell apart in his absence. Burma's other armies faced similar setbacks, and the invasion crumbled.

Two years after the Burmese marched against Bangkok, they sent a huge force against Lan Na, the northern kingdom centered on the city of Chiang Mai. Rama I responded to this threat by sending troops northward under the command of his *uparat*, who fought off the Burmese armies then attacking the kingdom of Lampang to Lan Na's south. At the same time, Rama I took his own force and drove on into Burma to attack the enemy at their center in Tavoy (Dawei). The northern campaign succeeded quickly, but Rama I was not able to sack Tavoy. No matter, he had pushed out the Burmese from the northern city-states that Thai rulers had commonly viewed as belonging to their tribute system. He fortified the captured areas of western Lan Na so that Burma would not be able to threaten his nascent state at Bangkok with another invasion from the north. The campaign also established his claim of suzerainty over the areas that would become the northern edge of the modern Thai state. Even though his campaign into Burmese territory stalled before he could destroy his rival, it yielded important benefits. In resisting Siam, the Burmese had drained their resources to the point that they could not threaten Bangkok in the immediate future. While Burma recovered and rebuilt its forces, Rama I, for the time being, had made Bangkok safe and could concentrate on building the city.

Rama I's most important goal was to maintain the supply of manpower he had won access to through military conquest and through treaties with friendly principalities. This was the key to Bangkok's survival. To do this, he enforced a system in which all commoners had their forearms tattooed with their registration numbers and the name of their local *chao*, or lord. The method involved penetrating their skin with a red-hot stiletto. The coercive nature of the system sparked resentment and resistance, but not necessarily the marks themselves. Thais were often tattooed heavily in this period. Tattoos tracked labor obligations, conscription, and taxation. The tattoos on their forearms would not have seemed overly conspicuous. Wrist tattoos allowed messengers free passage through the kingdom. Tattoos also tracked the status of the enslaved and the indentured, and their freedom when granted. Some criminals bore tattoos on their faces to denote serious transgressions. More elaborate were the Buddhist and magic (*sayasat*) tattoos that were meant to protect them from injury and illness. These were intricate yantra diagrams, mythical and natural creatures, words and letters of the Khom (ancient Khmer) alphabet, and sometimes dazzling combinations of all of these. With this system in place, Rama I called on all males to provide four months of corvée labor – unpaid, unfree, intermittent labor – per year. They would dig drainage and transportation canals, clear timber from forests, build palaces, and, when needed, go to war. The penalty for falsifying an official tattoo was death. Later, Thai subjects would have the option of avoiding this corvée labor by paying a tax in money or products such as ivory, beeswax, teak, sappan wood, stick lac, and cardamom.

Rama I set about rebuilding important religious, social, and government institutions. The heart of this new kingdom would be its Buddhist institutions. The temples provided not only the spiritual and moral guidelines necessary in the early uncertain years, but also served as the new kingdom's network of schools and training centers for the male population. Addressing what he saw as increasingly lax adherence to Buddhist tenets, he reformed the Buddhist order by issuing decrees designed to impose stricter discipline on the monks. He promoted the more devout and learned members of the Buddhist clergy to leadership positions. Beginning in 1788, he tried to discourage the more mystical factions by commissioning a new and more orthodox edition of the *Tripitaka*, the Pali-language collection of Buddhist scriptures. He also imposed similarly conservative policies on the government of the royal court. Rama I organized his government in imitation of Ayutthaya's, with six main departments (*krom*) and numerous other small offices. The principal departments were responsible for both geographical areas and specific state functions.

As a measure of Bangkok's stability and confidence during this first reign are its foreign relations at the time. Siam got deeply involved in the politics of its neighbors beyond the Tai principalities immediately surrounding it, especially in the Lao kingdom of Vientiane and in Cambodia. The other important measure was economic. Bangkok reclaimed Siam's former role as a chief player in the pan-Asian sea trade that passed through Southeast Asia. Siam had been deeply enmeshed in this system during the Ayutthaya period when many of the junks were of Chinese design but made in Siamese shipyards from the region's plentiful timber. This had been going on for hundreds of years, so it was natural for Rama I to encourage his princely siblings, relatives, nobles, and merchants to rebuild the commercial infrastructure that would allow Siam to trade rice, sugar, and forest products for the prized goods moving through Southeast Asia. With its military might and economic vitality now established under Rama I, the new Thai kingdom at Bangkok was a viable political entity that could rightly claim to be Ayutthaya's successor. Within a few decades of its utter ruin, Siam had done more than merely return from death. It now looked like it had the potential to become the wealthiest and most powerful kingdom mainland Southeast Asia had ever experienced.

CHAPTER 2

KING MONGKUT: THE THREAT OF WESTERN IMPERIALISM

The Western world came to know Siam's King Mongkut as a bald and argumentative buffoon, a stomping hothead who, despite his uncouth demeanor, captures an English governess's heart when he learns to waltz and banter like a dancehall gigolo. The real Mongkut bears only the slightest resemblance to the caricature created by Yul Brynner for the 1956 film version of Rodgers and Hammerstein's musical *The King & I*, which was based on the two memoirs of Anna Leonowens about her time in Siam in the 1860s as a tutor to Mongkut's children. It is true that Mongkut was mostly bald, and he did sometimes lose his temper when dealing with state affairs, but the rest of the Hollywood portrayal is pure fantasy. King Mongkut was one of his age's great minds, a ruler of high energy and talent who pursued initiatives that satisfied the demands of Western colonial powers while keeping them at a safe distance. He was a polymath, polyglot, religious reformer, and historian. He was, perhaps, even more than that.

A King-in-Waiting

King Mongkut (Rama IV, r. 1851–68) should have become king earlier than he did, but circumstances beyond his control delayed his kingship. The delay in his rule, and the extraordinary education he acquired in the intervening years, were enormous blessings for him and Siam even if it did not seem so at the time. Mongkut was the oldest surviving son of King Phra Phuttaloetla Naphalai (Rama II, r. 1809–24), born to his queen Sri Suriyendra. Upon his father's death in 1824, Mongkut had the best claim by birthright to the throne. His mother's royal blood put him at the top of the list of eligible candidates, especially over those half-brothers born to concubines and consorts. Mongkut's problem was his age. He was only twenty and thus judged too young to assume the weighty duties required of a monarch. The crown was passed instead to his older half-brother, Prince Thap, who reigned as King Nangklao and later came to be known as Rama III (r. 1824–51). Although Prince Thap's mother was only a noblewoman, he was sixteen years older than Mongkut. Nangklao was the safer bet to lead Siam in a perilous time. With the British gobbling up sections of Burma, and with an expanding Vietnam making claims on Cambodian territory that Siam had formerly considered its domain, the court saw dangers in entrusting the throne to someone as inexperienced as Mongkut. The court's consensus was that Mongkut would do better to wait until he was older before attempting to rule Siam.

The passed-over prince found himself in a difficult position. What do you do when you possess all the right qualifications to be king but are denied the title because of your age? His mere presence in the court would have been a threat to Rama III and his supporters. The new king's rule would potentially have been hampered by the faction that had favored the younger candidate. Mongkut would have been a focus for those who opposed Rama III and his policies, a human nexus of plots and intrigue. He might have found himself drawn into the conspiracies of those who plotted against the ruler. Mongkut was a monk at the time of his father's death, fulfilling his temporary ordination that nearly all Thai males served on the cusp of adulthood. To protect Mongkut and to ensure the stability of the court, he was encouraged to remain a monk. This meant abandoning the princely life he had known since birth. He would have to disappear into the *sangha*'s ranks. As it is, his time in robes proved to be the defining factor in tempering his character, developing his amazing intellect, and introducing him to a world of ideas from beyond Siam's court.

Mongkut was in his second stint as a monk when his father passed away. He had first donned robes at the age of seven as a *samanen* (novice). Although these experiences gave him a long familiarity with the austerities of a *bhikkhu*, his new life would have demanded emotional, intellectual, and even physical adjustments for the twenty-year-old prince. Mongkut left behind a wife, children, and the palace's sumptuous comforts when he agreed to remain in robes. For twenty-seven years, Siam's future king lived as a studious and somewhat anonymous monk in the kingdom he would one day inherit. He endured the daily rigors of a mendicant, awakening in the small hours for prayers, chanting, and meditation, before setting out to collect food. The practice is known as *bintebat* in Thai. Monks leave their monasteries and temples around 6:00 a.m. to collect food from the community that supports them. Although some Westerners describe the monks' metal bowl as a "begging bowl," the monks most certainly do not beg. Instead, they offer laypeople the opportunity to earn merit (*thambun*) by contributing food (*saibat*). Mongkut walked through Bangkok's streets to collect food from the people who would someday revere him as their king. He met many others in the temple as they came for prayer, advice, or ceremonies. While some may have known the identity of this royal prince-turned-monk, most did not. He was able to look into the eyes of Siam's humblest subjects. He absorbed their sorrows, worries, and exultations. In his interactions with the other monks and the devotees who came to the temple, he learned about the circumstances of common people. He acquired a firsthand understanding of their struggles to stay alive and to maintain a spiritual serenity in the face of life's challenges. He even endured insults and attacks by the court members who opposed his ascension and remained on guard against his return. There are stories told of how his royal rivals, those members of the court allied with Rama III who opposed Mongkut, would pour boiling soup into his metal bowl to burn his fingers. Mongkut endured these trials and others.

Transforming the Practices of Buddhism

Mongkut used his time as a monk to acquire an education. He gained knowledge in subjects that would not have been available to him had he remained in the palace. For his first seven years as a monk, he studied at Wat Samorai, north of Bangkok. During this time, he became a highly respected scholar of Pali, the sacred language of Buddhism, and Buddhist doctrine. While studying Buddhism, he became increasingly bothered by what he saw as the unorthodox ideas, especially superstition and magic, that had made their way into Buddhism over the previous few thousand years. Mongkut would have been aware that many of these un-Buddhist ideas had been there for a long time and were now wholly conflated with Buddha's teachings. He sought to remove all the non-Buddhist elements, such as folktales and incantations, that had been woven into the Thai Buddhist practice. He also saw that Siam's ordination and meditation practices were at odds with the teachings of the *Vinaya*, the monastic code that guides all monks' actions. Some of his understanding of a more orthodox practice of Theravada Buddhism came from a monk he met who was from the Mon areas of southern Burma.

Troubled by his discoveries, Mongkut set about transforming the practices of Buddhism at Wat Samorai. In the early 1830s, he changed the monks' dress by switching to robes that covered both shoulders. He altered the daily practices, the chanting, meditation, and study, of the monks to make them more in line with the *Vinaya*. He also had monks take only one meal a day instead of the two eaten by monks in other orders. Later, he became the abbot (*chao awat*) of Wat Bowonniwet Vihara, a temple that Rama III had constructed, possibly to keep a closer watch on Mongkut and his religious reforms. He served as the chief monk there for the next fourteen years. His leadership position helped him promote the changes among like-minded monks. These practices became the basis for a reform movement called Thammayut (Dhammayuttika Nikaya). Over the next few decades, Thammayut monks would continue to challenge the deviations and accretions that had so bothered Mongkut while he was a monk. Eventually, in 1902, Mongkut's son and successor, Chulalongkorn, changed the law to recognize Thammayut as a distinct denomination independent of the more popular Maha Nikai order. Along the way, the Thammayut movement, and the friction it generated with the Maha Nikai, helped shape Thailand's political affairs. More narrowly, Thammayut revitalized the Thai forest monk practice in which monks wander the forests and countryside seeking enlightenment through meditation.

Mongkut did not limit his studies to Theravada Buddhism but was also interested in other religions, languages, and the natural sciences. He befriended the French Catholic prelate in Siam, Bishop

Jean-Baptiste Pallegoix, whose church was near Wat Samorai. Mong-kut and the bishop discussed theological matters and exchanged language lessons. Mongkut taught Pallegoix Pali while Pallegoix taught Mongkut Latin. Always fascinated with languages, Mongkut also learned Lao, Khmer, Mon, and other Southeast Asian tongues. He became friends with Protestant missionaries who taught him English and who debated theological matters with him. He was particularly close to a remarkable figure named Reverend Dan Beach Bradley, or "Mo Bradley" (Dr. Bradley) as the Thais called him. Bradley was a medical missionary from central New York who had many scientific, civic, and public health interests. Mongkut threw himself into the sciences – geography, physics, mathematics, biology, and chemistry – and became somewhat knowledgeable about each field. He was attracted to astronomy. Knowledge of the stars' movements was often seen as the key to unlocking the secrets of nature. Astronomy aided success in agriculture and navigation, two components that would facilitate commercial exchange with foreign powers and contribute wealth to the kingdom. He also recognized that the military power of Western imperialists rested upon a foundation of superior scientific knowledge.

Finding the Sources of Thai History

The Western colonialists' intrusion into the power structures of traditional Southeast Asian kingdoms transformed how many rulers viewed education in general. In the past, for example, many Thai princes learned their future occupations by studying at their fathers' sides. Their education was limited to seeing how their fathers conducted themselves in the courts, parlors, palaces, and embassies. The superior technology demonstrated by the Western powers as they defeated the indigenous kingdoms in battle had encouraged some of the more open-minded princes to seek out Western knowledge in topics such as military sciences and shipbuilding. Mongkut's position outside the court meant that he could pursue that knowledge wherever he came across it.

Mongkut also learned about Western ideas of history during this period. He realized that Siam's own historical understanding, its recording of historical events in royal chronicles, was dramatically different from the West's. This difference in historical approaches encouraged Mongkut to investigate new avenues of knowledge about Siam's past. His status as a monk at the time meant that he had the opportunity to travel to other temples throughout the kingdom and talk to monks from the tributary states surrounding Bangkok. He learned about the customs and practices and histories of the areas beyond the Chao Phraya valley. He collected information about the histories of the various Tai kingdoms. He acquired artifacts, such as inscriptions and steles, that had been created in the premodern period. With them, he began to piece together the stories, themes, and episodes that would someday become the master narrative of Thailand's nationalist history. In 1833, while traveling to Sukhothai, he came across the Ramkhamhaeng Inscription. Later dated to 1292, the inscription is the most important, and most controversial, of Mongkut's discoveries. The four-sided stele bears a declaration by a ruler of Sukhothai, Ramkhamhaeng, in the oldest surviving example of the Thai script. With the help of a group of similarly talented linguists, Mongkut deciphered the ancient text. It tells of Ramkhamhaeng's bravery in battle, his ascension to the throne, the guardian spirits of the realm, and the kingdom's wealth. Ramkhamhaeng boasts that his Sukhothai has "fish in the water, and rice in the fields," a line memorized by every Thai pupil today. It also contains a description of the Sukhothai tradition by which every man (or more likely every nobleman) had the right to petition the king directly to remedy an injustice. For nationalist historians, the Ramkhamhaeng Inscription's text has become the opening words of the story of Thai civilization. Its invocation of an idealized thirteenth-century kingdom has served as a touchstone for many Thai leaders, especially those inclined toward reactionary policies. A few notable Western scholars have challenged its authenticity, claiming that the 14 x 45-inch pillar is likely a forgery created hundreds of years after the events it describes. The general scholarly consensus is that the stele is genuine.

Mongkut's Court

Mongkut became king in 1851. It was a time of significant change in Southeast Asia. European imperialism, and British imperialism in particular, was forcing a profound transformation of the kingdoms in the region. Mongkut was on the throne when Britain began its three-part conquest of Burma. Initially, Siam's rulers welcomed the military defeat of its most noisome neighboring rival. The British piecemeal destruction and subjugation of Burma's kingdoms in 1826 and 1852 would have been hailed by Siamese leaders as just desserts for Burma's leveling of Ayutthaya. But the rapid destruction of such a formerly powerful foe also gave Siamese leaders pause when they were forced to consider how they would fare militarily against such a powerful foreign power if Britain were to go to war against Siam over territorial or trade disputes. Siam was in a precarious position. In only half a century, Britain had taken Singapore, parts of Malaya, and lower Burma, and was about to seize more. In Vietnam, the French had just started shelling Vietnamese cities from gunboats as reprisals for the persecution of French missionaries and their converts. As parts of Southeast Asia fell to European powers, Siam became a potential target. In the schemes and dreams of European traders working in Southeast Asia, the idea of Siam becoming a colony was openly discussed. Some Europeans said they would need only the right incident, and their countrymen could rush in and claim Siam as a colonial possession, a dazzling prize to add to their growing territories across the map.

While Mongkut bore little resemblance to the impulsive tyrant that Yul Brynner portrayed him as, he could be stubborn, severe, and, sometimes, explosive in his anger. Despite the occasional outburst, Mongkut usually displayed a calmness that bordered on the severe. It was the demeanor of someone who had spent many years as a monk. Perhaps it was a powerful screen. Wise kings learn early that their likes and dislikes can be manipulated by schemers intent on controlling a king for their own benefit. Cautious and strategic-minded kings will adopt an air of impassivity, a blank mask, that they wear to separate themselves from those who would use them. Mongkut's severity was intensified by illness. It is likely that he suffered from Bell's palsy, a pinched facial nerve that can paralyze the face. He also had artificial teeth made from sappan wood, a likely source of physical discomfort. These red-hued dentures were further reddened by a habit he shared with much of his kingdom of chewing the mildly narcotic and badly staining betel nut.

Upon assuming the throne, Mongkut took measures to secure control over the kingdom's commerce, diplomacy, and defense. First, he elevated two trusted brothers and their adult children to important positions in the court. The brothers were Bunnags, members of an important aristocratic family of Persian descent who had manipulated their way into Thai court politics for generations. The elder of these brothers had probably played the decisive role in handing the crown to Mongkut, and the new king trusted him and his family over his fraternal rivals. The Bunnags would direct Siam's commerce and defense as the two elements came increasingly under foreign, specifically British, scrutiny.

British and French Interest in Siam

Mongkut's first major challenge came soon after when the British demanded a new treaty with Siam. Treaties had existed between the two kingdoms for some time, but these initial accords regulated mostly diplomatic protocol. By the mid-nineteenth century, the British wanted a new treaty to regulate commerce, encompassing British subjects' legal rights while pursuing trade in Siam's sphere. The British sought these treaties to clarify not only its position with Siam but also to prevent it from stumbling into conflict with other Western powers conducting similar commercial enterprises in the region.

In 1850, the year before Mongkut became king, Sir James Brooke, the so-called "White Rajah of Sarawak," had departed Siam greatly angered after he failed to press Rama III into signing a treaty. Mongkut was similarly cautious. He made it known to London's envoys that he was quite particular about when, with whom, and under what conditions he would sign a treaty with the British. He indicated he would work with Sir John Bowring, the British governor of Hong Kong, because Bowring did not come from British circles in India and Malaya, where Siam was often the target of covetous and angry statements by British traders. Mongkut's time studying with and talking to Christian missionaries from Britain, the United States, France, and other countries had prepared him for understanding the rhetoric used by the colonial powers when negotiating with Asian rulers. He was also ready for the self-importance with which Britain's envoys viewed themselves.

Mongkut did not risk giving the British any pretext for pursuing wars like those they had launched in Burma. Instead, Mongkut had his most trusted officials deal with the British. Mongkut stayed away from the negotiations, but he met with Bowring throughout his stay. Together they ate lavish meals, drank European wine, and enjoyed after-dinner cigars. He treated them to his favorite entertainments, including theatrical productions of the *Ramakien*. The highly stylized dance-dramas lasted late into the night, which may have helped to wear down the British delegates' resolve. Mongkut was aware of how the British had treated what they viewed as petty rulers in India and Africa. He sought to convince them that he was as worthy of respect as Queen Victoria without acting so grandiose in his court conduct as to inspire British chauvinism. The weeks of negotiation yielded a treaty, the Bowring Treaty, that was able to satisfy Mongkut's conservative rivals in the court, as well as his progressive allies, and, most importantly, the British themselves.

The treaty stabilized import and export duties, preserved the Siamese court's monopoly on domestic opium sales, gave British traders the right to deal directly with Siamese merchants, and upheld the legal protection of extraterritoriality that the British had enjoyed before Bowring's arrival. This special status would gall future generations of Thai leaders. British subjects enjoyed a kind of diplomatic immunity to Siam's laws. Instead, if they were accused of committing a crime, they were tried by British judges according to Britain's laws. It was a unilateral arrangement that did not extend the same rights to Siamese subjects who committed crimes in British territories. It also applied to Britain's colonial subjects working and living in Siam. Shortly after finalizing the Bowring Treaty, the extraterritorial privilege was extended to all Western powers. The arrangement would survive in Siam in one form or another until the 1930s.

Many in the Siamese court doubted the wisdom of this treaty. The scores of princes and nobles who earned their income from a closed trading system feared the new arrangement would impoverish them and diminish their financial autonomy, forcing them into dependency on the court. Mongkut himself was not pleased with some of the treaty's details, but he acquiesced to the final agreement. With Britain and the other colonial powers pressing in, Mongkut realized he had little choice but to strike some accommodation on trade with the Western powers. Mongkut did two things that helped the Siamese position. First, he insisted the Europeans treat him as they would a

European monarch. In his conduct and correspondence, he positioned himself as superior to those Asian despots that the European powers were toppling or co-opting across Asia. Second, he negotiated similar agreements with the other Western powers. The lessening of jealous tensions allowed the Western imperialists to benefit equally from the new and more open Siam. The treaty with Britain also freed Siam from China's historical claims of suzerainty over the kingdom. With Britain as its principal trading partner, Siam was no longer required to be subservient to the Qing court. Mongkut sent his final tribute mission to China around the same time that the Bowring Treaty came into effect.

The Bowring Treaty transformed Siam gradually. The court retained its system of internal taxation for the kingdom, continuing to rely on agents who were entrusted to collect a set amount of taxes to be paid to the appropriate government department while keeping all monies above that established amount. But with exports and imports affected by the new agreement, Siam's foreign trade culture changed, especially in the capital. Western traders and their agents built warehouses, wharves, shipyards, banks, insurance firms, and other enterprises in Bangkok's southern sections. The number of foreign trading vessels calling at Bangkok increased dramatically. With the arrival of more foreign sailors, traders, and officials came new ideas and technologies. Communication improved with the construction of a telegraph network. Siamese exports of agricultural products found new markets beyond Asia. Westerners pressed the Thais to build a new road in Bangkok that would link their consulates and commercial offices with the palaces. Thanon Charoen Krung ("Road that Makes the City Prosper") is still called "New Road" in English a century and a half after its creation. Over the years, it carried horse-drawn carriages, then rickshaws, then horse-pulled trams and electric trams, and then (in the next reign) automobiles. The changes around Bangkok's ports and legations also found their way into the Siamese interior as Mongkut imposed new taxes to make up for revenue lost under the Bowring Treaty.

While King Taksin and the first three Chakri monarchs had worked throughout their reigns to expand the Thai empire, Mongkut had to work to keep it from shrinking, or even disappearing. Mongkut had continuous reminders of his perilous position. The British use of the gunboat *Nemesis* and other powerful ships to subdue Qing China in the Opium Wars (1839–42, 1856–60) was a startling demonstration of Western military power for Asian rulers like Mongkut. Similarly, the French used warships to shell Saigon and other Vietnamese cities (1859–62) to grab territory there. Locally, Mongkut risked conflict with Britain while fighting in the Shan States not far from territory claimed by the British in the Second Anglo-Burmese War (1852–53). Even more dangerously, he nearly stumbled into a war with the British in Malaya when, upon the death of a sultan in the southern area over which the Siamese claimed suzerainty, the Siamese attempted to place their own candidate on the throne. The British sent gunboats that bombarded the city and drove out the Siamese-sponsored candidate. All-out war with Siam was averted, but the British home government, which supported the military action, made it clear that Siam's area of political influence was no longer as large as Mongkut had once imagined it to be.

Mongkut also nearly fell into conflict with the French. Like his older half-brother Rama III had done in the previous reign, Mongkut wanted to press Siam's claims over western Cambodia. The history-minded Mongkut was fascinated with the ruins of the old Khmer Empire around Angkor Wat. In 1859, he sent an army of 2,000 Thai soldiers to Cambodia's Siem Reap Province. Their mission was to dismantle one of the ancient stone temples there and bring it back to Siam so it could be rebuilt in Bangkok. Mongkut intended to demonstrate to his subjects and foreign visitors that the remains of the territory of the great Khmer empire belonged to Siam. Some sources say he wanted Angkor Wat itself, while others suggest he would have taken a smaller building. No matter the goal, the mission went badly. The Thai crew found Angkor Wat to be too large to dismantle and transport. Needing a substitute, they tried to take two towers from the gloriously tree-tangled ruins of Ta Prohm. When local people learned of the larcenous mission, they attacked the Siamese team, killing some of them. Mongkut got nothing from the expedition. As a consolation, he had a small model of Angkor Wat built at Wat Phra Kaeo, just over from the Temple of the Emerald Buddha. It remains there today, an intriguingly trompe l'oeil model that has become a favorite spot for tourist photos.

With the death of Cambodia's King Ang Duong in October 1860, King Norodom assumed the throne. To do so properly under the suzerainty principles that Siamese claimed over Cambodia, Norodom should have had Mongkut invest him with his title and regalia. Making the situation more poignant was the personal connection between Norodom and Mongkut. Norodom had been ordained as a monk at Bangkok's Wat Bowonniwet Vihara while Mongkut was the abbot. Norodom still recognized Siam's claims over Cambodia, but his close relationship with the French complicated matters. While Norodom was traveling to Bangkok to receive his royal accoutrements, the French took control of the Cambodian palace. Norodom rushed back to Cambodia to hammer out an accommodation with the French. Mongkut was incensed by the snub. The Siamese had fought a costly war just fifteen years earlier to prevent Cambodia from falling entirely under Vietnamese control. Norodom's actions toward the French looked like a betrayal, and Mongkut refused to release his regalia. The tussle over Norodom's ascension was only solved after drawn out and tense negotiations between Siam and France, but it came with a heavy cost for Mongkut. After years of diplomatic pressure by France's consul to Siam, Mongkut agreed to place Cambodia under joint French-Siamese supervision. It was a face-saving solution. In real terms, it marked a pronounced weakening of Siam's power in Cambodia. The French threat to Siam's independence came into focus during the negotiations. So clear was France's growing covetousness that Mongkut had begun to accept the idea that his kingdom would eventually fall to one European power or another. Mongkut favored the British, and he began to reach out to the British as possible protection against the French, even if it meant the loss of Siam's sovereignty.

Taken together, the actions in Cambodia and Malaya foreshadowed greater challenges that would befall Siam a generation later. The combination of French covetousness and gunboat diplomacy would deal Siam a devastating blow three decades later in the Lao territories. Siam's rulers would have to adapt to European ideas and technology to survive intact. During this phase of increasingly intense contact with the European colonial powers, Siam's rulers underwent dramatic changes in their understanding of what constituted a political realm. They began to see their kingdoms in terms similar to how the European powers understood the sovereignty of states and, increasingly, nations. Traditionally, the kingdoms of mainland Southeast

Asia had been borderless states. They did not define themselves with fixed boundaries illustrated on a map or globe. While established in Europe for hundreds of years, this concept did not make sense in the context of Southeast Asia. In the land-rich and manpower-poor realms of the region, it was neither important nor desirable to lay claim to vast expanses of territory. Nor did the Siamese understand treaties in terms of specific limitations on the extent of their power as defined by what Europeans were now calling national boundaries. Traditionally, Southeast Asian rulers had accepted expressions of loyalty and dependence from the weaker states that surrounded them. That is, they claimed groups of people in surrounding polities, but they did not conceive of them as falling within an imaginary boundary line that encircled them. These weaker polities would have acknowledged the supremacy of a stronger kingdom, but they did not necessarily accept its exclusive suzerainty. Instead, they may have offered tribute and loyalty to other strong states nearby simultaneously. This system of overlapping and interconnected circles of power spread out over the Southeast Asian landscape has been labeled "the Mandala System" by the Anglo-American historian Oliver Wolters. The Siamese did not have Western-style maps. Instead, they mapped territories in palm leaf manuscripts that contained stories, symbols, and pictures that described pilgrimage destinations and other religious sites within their realm. Their ignorance of Western-style geographic conventions left Bangkok's rulers vulnerable to British and French imperialists eager to press territorial claims.

New Spacial Knowledge

The Thai-American historian Thongchai Winichakul has illustrated and analyzed Siam's evolving notions of space and its geographic representations in his 1994 study, *Siam Mapped: A History of the Geo-Body of a Nation*. Thongchai's book was groundbreaking in its exploration of how this new spatial understanding was applied by Mongkut and his successors to create both a bounded nation with borders as well as the common characteristics and traditions to define the people within. To illustrate the newness of this knowledge, Thongchai includes an anecdote from the second quarter of the nineteenth century, the period of Rama III, in which Siam's rulers were first learning about Western maps and their representations of space. The Siamese king offered to show a group of English envoys a map of his territory and that of Burma. The map composed by one of his ministers was supposed to impress the visitors with Siam's brilliance in mapping and painting. The British envoy Frederick A. Neale described his group's efforts to conceal their laughter when the king brought out his so-called "map." It was an illustration that depicted what looked to the British like a demonic figure in a loincloth and crown holding a pitchfork in one hand and an orb in the other. The figure was made out of silver paper cut out and pressed against a red patch on the page. The strange figure was surrounded by ships. Above the kingly shape was a tiny black outline of a human form. The Siamese explained that this diminutive figure was Burma. The drawing was like no map these Englishmen had ever seen. The chart that the English viewed that day was really an illustration of Thai power that had been adapted from Buddhist cosmological schemes called the Traiphum, or "Three Worlds." Thais in this period were still representing political space in religious symbols. And it was in the period of Mongkut's reign and that of his successor Chulalongkorn that they were to learn how differently the British and other Western peoples thought about space.

Having signed these new treaties with the British, Siam now had to understand political realms as the British did. The British played a role in defining Siam's geo-body. The Siamese used British surveyors to mark out their territories. Among the earliest and most important was the study conducted by Europeans who surveyed Siam's presumed territory in the late nineteenth century. These treaties, maps, and surveys all played an essential early step in creating what would become the ingredients of Thai nationalism in the twentieth century.

Siam, while concerned about the territorial and commercial claims of the European colonial powers, approached these interactions with confidence and strength. Its leaders recognized the potential threats of interaction with the Western powers, but they also recognized its promises. Many in Siam embraced the scientific and technological advances coming out of Europe and the United States. Mongkut was one of them. He delighted in collecting Western scientific instruments and gadgets. They were a large part of the gifts that foreign diplomats gave to Siam during his reign, partly because he was always so eager to get his hands on the latest telescopes, microscopes, magic lanterns, or other optical devices being made in Europe.

It was his interest in science that led, almost directly, to his death. Astronomers concluded that a solar eclipse would be observable in Southeast Asia at some point midway through 1868. Mongkut greeted the news with great enthusiasm and set about predicting when and where it would become evident. Other members of Bangkok's foreign community and from around Asia likewise had their own predictions based on available calculations. So excited was he by the coming astronomical phenomenon, he wanted to observe the eclipse firsthand. He also wanted to stress to his court and kingdom the scientific explanation of the astronomical event rather than the superstitious explanations. He invited some court officials and royal family members, including some of his children, to view the event with him. The difficult part was that they would not be able to view the solar eclipse from Bangkok. They would have to travel south down the Malay peninsula to Hua Wan.

Mongkut led a large expedition to see the celestial event. The party included his eldest son and presumed heir apparent, Prince Chulalongkorn. They were joined by a party of European diplomats and other Westerners, including some astronomers in Siam at the time. On the fateful day, it was raining. But, by seemingly divine intervention, when it came time for the eclipse to appear, the rain stopped, the fog lifted, and the clouds finally dissipated: the eclipse showed itself. As it was reported robustly in Siam afterward, Mongkut's scientific acumen was demonstrated by his accurate calculations and successful eclipse viewing party. But he also paid a terrible price for his triumph. While encamped in the southern jungles, Mongkut and Chulalongkorn contracted what was called "jungle fever," probably malaria. Both returned to Bangkok so sick that they were not expected to recover. Mongkut never did. The illness took him on October 1, 1868.

The Enigma of Anna

Today, if people in the West know anything about King Mongkut, it is usually because of Anna Leonowens. The two memoirs she wrote about her time as a tutor to Mongkut's children in Siam in the 1860s became the basis for not only the Western view of Mongkut but many lingering misperceptions about premodern Siam as well. Leonowens' memoirs, *The English Governess at the Siamese Court* (1870) and *Romance of the Harem* (1874), were bestsellers in the United Kingdom, the United States, and Canada for many years. The memory of Leonowens' account faded somewhat in the early part of the twentieth century. But in 1942, an American named Margaret Landon came across the volumes while living in Siam. Landon, along with her husband Kenneth, was in Siam to work as a Presbyterian missionary. Fascinated by the memoirs, Landon rewrote the tales into a kind of romanticized novel. She published it under the title *Anna and the King of Siam* in 1944. Landon's volume was a huge and immediate success. In 1951, Richard Rodgers and Oscar Hammerstein II transformed the story into a Tony-award winning Broadway musical, *The King & I*. The 1956 film version of the musical brought Yul Brynner an Oscar for his energetic portrayal of a fiery and stubborn King Mongkut who is ultimately tamed by the English governess' charms and logic. Leonowens' story would be an inspiring example of cross-cultural communication and friendship except for one thing: the account was full of lies, inaccuracies, and misunderstandings. And because of that, Thailand's people still have not forgiven Leonowens for what they see as her betrayal of Mongkut.

Anna Leonowens was a figure as complex as Mongkut himself. The details of her life are as incredible as anything a writer's imagination could conjure. She was not, as she described herself in her writings, an Anglo-Welsh woman who had come to Asia as the wife of a British army officer serving in India. She was, in fact, an Anglo-Indian, a person of mixed Indian and European parentage, who had been born in India. Her father was a non-commissioned officer and her mother an Anglo-Indian woman. She grew up among the British colonial barracks of western India. She was married young to an English civilian clerk in the British colonial service. He brought Leonowens and their two surviving children to various towns in Asia and Australia as he searched for work. When he died prematurely on the island of Penang in British Malaya, Anna was left to fend for herself and her children. Although not shunned, she was not fully embraced by the British expatriate community of Singapore because she was mixed-race. Somewhere along the way, Leonowens realized that her fortunes, and those of her children, would improve if she could pass herself off as an English gentlewoman who had fallen on hard times. She took various teaching jobs in Singapore before being hired by Mongkut's representatives to tutor the king's children in 1862. The Siamese officials had likely selected Leonowens precisely for the same reasons that the British expatriate community could not fully embrace her. She was bright, independent, and open-minded when such qualities were not valued in women. And unlike many Europeans in Asia at the time, she did not possess the missionary's impulse to convert the indigenous people to Christianity. If anything, her childhood in India most likely left her with an appreciation for numerous belief systems. Mongkut had initially hired the wives of a few American missionaries to teach the women of his court. But their inclusion of Christian proselytizing tracts had discouraged him from continuing their employment. Leonowens seemed a safer alternative.

Leonowens had a successful, albeit turbulent, tenure as royal tutor. She gave Mongkut's children, including Prince Chulalongkorn, a British-style secular education that included Western sciences and mathematics. She also served as Mongkut's English language advisor, a position of considerable status at the time. In this capacity, she apparently vexed the Siamese ruler with her opinions and spiritedness. Mongkut's only recorded comment about Leonowens describes her as "particularly difficult" in that day's diary entry. As in Singapore, she was not embraced by the expatriate community of Siam. But serving the ruler of an independent Buddhist kingdom, Leonowens was not reliant on that social sphere. She lived outside the palace walls and developed a circle of friends from both the Siamese court and the more open-minded Western expatriates. She was abroad when Mongkut died in 1868. The young Chulalongkorn, still gravely ill himself and under the control of a regent, did not rehire her.

While living in North America, Leonowens published two accounts of her time in Siam, both to high acclaim. Her descriptions of Mongkut and Siam have been transmitted and magnified to Western audiences by Landon's novel, the Broadway musical, an American cartoon, a weekly situation comedy, and various other cinematic adaptations. Leonowens' view of Mongkut's court has become the most famous portrait of nineteenth-century Siam. Although her insider status would have provided her with an almost unparalleled view into the world of Siam's inner palace, her books, and Leonowens herself, have been tainted by the inclusion of inaccurate details and outright lies. In them, Leonowens portrays Mongkut as intelligent, but she stresses his volatile temper as his main characteristic. She seems to overstate her role as a reformer by suggesting she was the civilizer of an Oriental despot and the cool-headed counselor to a hot-headed man. She claims credit for the introduction of many of the progressive changes Mongkut and Chulalongkorn made during their reigns. But it was her description of Mongkut's relationships with the women of his harem that was the most damning to the king's reputation.

Leonowens' portrays Mongkut as something akin to a sadistic slaveholder who presides over 9,000 captive women. She suggests that he enjoyed torturing them and that he even had some publicly executed for minor offenses. The earliest Western historians working in Siam doubted the veracity of Leonowens' account. They pointed to the form of execution – death by fire – that Leonowens claims to have witnessed as her most obvious inaccuracy. Burning at the stake was not a form of execution used by the Siamese. Nor is there any other existing account describing such public executions. Mongkut's twenty years as a Buddhist monk left him with a reverence for life that is at odds with Leonowens' depiction. She describes Mongkut as having disobedient concubines cast into a subterranean dungeon when such an architectural engineering feat as a basement would have been impossible in Bangkok's high-water table. Likewise, she describes Mongkut sacrilizing a new gate by having a man butchered and dumped into the hole dug for the first gatepost. Such practices did exist in a much earlier era, and would have been talked about while Leonowens was there, but Mongkut certainly did not indulge in human sacrifice. Modern scholars have identified the sources of many of Leonowens' fanciful claims, most of them stories from previous reigns, contemporary novels, silly songs composed by expatriates, or news items from other Asian kingdoms that she appropriated for her book. Although most of Leonowens' questionable assertions have been debunked by scholars such as Abbot Low Moffat and others. One biographer, the American literary scholar Susan Morgan, defends Leonowens' account by arguing that the governess was describing the "emotional truth" of court life for the concubines rather than the literal one. The historian Tamara Loos has studied the palace laws governing the conduct of women like those given to King Mongkut as part of a more extensive system designed to maintain political hierarchies among Siam's elite. She provides a far more complex and compelling analysis of the definitions of sexual transgressions based on gender, family connections, and social rank than that described in overly romantic terms by Leonowens. Loos' research provides an important historical and cultural context, and a corrective one, to the many outlandish myths generated by *The King and I* phenomenon.

How should history remember Anna Leonowens? As a fraud and a liar? As a tough and resourceful survivor who created a new identity in order to care for her family during a misogynistic age? As a creative genius whose work has touched the hearts of millions worldwide? No matter what one might think of Leonowens, her toughness and accomplishments are probably equal to the multifaceted Siamese king whom she served.

Staving off Colonization

One of the most common questions asked about Thailand is: why was Thailand the sole Southeast Asian country that avoided being colonized by a Western power? There is no one answer. Some say that the collection of good leaders during this age – Mongkut and his son Chulalongkorn, as well as the princes and officials upon whom they relied – had enough savvy and talent to stave off European colonial demands. They devised strategies that combined rapid modernization and the adoption of Western civilization makers that kept the European powers at bay. This explanation gives credit to Thai abilities. The other answer is that the Europeans themselves wanted Siam to remain uncolonized to serve as a buffer between the British colonies of Malaya and Burma with those of the French colonies of Laos and Cambodia. At a time when European nations had launched destructive wars against each other, these powers saw the dangers that might erupt if they were to collide in their Asian colonies. The third explanation is strange but intriguing. Some Western scholars contend that Siam was colonized, but not by a Western imperial power. They argue, persuasively, that Siam colonized itself. They claim that Bangkok styled itself after a European imperial power – Great Britain is the most likely model – and set about colonizing the autonomous and independent polities over which Bangkok had long claimed suzerainty. The process they call self-colonization or crypto-colonization unfolded during the reign of Mongkut's successor, the boy prince who survived that grave illness: King Chulalongkorn the Great.

CHAPTER 3

KING CHULALONGKORN: CIVILIZATION AND THE MODERNIZATION OF SIAM

Many Thai books about King Chulalongkorn (r. 1868–1910) border on hagiography. The enduring reverence they indicate has colored popular perceptions of the Siamese king, even in Western histories. Today, some Thai people worship Chulalongkorn as a demigod who bestows magical blessings on his devotees. The sources for this devotion are the remarkable accomplishments of his long and eventful reign. In four significant areas, he transformed Siam into a nation-state that was strong and "modern" at a time when it was under threat from Western colonialism. He updated the Siamese government's bureaucratic and administrative systems to make them more effective in addressing the era's challenges. His policies improved the education, training, and professionalism of the kingdom's leaders, especially his princely brothers, who came to dominate control of the most powerful ministries. These far-sighted princes, many of them educated in Europe, understood Western attitudes far more keenly than the previous Siamese generation. In making a nation from a collection of kingdoms, Chulalongkorn improved the communication and logistical networks throughout Siam by importing Western technology and hiring foreign engineers to guide the construction of roads, ports, and railways. He oversaw an improvement in the Siamese armed forces, laying the foundation for a strong army and navy. But while Chulalongkorn did a lot that can be considered positive for Siam, it is a mischaracterization to portray him as superhuman. Instead, we can more accurately see him as a resourceful monarch who used his wits to maintain his throne while protecting his kingdom's independence. His endurance in the face of adversity guaranteed Siam's survival in the most dangerous age of Western colonial expansion in Southeast Asia.

A Cultlike Status

Chulalongkorn is unique among Chakri kings for the almost cultlike status he enjoys among the Thai people today. The anthropologist Irene Stengs has researched this phenomenon. Her study of Rama V's deification, *Worshipping the Great Moderniser: King Chulalongkorn, Patron Saint of the Thai Middle Class*, describes the hold that his life story has on the imagination of many Thai people. Wherever you go throughout Thailand, you will see Chulalongkorn's image adorning homes, businesses, offices, schools, taxis, and shrines. He is instantly recognizable as a heavyset king with a kindly face and a prominent mustache. His admirers believe he possessed extraordinary Buddhist merit. They assert that Chulalongkorn continues to protect Thailand from peril. The geographical center of their cultlike worship is Bangkok's Royal Plaza, where devoted crowds gather to pay their respects at a statue of King Chulalongkorn astride a horse. Chulalongkorn himself rarely traveled anywhere on horseback, but he was said to have admired the equestrian statue of Louis XIV while in France. The lack of historical accuracy does not deter his admirers. They believe that the king's spirit descends from the heavens at 10:00 pm on Tuesdays to inhabit the statue. His devotees offer garlands, incense, sweets, liquor, and other gifts. Some buy dried grass for his horse. They bring portraits, medallions, coins, and charms bearing his likeness to be blessed by the *barami* (karmic power) emanating from the statue. As with this celebrated landmark, he is rendered as nearly godlike in the images of devotion created of him. His portrait hangs in glitzy boutiques and open-air markets. You will find Chulalongkorn's face inside amulets dangling from necklaces and as a colorful sticker affixed to a speedy motorcycle zipping along Bangkok's boulevards and upon the cover of more books than almost anyone in any Thai bookstore. Chulalongkorn's power to safeguard Siam's independence in the nineteenth century extends in death to protecting Thailand's citizens in the twenty-first century.

An Interim Regent

While the source of Chulalongkorn's historical reputation is his resistance to Western imperialism, it was the Western community in Bangkok that played a critical role in his ascension. Likewise, the fragile state of his health shaped the character of his early reign. Chulalongkorn was still quite sick when he was named king. The fifteen-year-old prince was weakened by the agonies of the illness that he and King Mongkut had contracted while in Siam's south to view a solar eclipse. While the two of them lay gravely ill, a royal council met to discuss succession. Historically, these royal succession councils consisted of high-ranking royalty, powerful nobles, and Buddhist monks. If the king had not explicitly named an heir, the royal council would convene to select the best candidate for the throne. Because Chulalongkorn's condition was still precarious, Mongkut did not push to have his son named as his successor. But he did say that if Chulalongkorn was chosen, he wanted Sisuriyawong, a trusted court official from the Bunnag family, to act as regent until the boy was old enough to fully assume the throne. As with the debates surrounding the selection of Rama III a generation earlier, the Siamese did not accept male primogeniture as the sole factor in choosing a successor. The succession council did not necessarily elevate the eldest son born to a full queen to become the new king. There was not a formal crown prince like those found in European royal courts. But a lot changed from the time of Rama II and Rama III. Owing to the Western influence that had grown during Mongkut's reign, there was a strong expectation among the expatriate community in Bangkok that Chulalongkorn, as eldest son, would become king. Mongkut signaled as much by training him for future leadership and by hiring Western tutors for him. In 1868, Sisuriyawong made the case for Chulalongkorn's selection by suggesting that the council had no choice. He pointed out that the increasingly powerful Western diplomatic presence had assumed that Prince Chulalongkorn would be next. To deviate from such expectations would make the next king appear less legitimate in Western eyes. A seemingly illegitimate king would have made Siam look weak and unstable. Sisuriyawong also had to counter rumors that he, a nobleman, was planning to seize the throne for himself. He made the council recognize that Chulalongkorn was the best option for Siam and himself.

Sisuriyawong's management of the transition generated risks for the new king. The first was that Chulalongkorn was at the mercy of an older, better-connected regent who could limit his power by promoting people and policies that were to his benefit and not to those of the young monarch as he convalesced from his illness. The other problem was that the new *uparat*, Prince Wichaichan, was older than Chulalongkorn, an odd circumstance considering that the *uparat* often became king following the reigning monarch's death. Adding danger to the unusual arrangement was that Wichaichan might have had monarchical ambitions. He had cultivated independent contacts among the British and French in Bangkok. He commanded an army that was larger than that under the control of Chulalongkorn. The two figures entrusted with helping the young king, the regent and the *uparat*, seemed dedicated to limiting his power and making him insecure. But just as Mongkut had waited out the danger of his youth by becoming a monk and traveling, Chulalongkorn found a way to keep himself safe while waiting to assume power. He recovered from his illness, then bided his time before coronation by traveling, observing, and learning.

Models for Modernity

Chulalongkorn went abroad as a young king. He visited India, Singapore, Malaya, Burma, the Dutch East Indies, and other colonized areas of South and Southeast Asia on several trips. He went abroad to learn modern governmental and administrative practices, but he viewed them through a Western colonial lens. He saw firsthand the intricate apparatuses that the British and Dutch had built to maintain their colonies, how these Western powers manipulated displaced local rulers to their advantage. He also learned how local rulers had adapted themselves to accommodate, and sometimes push back against, the Western imperialists. These trips turned out to be a significant part of his education and played an essential role in the development of Siam as a nation. As the political scientist Benedict Anderson has pointed out, when Chulalongkorn eventually came into his own and began building what he saw as the modern nation of Siam, his model was not France, Britain, the Netherlands, or any other European country but, rather, the colonies of these European powers. He would draft policies and create institutions that would make Siam look more like its colonized counterparts in Asia than the European powers that controlled them. In other words, the institutions Chulalongkorn created may have been better suited for a colonized country than for an independent nation. But the models he imitated were relevant. In building a nation, Chulalongkorn would have to gain control of outlying city-states and principalities that had never belonged to Siam. He would have to send out his officials, his representatives, and, eventually, his soldiers, to assert Siam's sovereignty over these areas.

Wide-ranging Reforms

When he returned from his tours abroad, he went into a *wat* to carry out a short stint as a monk. Upon returning to secular life, he began a series of wide-ranging reforms that better protected himself from usurpers and transformed Siam along the lines of the Western colonial states. In 1874, he turned twenty and gained full status as king. Though still young and vulnerable, Chulalongkorn acted to strengthen his control over the kingdom by reforming the Siamese government's vital elements. In May of that year, he created two governmental bodies designed to give him more control over Siam's resources and administration: a State Council and a Privy Council into which he drew younger and more loyal supporters than those who had come to dominate senior positions in the court. He hoped that this new group would help him stand up to the old guard that controlled state matters during his minority. The State Council's principal mission was assisting him in overhauling two critical areas, taxation and human labor. The State Council helped Chulalongkorn draft new laws and assess existing systems more in line with the ones he had learned about while traveling abroad. With these changes, he began marshaling his power and initiating the process by which he would transform the Siamese court into something more like a modern Western government. All the changes they made removed power, money, and labor from the control of various princes, lords, and nobles who diluted Chulalongkorn's authority. Chulalongkorn and his council placed that power and wealth more squarely under the control of the monarch as the unrivaled center of the kingdom.

The first area he concentrated on was taxation. The reproductive habits of Siam's royal family created serious financial problems for the court. Princes had multiple consorts with whom they produced many children, sometimes dozens. As the Siamese royal families grew exponentially, the princes required ever more income to maintain their households. In Chulalongkorn's time, this need for revenue amongst royals became especially acute. He worked to overhaul the system by which money was collected and distributed to give more control to the palace or, rather, to himself in this process. The other important, and related, matter that Chulalongkorn and his State Council addressed was slavery. At the time of Chulalongkorn's crowning, about one-third of Siam's population was a slave of some kind, including war slaves, debt slaves, and those families born to slavery. These slaves were a source of wealth for Siam's elites. Freeing Siam's slaves overnight would have proven socially explosive and economically ruinous for those who wielded power in the kingdom. Chulalongkorn would have made enemies of the many powerful men whose wealth and power relied on slave labor, including those in the court around him. But Chulalongkorn was resolute in his determination to end it. Moving carefully to avoid potential conflicts, he instead began a process by which he would end slavery gradually. In 1874, Chulalongkorn issued a decree making it easier for debt slaves to buy their freedom. Other policy changes regulating labor followed in the decades to come. It would be thirty years before the Siamese court fully abolished slavery in all forms, a long time for those who suffered the agonies and indignities of labor bondage. As Chulalongkorn's admirers often point out, this pace of abolition did not spark bloody conflict like that which roiled the United States and Russia in this age. Some authors erroneously credit Anna Leonowens's influence on Chulalongkorn for his decision to end slavery. Such a connection has not been established. But if such influence was there, it did not extend to the institution of the royal harem. Chulalongkorn maintained the system of polygyny common to Siamese rulers, an arrangement of which Leonowens was highly critical. Chulalongkorn had 91 wives of whom 52 bore his 77 children.

Chulalongkorn's other reforms from this period were equally revolutionary. He traveled to the countryside, sometimes incognito, to examine the conditions of rural people firsthand. Some of the changes he made directly affected his relationship with his subjects. He ended the custom of having all subjects prostrate themselves before him, although most still did. He allowed his image to be used on currency, stamps, and later, postcards. He ended the prohibition of commoners touching members of the royal family. The inspiration for this reform came about from tragic circumstances. On May 31, 1880, while traveling up the Chao Phraya River to the so-called "Summer Palace," Bang Pa-in in Ayutthaya, Chulalongkorn's first queen and her daughter fell from a capsized royal vessel into the river. Courtiers and other onlookers stood by helplessly as Queen Sunanda Kumariratana and her child drowned before them. Compounding the loss, Queen Sunanda was pregnant at the time. Heartbroken by the tragedy, Chulalongkorn had a funerary memorial to Queen Sunanda built on the grounds of Bang Pa-in Royal Palace. To prevent another such loss, he lifted the ban on commoners touching royalty. But such taboos are slow to die. Many Thai commoners still fear physical contact with royalty. Memoirs written by foreigners in the twentieth century include many examples of Thai people shrinking in terror to avoid contact with a member of the royal family. The drowned queen has a devoted following in death. Today, Thai people venerate the spirits of Queen Sunanda, her daughter, and her unborn child at the Bang Pa-in memorial and its vicinity.

Chulalongkorn recognized that Siam's military forces would be no match for the armies and navies of the Western powers' colonial forces. To begin the process of improving his fighting forces, Chulalongkorn established new administrative structures governing the troops under his command. He made them more financially secure and better educated. On top of more up-to-date military training methods, the troops studied modern governmental administration so that they could also serve in the court's various departments. His military modernization started with the troops closest to him. Chulalongkorn may have had the West on his mind when he made military reforms, but he recognized that the *farang* imperialists were not necessarily his most immediate danger.

Internal Threats

The most alarming threat to his power, and his life, came during an incident known as the Front Palace Crisis of 1874. Over the previous few years, some of Chulalongkorn's more youthful and progressive advisors in the Privy Council had begun to agitate for change, among these a reconsideration of the selection of Prince Wichaichan as *uparat*. With Chulalongkorn healthy and more mature, these advisors thought it important, and safer, for him to choose his own front palace king, or perhaps even to eliminate the position. As rumors about an impending change swirled about court circles, Wichaichan continued to arm and train his troops. Disconcertingly for Chulalongkorn, Wichaichan gave his soldiers better firearms, including British-manufactured field guns, than those used by the king's troops. His acquisition of a large and sophisticated arsenal appeared provocative. Was he threatening Chulalongkorn to scare him into keeping him on as heir presumptive? Was he planning a palace coup d'état? The two seemed headed for a showdown when an event occurred that transformed the simmering court intrigue into an international incident.

Late at night on December 28–29, fire erupted in the Grand Palace's gasworks, threatening to trigger a great explosion at the royal armory and gunpowder storage buildings nearby. The late-night fire was suspicious. Historians have long suspected that it was intentionally set as part of a plot to overthrow Chulalongkorn while he remained weak and uncertain. No matter the cause, the danger posed by such a blaze was real and immediate as an explosion could have killed many in the palace. As the fire blazed, all available men of the court except those from Wichaichan's army rushed to the site of the fire and worked to extinguish it. As the ad hoc fire brigades were bringing the flames under control, Wichaichan turned up at the palace gates accompanied by his troops. He demanded that he and his forces be let inside, ostensibly to help put out the fire. Sensing trouble, Chulalongkorn's men refused to unlock the gates to admit them. As the argument intensified and tempers flared, both sides rushed more men to the scene. Chulalongkorn rallied thousands of troops to his side. They bottled up Wichaichan and many of his soldiers in the Front Palace. To some, the argument looked like it had the potential to launch not only a coup but perhaps even something akin to a civil war between the factions' armies.

In the chaotic events that unfolded that night and into the next day, Chulalongkorn showed his resolve. He demanded that Wichaichan order his troops to stand down and then surrender. The former regent, Sisuriyawong, attempted to broker a compromise. But so great was the suspicion on both sides that the negotiations failed to resolve the impasse. In desperation, Wichaichan escaped from his besieged palace and, claiming persecution, begged the British Consulate to protect him. He asked for British help in getting him restored as second king and having his palace returned to him. Chulalongkorn refused to enter into such a deal because it would undermine his sovereignty. In the midst of the month-long standoff and negotiations, both the British and the French sent warships into Bangkok's harbors. The British eventually rejected Prince Wichaichan's pleas for help and, under instructions from their home government, reiterated their support for Chulalongkorn as the sole legitimate monarch of Siam. The king allowed Prince Wichaichan to return to his palace, but prevented him from reconstituting his private army. Chulalongkorn had survived this early threat to his power and emerged looking stronger.

The short-term results of this fight can be understood in somewhat contradictory terms. On the one hand, Chulalongkorn had demonstrated that he could stand up to a strong and ambitious rival and remain intact and secure. Ultimately, his kingship won the support of the foreign powers Britain and France that could have easily exploited any potential weakness to press their demands. On the other hand, the old guard within the court blamed Chulalongkorn's young reformers for the upheaval, accusing them of destabilizing Siam by provoking Wichaichan into a match of political brinkmanship. The court elders forced Chulalongkorn to back down from some of his more radical financial and judicial reforms. The retreat delayed for the time being the modernization of Siam's administration that he sought. The court's conservative members pressed Chulalongkorn to return to a royal balance of power among nobles and princes similar to that which was maintained during the reign of his father. Chulalongkorn acquiesced to some of the requests. But that did not stop him from reforming other areas of the Siamese state.

Modernization Continues

In the late 1870s, Chulalongkorn reformed the armed forces. At the time, most Thai soldiers belonged to the various regional lords who had traditionally contributed men to the center's military campaigns. Chulalongkorn aimed to develop his own armed forces, those that protected the king and the palace, into something like a modern national army that could defend Siam from foreign powers while asserting Bangkok's sovereignty in the former vassal states. To attract better soldiers, the king's military commander came up with an enticing arrangement. In return for five years of military service, the recruits received good pay, training, and, most importantly, exemption from the mandatory tattooing that obliged most commoners to provide corvée labor to the government, a nobleman, or a local lord. Although corvée labor obligations had shrunk from six months to one month for most commoners over the previous two decades, the mandatory labor remained an onerous burden for most subjects. The military service scheme was popular. The new army attracted many thousands of young men who preferred service as soldiers in the king's forces to a lifetime of labor obligation for a regional lord. As manpower flowed away from the provinces and into the capital, powerful regional lords resisted Chulalongkorn's drive. Some actively worked to undermine his effort by encouraging men to desert. Ultimately, Chulalongkorn worked out an agreement with the local lords most affected by the scheme. But the new force was still a far cry from the modern army he sought, and weaker than those assembled by the Western powers in Asia. Chulalongkorn's lack of a single, unified army at his disposal and under his command had its consequences in the coming decades. It may have cost him a large piece of his kingdom.

While the old guard at court felt threatened by Chulalongkorn's efforts at reform, some young officials expressed fear that Chulalongkorn was moving too slowly. They wanted Siam to modernize more quickly so that no Western power could cite Siam's antiquated governmental systems as grounds for seizing the "uncivilized" kingdom as a colony. To demonstrate its civilized status, Siam would need political systems similar to those of the Western powers, while also demonstrating advancements in technology, military power, and education. As Chulalongkorn faced calls for reform from within, he brought a small crisis upon himself. In 1885, he asked Prince Prisdang, Siam's minister to Paris, for ideas about how to keep the Western powers from claiming Siam as a colony. Prisdang organized a group of princes and nobles posted to Europe to draft a reform program that they then presented to Chulalongkorn. They recommended that Siam become a constitutional monarchy like Great Britain, and they wanted Chulalongkorn to name an heir as the British monarch did. They proposed a cabinet of ministers chosen for their abilities, not for their families, who would control departments like those found in most European governments. They wanted military reforms that would use conscription to constitute a national army and a navy. To make such a system work, they proposed Siam grant the right to vote to all subjects within the kingdom. Furthermore, they recommended an assortment of civil liberties that would encourage public participation in governmental matters. The group believed that without such reforms, Siam would be vulnerable to subjugation by a Western power.

Chulalongkorn reacted negatively to the suggestions. While he had earlier encouraged calls for reform, the proposals put forward by the European-based princes rattled him. They threatened his power too directly. He felt betrayed by these European-based diplomat princes, who seemed to be threatening him in the guise of protecting him. Previous kings may have dealt with such a challenge to the monarch's authority with harsh reprisals, but Chulalongkorn was measured in his response. He acknowledged that the group was sincere in their desire to improve the kingdom, but signaled his displeasure by recalling the prince who led the effort. Siam would not be a constitutional monarchy, Chulalongkorn made clear, and its reforms would come from the king. Pressured from within, Chulalongkorn used the ostensible threat to his authority to make the changes he wanted. With the death of Prince Wichaichan, he abolished the position of *uparat*. In its place, he would have an heir. He hoped the move would lessen the manipulation that the Bunnags and other powerful families had exercised over succession. Then he went after other long-standing prerogatives of the noble families.

Chulalongkorn turned to his younger brothers and half-brothers as his allies against the network of powerful aristocratic families who had formerly dominated much of the administration. He gave them control over a set of newly created departments that would act more like government entities in the West while easing out the nobles who dominated the old positions. He put the young princes in charge of the Departments of Education, Justice, Public Works, and the Privy Seal. The most consequential was the Department of the Military. He created professional schools for commissioned and non-commissioned officers. He oversaw the creation of a code of military justice similar to those of the Western powers. He made the acquisition of modern weapons a priority, and bought some of the best German rifles of the day.

By 1892, Chulalongkorn took the next step toward modernization by creating a cabinet of ministers similar to the one that the reformist officials had suggested seven years earlier. He transformed the surviving *krom* of the old system into modern ministries with a cabinet minister in charge of each. He established Ministries of Agriculture, of the Interior, of the Palace, of Justice, of the Capital, and others. As he had done with the departments created a few years earlier, Chulalongkorn appointed his princely brothers to run nearly all of them. He gave the remaining ministries to noblemen he trusted. The arrangement ensured that Chulalongkorn had ministers who were more loyal than the officials who had run Siam a generation earlier. But assigning ministers based on blood ties and loyalty had consequences. Most of the new ministers lacked administrative experience. Predictably for siblings, they also squabbled among themselves to a greater degree than had the aristocratic families they replaced. Chulalongkorn may now have been safer from internal resistance, but he had put his kingdom into the collective hands of a cabinet of green ministers who were often fractious and dysfunctional. It turned out to be a terrible time for such disunity at the top.

"Loss" of Laos

Many Thai people today talk bitterly about how Thailand used to "own" Laos in the period before the colonial era. They will point out that the loss of Laos to France through gunboat diplomacy deprived modern Thailand of much of its rightful territory. They argue that France's greed denied Thailand from becoming the far larger and more powerful super-state it should have become. The diminished state they ended up with from the early twentieth century onward is little more than half of what they should have claimed as their nation. Like a lot of historical myths, this characterization has its roots in genuine historical episodes. But it is also necessary to point out that it is built on faulty understandings of sovereignty and administration in the premodern era. First, there has never been a single Laos. The name Laos is itself a strange and mysterious creation. It is a plural designator created by Europeans to signify on maps the many kingdoms of ethnic Lao people found in what are now northern Thailand, Laos, and western Vietnam. Moreover, Siam never truly ruled any of these Lao kingdoms in the way that, say, England's London-based parliament has ruled Scotland within the United Kingdom after the 1707 Treaty of Union. The Siamese courts at Ayutthaya and Bangkok had long claimed suzerainty over the many kingdoms of the Lao people on both sides of the Mekong River. The Siamese extracted tribute, labor, and loyalty statements from the various Lao polities in exchange for recognition, stability, and peace. Usually, this relationship was cooperative and harmonious. The Lao sent upland forest products down to lowland Siam for trade onward to the rest of Asia. Bangkok requested their labor for public works projects and war. But, on occasion, there were fights.

In 1826–27, Chao Anouvong, the king of Vientiane (r. 1805–28), joined with his son, the ruler of Champasak, to rebel against Bangkok. Over the years, Anouvong had become disaffected with his previously solid relationship with Bangkok. One reason might have been his own ambitions in restoring a specifically Lao circle of interdependent states, a Lao mandala, free of Bangkok's meddling. He might have been interested in sewing together the culturally similar Lao states of Luang Prabang, Champassak, and even Chiang Mai, which despite being considered an integral part of Thailand today was historically more like the Lao kingdoms around it than it was like Ayutthaya or Bangkok. He was also dissatisfied with Bangkok's increasingly imperious ways. He resented Rama I's demands that all subjects of his empire be tattooed for labor management purposes. During the first and second Chakri reigns, the area of tattooing had expanded beyond the traditional Thai domains to include ever more Lao-speaking peoples. He also wanted the Emerald Buddha returned to Vientiane. Anouvong may have also been insulted by the shabby treatment he and his family received when they came to Bangkok to attend the funeral of Rama II. No matter the reasons, Anouvong not only rebelled against Bangkok, he gave his best effort to destroy it.

In early 1827, Chao Anouvong put his armies into territory that Bangkok saw as its sphere of influence. He crushed some of Siam's vassal states in what is now northeastern Thailand, capturing the population as war prizes to be resettled around Vientiane. His armies got as far as Korat before Bangkok was able to halt their advance. After bloody battles in the lower Khorat Plateau, Rama III's forces gained the upper hand on the rebellious Lao. With his armies in disarray, Anouvong fled to Vietnam. When he returned to Laos with a small force he had put together in exile, Bangkok's armies rushed out and captured him. They hauled him to Bangkok as a war prisoner. The Thais put the former Vientiane king on public display in a cage, his torment and degradation a warning to would-be rebellious tributary rulers entertaining thoughts of challenging Bangkok's hegemony. After a few days of terrible suffering, Anouvong died. The Thais displayed his corpse from chains beside the Chao Phraya River. Over the next few decades, Bangkok maintained suzerainty over the Lao kingdoms without exercising direct control over their affairs.

In the mid-nineteenth century, French imperialists in Southeast Asia recognized that only loose strands held these Lao states to Bangkok's center, and they searched for means to delegitimize Siam's claims over them. Although the Lao kingdoms themselves did not seem to possess great material wealth, they stood in the way of French ambitions in China. The French, especially after securing control of the bulk of Cambodia from Siam in 1867, had dreamed of finding a back door into southwestern China. French colonial adventurers craved access to the imagined riches that such direct trade might yield. If they could claim Laos, they would have a river route into China's Yunnan Province via the Mekong, and from there they could trade with China's densely populated Sichuan Province.

The French tried various methods to gain the Lao territories. From the moment they claimed protectorship over the northern two-thirds of Vietnam, they scoured Vietnamese court documents for past historical claims by Vietnamese lords over some of these territories to their west. They found a few such claims, but they were thin and mostly wishful thinking on the part of the Vietnamese rulers who had declared them. The French sent several expeditions into these Lao territories to search for a navigable river or overland route into southwest China. Henri Mouhot led several expeditions in the 1850s and early 1860s. The Lagrée-Garnier and Aymonier missions also searched for this route in the 1860s. The reports and correspondence generated by the French explorers contain anti-Siamese rhetoric indicative of their frustration with the Siamese claims to the Lao states. The French would write to their home government and to readers in weekly magazines about the Lao people's alleged desire to free themselves from the "Siamese yoke." This was more French fabrication than reality. It was propaganda meant to inspire the French back in the metropole to support wresting these lands from Siam. The French who worked to displace Siam needed the right incident that would deliver the Lao states to them. When those incidents did not materialize quickly enough, they provoked them.

From the mid-1860s onward, northern areas of Laos had fallen victim to Chinese bandits known as the Ho (pronounced "Haw"). The nucleus of these Ho bandits were soldiers and refugees from the Taiping Rebellion that had ended in 1864. As they roamed about northern Laos, these former soldiers sacked towns and villages in search of plunder. They often targeted the conical-shaped *chedi* (stupas) within the grounds of Buddhist temple complexes because they usually contained gold objects and gemstones along with the bones and other relics they honored. The French representatives in Cambodia, Vietnam, and Siam seized on these reports of theft and destruction. They repeatedly criticized Siam for not doing enough to maintain law and order in these Lao states. In response, the Siamese sent their best troops north in 1885 to confront the battle-hardened Ho. Chulalongkorn's army and its modern weapons proved capable of asserting Siamese authority over lands terrorized by the Ho. After a couple of setbacks, the Siamese forced some of the Chinese bandits out of the towns they claimed, while other Ho leaders negotiated truces.

The French sought to maximize any incident that might give them the opportunity to claim the Lao states. In 1887, Auguste Pavie, one of the French colonial functionaries who had been heavily involved in the French takeover of Cambodia, was serving as France's vice-consul to the Lao kingdom of Luang Prabang when word of an imminent attack by a surviving army of Chinese bandits reached the city. The Siamese military official in charge of protecting Luang Prabang dismissed the threat as unsubstantiated and left the city for official duties in Bangkok. When the Chinese bandits did attack, Pavie and his men swooped in to rescue the king of Luang Prabang and his Siamese government advisor and escorted them to safety in Siamese territory. Upon returning to Bangkok, Pavie criticized the lax control of Siamese troops over Luang Prabang and spoke contemptuously of Siamese claims of suzerainty over all of Laos. Pavie made it clear to all who would listen, both in French Indochina and back in Paris, that Siam would never be able to hold on to Laos in a military contest.

Pavie led an expedition that annexed the Tai *mueang* areas to the west of the Black and Red rivers in what is now northern Vietnam. In extending the frontier of Vietnam further west, he put ethnic Tai lands and the peoples who had occupied them for centuries into Vietnam, where they remain to this day. From there, he acted to extend French protectorship further west across central Laos. Later, in 1890, he led a scientific mission into Laos that dispatched scores of French colonial officials, including scientists, soldiers, explorers, and various functionaries, throughout Laos. Officially, the goal was to gather scientific information about the territories of northern Indochina. But to the Siamese, it appeared to be another effort to claim more territory for France.

The Siamese were concerned by the presence of the French. They sent government officials and troop reinforcements into towns along the Mekong River in what is now Nong Khai and Ubon Ratchathani in Thailand, and Champasak in Laos. The move outraged the French. The French minister to Bangkok protested the additional Siamese troops and officials as an illegal act and a provocation. The tension between Siam and France heightened with each passing month. In late 1892, the standoff came to a head when the French consul to Luang Prabang died, apparently driven to suicide by months of stressful negotiations with the Siamese. Outraged by the consul's death, the French sprang into action. The governor of French Indochina, Jean Marie Antoine de Lanessan, sent three residents (civilian administrators) and a hundred Vietnamese soldiers to occupy the towns and drive off the Siamese troops. From March until July, the two sides clashed. The French concentrated on pushing the Siamese from the forts they had built around the Khone Falls in southern Laos. The Siamese suffered hundreds of casualties and many deaths. The French side saw dozens wounded and several French officers killed before getting the upper hand militarily and moving quickly to press their advantage.

Back in Bangkok, the French demanded reparations. They rushed two gunboats to the mouth of the Chao Phraya River and demanded permission to sail them up to Bangkok. When Siamese officials refused, the French shot their way past Siam's main fortress at Paknam and other defenses that protected the approach to Bangkok. Fire from the Siamese fortress and naval vessels disabled one French steamer on the river, but the gunboats easily reached the capital. With its gunboats in position to enforce a blockade, the French demanded all of Laos. A blockade would rob the Siamese government of its chief sources of income from the seaborne trade that fed the port. The French had the power to level the heart of Bangkok, its palaces, temples, and commercial quarters, with the guns of their ironclad ships. Economically and militarily, the French would make Siam suffer if its conditions were not met. Siam's minister of foreign affairs, the capable and talented Prince Devawongse, a son of King Mongkut and half-brother of Chulalongkorn, rushed down to the French ships. With French military might menacing the capital, Devawongse had little room to negotiate. He ordered Siamese troops out of territories east of the Mekong, and thus ceded all of Laos to the French. The French wanted more, though. They demanded two million francs in compensation for the French officers killed in the skirmish, as well as other payments derived from customs duties in western Cambodia. They also demanded the right to occupy Siam's eastern provinces of Chantaburi and Trat, areas adjacent to French-controlled Cambodia, until Siam met their demands and called on Siam to remove its officials and soldiers from a twenty-five-kilometer zone running along the western bank of the Mekong. Finally, the French claimed extraterritorial powers over the Lao, Vietnamese, and Cambodian people living in the contested regions, a development that, potentially, put hundreds of thousands of French subjects in Siam. Unable to counter the French military threat, and lacking diplomatic support from the British, Siam accepted many of the demands. The French threat would remain over Chulalongkorn as he rushed to reform Siam's administration and modernize its institutions, especially its military.

The British, whom Chlalongkorn had relied upon to counterbalance the aggressive actions of the French, did little to help. In the middle of this tense time, the British had grown frustrated with Chulalongkorn, fearing that his resistance to French demands might draw them into war with their chief European rival. The British continued to see Siam as a buffer to be maintained between French and British colonial possessions, but they did not see Laos as vital to Siam's integrity. The British were more fixated on the areas where Burma, Siam, and Laos came together. London had grown nervous about French gains in mainland Southeast Asia, but they were not willing to fight France to restore Siam's vassal states east of the Mekong. Chulalongkorn felt let down by the British and lost much of the trust he had had in them. He continued, nevertheless, to employ many British advisors in his government and sent two of his most talented young sons to study military sciences at Britain's army and navy war colleges. But interestingly, the court added many Danish, German, Belgian, Italian, American, and other Western advisors to its government after 1893. Bangkok appeared to have sought safer alternatives to the unreliable British who had formerly held sway.

Many histories describe this period as the darkest in Chulalongkorn's reign. They write that he fell into a deep, year-long depression during which he withdrew from all government business. Grave rumors of his ill health streaked through the Western diplomatic community, although this gossip may have overstated his debilitation. They gleaned information from palace contacts about the king's devastated condition. But Chulalongkorn was probably more resilient than they believed him to be. This loss of territory and sovereignty – and face – to the French surely affected him profoundly. But he did not stop working. Historians point to the hundreds of letters he signed during that dark year as evidence of his resilience.

Embracing Western Culture

By 1897, Chulalongkorn felt sufficiently secure to leave his kingdom for a voyage to Europe. He visited France, Italy, Russia, and the United Kingdom, among other places. In *Lords of Things: The Fashioning of the Siamese Monarchy's Modern Image*, historian Maurizio Peleggi describes the Siamese court's embrace and absorption of elite Western cultural commodities during this period. He shows how Chulalongkorn projected authority over the burgeoning nation by embracing global culture, most of it Western in origin. Externally, Chulalongkorn displayed Western civilization markers that would place Siam as something close to an equal of the European nations. In clothes, food, art, furniture, boats, and other symbols, he imitated the tastes of Europe's royalty and aristocrats. Dating from his first trip abroad some two decades earlier, Chulalongkorn had started to incorporate Western dress into his wardrobe. On the second trip, he went abroad in full Western attire. He aimed to use the journey to project himself as a king and a family man in the European model. Chulalongkorn worked to control the image of Siam absorbed by Western governments and their people. He also wanted to bolster diplomatic ties among his European counterparts by personally meeting with the major European heads of state. He hoped such ties would help him check potential future French threats to Siam's continued independence and perhaps even bring about the cancelation of French claims of extraterritorial powers over Lao, Cambodian, and Vietnamese peoples living in Siam. He visited numerous cities throughout Europe, including Rome, Vienna, Warsaw, St. Petersburg, Hamburg, Brussels, the Hague, London, and Paris. The trip was a success. Chulalongkorn was pleased with how he was received by Europe's leaders and delighted by all that he learned about Europe's technological advances and cultural trends. The trip inspired him to build a new royal residence on the outskirts of Bangkok's old district, a palace surrounded by fields and gardens that he could stroll through. The site, which he named Suan Dusit (Heavenly Gardens), became the primary palace of all subsequent Chakri monarchs. During his trip, he also learned much about the limitations of the Western powers to solve problems like those facing him across Siam. In touring these countries, Chulalongkorn came to understand that the European model he had idealized was not without its flaws. He was struck by the problem of extreme poverty that many European countries had failed to remedy. The slums of London astonished him so much during his first tour of them that he insisted on going back for a second visit.

After returning from his second trip to Europe in 1902, he undertook more reforms meant to unify all people under his realm. One of the most critical sets of changes was designed to ensure that every Thai child could get a basic education. He insisted that, as part of their education, all Thai children study the history and culture of their country and come away knowing that they are the subjects of the king of Siam. He also scrapped the old system of military obligation. In its place, he enacted, finally, a form of military conscription similar to that of Britain. He oversaw changes in the areas of health, science, law, banking, and taxes, which helped to dramatically reshape Siam in the final decade of his reign.

Establishing a Centralized State

The princely sons of Mongkut and Chulalongkorn played important roles in carrying out Chulalongkorn's vision of a singular centralized state that was administered from Bangkok under a unified code of law. The most important of these minister princes was Prince Damrong Rajanubhab, a half-brother of Chulalongkorn, who became Siam's first minister of the interior in 1894 at the age of thirty-two. Damrong's first and most vital task was to wrest power from the local lords who ruled these areas and transfer it to a cadre of Bangkok-educated officials who served the central government. Up to this point, Bangkok's rulers had divided the surrounding areas into inner provinces, outer provinces, and tributary states. The Chakri court gave more latitude to local rulers the farther they were from Bangkok. To make Siam more like a Western power, Damrong had to establish a centralized bureaucratic administration that was rational and transparent. To accomplish this, he organized Siam's lands into *monthon*, giant regions, which were then divided into smaller political units as provinces, towns, districts, subdistricts, and villages. Damrong's job was made difficult by the well-entrenched networks of kinship, obligation, loyalty, and cultural chauvinism that had been spun around these ruling families for generations. His task was to dismantle them quickly and thoroughly without sparking a rebellion or civil war. He was helped in this effort by the desire for more freedom among many people in these principalities. Many farmers and traders sought release from the sometimes arbitrary and corrupt power that these local lords exercised over their subjects. Damrong's reforms received enough support from these regional populations to accomplish the goal of a centralized and unified Siam. But the process was not without resistance.

In the course of Damrong's ongoing reforms, Bangkok endured

several rebellions in areas that had formerly enjoyed considerable autonomy from the Thai of the Chao Phraya valley. All occurred in different and distinct regions, and each had its own peculiar characteristics. But all of them were similar in their focus on resistance to joining a Bangkok-based core, and all coincided with the push by Damrong's Ministry of the Interior to bring them into line with the central government's administrative apparatus. Three of these rebellions, for example, occurred in 1902. In Siam's deep south, the sultan of Patthani, the nominal ruler of Muslims in that area, resisted integration into Chulalongkorn's new state. Specifically, he opposed the transfer of traditional revenue streams that had once passed through his offices to that of the new Siamese government. In his defiance of Bangkok, he appealed to Britain for assistance. His efforts at remaining independent failed, and for his rebelliousness he was arrested by Siamese soldiers and hauled off to exile in the northern (and Buddhist) city of Phitsanulok. In Siam's northeast, mystics claiming foreknowledge of imminent calamities that would devastate the region for years to come drew bands of fervent followers who resisted both Bangkok's authority and that of French officials in Laos and Cambodia. One of the mystics, a figure called Ong Man, led a rebellion against Siamese representatives in the towns and villages around Ubon Ratchathani. Ong Man claimed to have supernatural powers that made him invulnerable to bullets and other modern weapons. After successfully capturing the town of Kemmarat and kidnapping its governor, Ong Man had attracted several thousand followers who rallied behind his message of political resistance and religious awakening. The unrest he inspired, known as the Phu Mi Bun Rebellion or the Holy Man's Rebellion, worried Siam's leaders because of its potential to pull Bangkok into further conflict with France. Bangkok rushed additional troops into the region, and after laying a trap for the millenarian army, killed many of Ong Man's followers. Although Siam successfully extinguished the uprising on its side of the Mekong, similar uprisings continued in the French-controlled territory of southern Laos until the mid-1930s. The third rebellion occurred in the north. There, a gang of Shan outlaws attacked Phrae and Lampang, looting the towns and driving off the police and officials. Taken by surprise by the speed and audacity of the Shan outlaws' rampage, Bangkok was forced to rely on a Danish advisor to organize a makeshift army of villagers and local militia to oppose them. The impromptu unit fought the robber gangs for weeks until Bangkok could send a large force north to quell the uprising.

With rebellions flaring in various regions and Chulalongkorn's health failing, Siam set about fixing its territorial disputes with France and Britain in border areas that remained ill-defined or contested. Bangkok ceded the important Cambodian provinces of Battambang and Siem Reap to France in exchange for two relatively small parcels of territory, one in Loei Province (around Dan Sai) and on the coast near Trat city. Siam also got the French to drop their extraterritorial claims over ethnic Lao, Vietnamese, and Cambodians in Siam. The deal greatly favored French Indochina over Siam. The lopsided settlement emboldened Britain to seek its own advantageous deal over similar territorial conflicts in Siam's south. Again, Chulalongkorn acquiesced to unfavorable terms, ceding Siam's claims on the Malay sultanates of Kedah, Perlis, Terengganu, and Kelantan in exchange for Britain dropping some of the extraterritorial legal privileges it had previously claimed for British colonial subjects in Siam. Why would Chulalongkorn accept such poor terms for treaties? Apparently, he was eager for a settlement that would neutralize potential flashpoints with his chief Western rivals. Sick with diabetes, kidney disease, and other ailments, the Siamese monarch worked to fix his nation's borders while he was still strong enough to oversee governmental affairs. These concessions also cleared up Siam's most vexing foreign relations matters ahead of Chulalongkorn's second trip to Europe, this one intended to help rejuvenate the king's failing health.

While tensions eased in the hinterlands and along the border, Bangkok faced upheaval close to home. In 1910, Chinese in the capital went on strike to protest a new government policy requiring them to pay the same annual poll tax as the Thais rather than the triennial tax formerly levied upon them. Chulalongkorn had begun to treat the Chinese as if they were citizens of Siam rather than temporary visitors. In principle, such a move was positive. This law and others helped pave the way for Chinese assimilation, something Thailand has done better than any other country in Southeast Asia. But the sting of the new taxes drove the Chinese secret societies to protest the new tax burden. The strike had a curious effect on different segments of the population: a newfound self-awareness on the part of both Chinese and Thais. The Chinese were aware of the power that their numbers gave them as they saw how they could affect the kingdom's revenue and well-being through labor action. But they also saw its limitations, especially when answered by a steadfast and robust response from the Siamese government. The Thais themselves became more aware of their social status as the ethnic majority of a multiethnic country that nonetheless counted some 10 percent Chinese within it. They also saw the potential power that the Chinese had for economic disruption in circumstances like the strikes of 1910. Many Thais in the capital resented the special status demanded by Chinese strike leaders. Their simmering antipathy would manifest itself in Thailand's social fabric more acutely over the next half-century.

Chulalongkorn died in 1910 after more than four decades on the throne. Thai histories often call this "the record reign" because his forty years as king surpassed the longest of the Ayutthaya monarchs by a few years. But it was more than a mere matter of time on the throne. Chulalongkorn's policies brought the king's authority directly into the lives of his subjects to an unprecedented degree. At the time of Chulalongkorn's death, nearly all Thais had one leader who ruled from Bangkok, not a set of competing kings, princes, and lords pressing overlapping claims of authority. He presided over radical changes in governance, finance, education, law, culture, and military structure. He made something like a nation where none had existed before. At the same time, he concentrated power around himself to make him arguably the most absolute of the Chakri dynasty's absolute monarchs. But he was not tyrannical or irresponsible. He tolerated internal dissent with more forbearance than almost any other king but was dogged in crushing regional rebellions. His achievements in international relations were mixed. He played a vital role in preserving Siam's independence despite intense pressure from French, British, and other Western colonial powers. But his clumsy handling of the 1893 crisis and its aftermath left Thailand with probably a much smaller geostate than it would have been under better leadership. Historians can debate the wisdom and efficacy of his actions and policies, but in the court of public opinion, in the hearts of many Thai people then and now, he was a brave visionary in a time of great peril. It is no surprise that many Thais embrace him as a guardian spirit for the nation and its citizens. They credit him with saving Thailand from an ignoble fate at the hands of Western imperialists by modernizing it. They find evidence that Chulalongkorn remains on hand to protect them from the lurking dangers of today.

CHAPTER 4

KING VAJIRAVUDH: A NEW THAI NATIONAL IDENTITY

Having established its borders and defined the physical outline of its nation by the first decade of the twentieth century, Thai leaders now had to assemble the complex abstract elements that people in the West called "nationalism." This can generally include the shared qualities, values, habits, rights, and experiences of the people within a fixed border. To maintain its idea of nationalism, a government needs programs that support and popularize it. In Siam's case, the task was complicated but necessary if the court was going to forge something akin to a nation. Bangkok's officials had to convince its citizens and subjects that they were better off governed by ministers in Bangkok than the leaders in, say, Vientiane, Chiang Mai, Nan, Phnom Penh, Hue, or even Paris. They had to demonstrate that Bangkok's uncontested control over these areas was logical, right, and even desirable. Their efforts inspired both goodwill and resistance across the territory over which the king now claimed sovereignty. The process of creating Thai nationalism involved numerous political, economic, and cultural elements, some practical and easily illustrated, others subtle and idiosyncratic. In the decades spanning the turn of the twentieth century, Prince Damrong, as minister of the interior, had worked hard to establish the administrative and bureaucratic apparatus for governing the diverse peoples living within Siam's borders. Damrong's administrative mission was delicate but straightforward. Getting the people to accept that they were a single people with a common political center, monarch, history, language, religion, and system of values was far more difficult. The process of creating a shared national identity was more challenging than delineating what defined its geographical borders and administrative structures.

Creating a Shared National Identity

Concocting Thai nationalism brought together contributions from countless segments of Siam's administration and society. But it was the king's experiences, inspirations, and opinions that laid the artificial foundations of Thai nationalism. He urged his subjects to develop something similar to Western cultural products and styles in a way that resembled the "civilizing mission" of some European colonial powers. At the same time, King Vajiravudh created Thai "tradition" by elevating various regional Thai products and practices as symbols of an idealized Thai national culture. Although some of the proposals he put forward did not survive long beyond his time, most did. His distillation of symbols, sentiments, and stories has endured to the present as accepted foundations of Thailand's national ethos. The nationalistic principles he advanced came together in a relatively short period at the start of the twentieth century. Although it is unwise to associate exclusively a historical period with the king who happened to be on the throne at the time, when it comes to the period in which Thai nationalism took shape, it was certainly dominated by the energies and vision of Vajiravudh. Vajiravudh invented Thai tradition, and the oxymoronic quality of that statement captures the difficulty of assessing the man and his accomplishments.

Vajiravudh's grandiose personality and obsessive interests can make him seem frivolous, childish, or even ridiculous. In reality, he was an amazingly complex figure of boundless energy and varied talents who projected his will onto Siam's modernizing program to an even greater extent than his father had, partly because he could. King Chulalongkorn had laid the groundwork necessary for the construction of nationalism that Vajiravudh pursued. The national institutions he created and the nationalist rhetoric he coined to describe them survive largely intact in Thailand because the majority of the kingdom's subjects believe they are true. The most obvious example is the three-part formula of national devotion every patriotic Thai is supposed to embrace and defend: nation (*chat*), religion (*sasana*), and monarch (*phra mahakasat*). This formulation of Thai nationalistic sentiment became the focus of Vajiravudh's fourteen-year reign. The best English-language study of Vajiravudh and principal source of this chapter is *Chaiyo! King Vajiravudh and the Development of Thai Nationalism* by the American historian Walter Vella. It is an enormously readable classic of Thailand's modern history that examines a mercurial, sometimes brilliant and sometimes quirky monarch who transformed Siam in many ways but was not remembered well upon his death.

Education and Ascension to the Throne

As with the ascension of Mongkut and Chulalongkorn, Vajiravudh's enthronement was not a certainty. Originally, Chulalongkorn had named an older son, Vajirunhis, as crown prince. Chulalongkorn carefully guided the education and training of Siam's heir apparent, and the boy had undergone elaborate rituals to ensure an auspicious reign. But after the sixteen-year-old Vajirunhis died of typhoid in 1895, Vajiravudh took his place as crown prince. Vajiravudh was in school in England at the time. His overseas education was part of the process that his grandfather King Mongkut had started when he hired Anna Leonowens to tutor the royal children in Western subjects. Mongkut's son Chulalongkorn took the process a step further by sending many of his children to Western European countries – France, Germany, and England – and the United States to be educated. Vajiravudh went to England in 1893 when he was thirteen. His father's plan was to have him study British military methods, specifically the use of ground forces. He studied with British tutors for a few years and threw himself into the life of a British public schoolboy, relishing football (soccer), rugby, cricket, and hunting. He loved the London theatre and saw many plays. So thorough was his immersion in British culture that his father admonished him to maintain his native language lest he forgot it. Chulalongkorn dispatched Thai tutors to keep him fluent in Thai. When he was not studying, playing, or going out, Vajiravudh was traveling. He saw France, Germany, Italy, and Russia as a student, and later the United States and Japan.

Vajiravudh first studied military sciences at the Royal Military Academy Sandhurst, then went to Oxford to study history and law. This concentration on law and history would guide his kingship and help shape the form of nationalism he promoted. He returned to Siam in 1903 after being abroad for nearly a decade. He spent the next few years learning the job he would someday assume, king of a Southeast Asian realm. It was not a smooth transition. Aloof and awkward, he lacked his father's genial temperament and his grandfather's forceful curiosity. Literature and drama were his passions. He composed essays and fiction, often under pseudonyms, and was particularly fond of dramatic arts. He wrote and acted in plays, and favored a small coterie of friends to pursue his interest in literature, drama, and sports.

Transforming the Kingdom

From the moment he was crowned on November 11, 1910, Vajiravudh set about transforming his kingdom. He sought to convince Siam's many ethnicities, regions, cultures, and faiths that they shared a common interest. His many writings, which he did under multiple pen names for the newspapers, aimed to make his subjects believe that their security lay in recognizing the common cultural elements that all people living within Siam's boundaries shared. Although this vision came from the West, Vajiravudh's concept of nationalism did not stress equality or democracy. He had a hierarchical and paternalistic view of nationhood that promoted the idea that everyone should give their support regardless of where they were on the social scale. Harmony and security would come to everyone through their acceptance of their place and their willingness to work hard to improve it.

Vajiravudh set the tone early for his reign with two important initiatives. The first was his creation of a paramilitary organization called the Wild Tiger Corps in 1911. He was inspired by the rise of highly nationalistic paramilitary youth movements, many with strong religious overtones, that had emerged in Europe. Britain saw the Boy Scouts' creation, Germany had the Wandervogel, and France's reverence for Joan of Arc drew young people on nationalistic pilgrimages. Vajiravudh wanted something similar, but on an elite level. He invited those from prominent families – many highborn officials and royalty – to join an organization formed around his personal and political obsessions. It was also a kind of private club like those he had known in England. Members paid dues, bought their uniforms, and gathered socially. When not in military-style training, they played games, competed in sports, listened to speeches, and debated issues. He also added a youth contingent called the Tiger Cubs, whose members engaged in activities similar to those of the Wild Tigers.

Vajiravudh was directly involved in every activity the members pursued, guiding them meticulously. He designed the Wild Tigers' black-and-yellow military-style uniforms, wrote their slogans, and composed their anthems. He created the loyalty oath that each member took and drilled them in preparation for marching in parades. Their purpose was to promote Thai nationalism as it was being defined by Vajiravudh and to demonstrate a model of intense devotion to the king. They carried out military training and exercises nearly every day, gathering at the palace or on royal parade grounds in the morning or, more commonly, in the late afternoon as the day's heat abated. They went on outings to important religious or historical sites. They were like an adult Boy Scouts built around a personality cult. Vajiravudh used the Wild Tiger Corps as both a sounding board and megaphone for his nationalist policies. They were examples of the idealized citizens he promoted to the nation – vigorous, modern, and patriotic. The king delivered his speeches about loyalty, citizenship, military prowess, and history to his Wild Tigers. The Corps also gave Vajiravudh a way to reach into the human machinery of Siam's bureaucratic administration and to control it with people devoted to him. His home guard ran the country and kept an eye on other bureaucrats.

The Wild Tiger Corps was not meant to supplant the functions of the army, but to become auxiliary troops in times of national emergencies. But even in this secondary role, they carried out military training similar to that of the army. One purpose of their extended camping trips to the provincial districts outside Bangkok was to train them in war games. These bureaucratic elites learned how to camp in the wilderness and endure the deprivations and challenges of a military campaign. Vajiravudh led them on these war drills and reveled in the camaraderie of camp life at day's end.

For all of the fun and fellowship it generated for its participants, Vajiravudh's Wild Tiger Corps was divisive. As an organization dominated by wealthy civilians, it sparked criticism and hard feelings from less well-to-do bureaucrats and military men blocked from joining. More importantly, members of the regular army resented the attention and resources lavished on the Corps. The military commanders tasked with building a modern military chafed at the celebration of what appeared to be the king's plaything, a kind of pretend army meant to occupy Vajiravudh's time and boost his ego.

The other early project was his second coronation. While the first had been a relatively low-key and traditional transfer of royal power attended by members of the court and the government, the second was a public spectacle meant to transmit his vision of kingship to the realm and beyond. In November-December 1911, he oversaw weeks of grandiose ceremonies that marked his ascension. Drawing upon traditional Brahmin and Buddhist religious rites, Vajiravudh staged numerous rituals and ceremonies designed to impart utmost auspiciousness to his kingship. They were also designed to project his plan for the reign as a dramatic spectacle of grand gestures and clear symbols. He showed his intention to cast himself as the star of Siam's national story while the subjects would be the audience and observers. Siam's growing press industry transmitted the pageantry and its intended message to segments of the population living outside Bangkok. The final segment of the second coronation was a series of receptions for foreign dignitaries who came to Siam as representatives of their nations' leaders. Vajiravudh depleted the kingdom's coffers to ensure that the diplomatic representatives received lavish hospitality and entertainment.

Like the Wild Tiger Corps, the second coronation also generated resentment among members of Siam's leading institutions. Their enmity almost cost Vajiravudh his crown in March 1912 when a group of army junior officers fostered a plot to topple the king. The intrigue was an amalgamation of three separate schemes undertaken by officers from different military entities. Sympathetic government officials joined them when they got wind of the plan. Despite their independent origins, all plotters shared a common aim to oust Vajiravudh and replace him with a Chakri prince of their choosing. In one plan, the goal was to name another of Chulalongkorn's sons, Prince Raphi Phatthanasak, as the first president of a Siamese republic. The other two groups favored making Siam a constitutional monarchy under one of Vajiravudh's brothers. They remained supportive of the Chakri bloodline as the logical source of Siam's leadership while also harboring disgust for Vajiravudh. They resented his focus on friends and associates while ignoring the merits of those who led the military and other institutions. They also saw Vajiravudh's pastimes of drama, literature, and games as unkingly, even dangerous. The king's lavish coronation struck them as an indulgent misuse of limited government funds. The cabalists saw the threat from Western colonialism as undiminished, while unrest in China demonstrated the possibility of similar chaos in Siam. Their plotting had reached the point where the leaders had agreed upon the location and time of the coup. But with more than a month to go before launching their rebellion, word of the plot leaked to security officials. Vajiravudh's court scrambled to quash the uprising before it could begin. After a two-month investigation, a special court sentenced the coup leaders to death and gave some associates jail sentences of twelve to twenty years. Vajiravudh commuted the death sentences to jail time and reduced the length of the prison sentences of the others.

Improving the Kingdom's Infrastructure

Rattled by the coup plotters, Vajiravudh worked harder to project his kingship as dedicated to the public good. In the immediate aftermath, he prioritized the construction of modern bridges, roads, railroads, and other infrastructure initiatives begun under his father's reign. He publicized progress on other projects such as waterworks and electrical power stations for the capital. A couple of years later, he pushed for improving the Royal Siamese Navy by acquiring a modern light cruiser. In this age, naval power was one of the most important metrics for measuring a nation's greatness. The ship would be both a practical and symbolic expression of Siam's improving standing in the world. Vajiravudh gave considerable amounts of his money toward the ship but also enlisted the public to make contributions. Writing under an assumed name, he contributed newspaper essays exhorting the public to contribute. He wrote historical plays that drew parallels between past efforts at defending Siam's independence with the acquisition of the ship. He had large signs championing the campaign erected around the capital. He even drew cartoons to promote the effort in the press.

As with the warship campaign, Vajiravudh vested a lot of energy into creating and promoting the symbols of Thai nationalism – flags, costumes, anthems, literature, activities – with bursts of energy that leave him looking both admirable and eccentric in the historic record. He built Siam's first university, Chulalongkorn University, and restructured the Siamese military branches along modern Western models. He also tried to modernize the people by giving them surnames. Until the early part of the twentieth century, the people of Siam saw no need for family names. Unlike the Chinese, whose reliance on clan names for social organization and cohesion dates back several millennia, the Thais never used them. People got by on their given name. Some members of the elite strata carried family names, but they were just as likely to be known by the title they carried. Having studied in the West, Vajiravudh believed that his kingdom would not be civilized unless its subjects had family names. The innovation would facilitate the new administration, such as registration of births and deaths, the collection of taxes, conscription, and other state functions that he imposed on Siam. He also wanted the last name to provide a clue to the socio-economic origins of its bearer. His time in England had impressed upon him the British consideration of class. He devised a system by which these new and socially indicative names would be applied to people. The names came from the occupation, place of origin, or interest of the recipient, always rendered in elevated terms derived from Pali, the language of Buddhism, or Sanskrit. Vajiravudh himself delighted in creating and dispensing these new last names. He generated many surnames for the people in his court, with some sources crediting him for creating and awarding some three thousand names himself.

It was difficult to convince the people of the rural areas, who comprised the vast majority of the kingdom, that they needed surnames. Local administrators were instructed to assign names to those in their area of responsibility. Some rural families forgot their new surname as soon as they misplaced the paper on which it was written. In some cases, this loss may have been deliberate. While not as hated as the tattoos, the imposition of family names by a distant court was met with suspicion. It was intrusive and augured further efforts at control. But some welcomed the change. It offered a chance at raising their social status, even if this elevation was illusory. There were commoners who forged their own family names by selecting words that alluded to royal blood they did not possess. In such cases, they had to change their new surnames to less august ones. It was a complicated process. Launched in 1913, the effort went on for many years. Even a decade after the law's enactment, many did not have last names.

The most striking visual change was the national flag. Vajiravudh himself designed the national standard. Siam's flag had been a bright red banner with an auspicious white elephant in the middle. It was a charming design that foreigners found easy to remember and easy to associate with Siam. But Vajiravudh was unhappy with it. Having lived in Europe, with the tri-colored, banded national flags of France, Italy, Germany, and, of course, Great Britain, Vajiravudh wanted a similarly designed national standard for Siam. One story goes that he was inspired to change the flag after an awkward encounter with peasants in Siam's countryside who hurriedly hoisted a homemade Siamese flag upside down on a crude flagpole so that the poorly cut-out elephant on the banner looked like a dead pig. The embarrassing display, the story goes, inspired Vajiravudh to design a flag that could be easily manufactured without having to rely on a flag-maker's skill to render a white elephant accurately. No matter its origins, the new banner was a departure from the evocations of kingship and Buddhism in the white elephant. Adopted right before Siam's entry into World War I, the new flag was a red, white, and blue standard of alternating bands whose symmetrical design made it impossible to fly upside down. It remains Thailand's flag today, even though evidence of lingering affection for the white elephant standard is found adorning bumper stickers, posters, coffee mugs, and T-shirts.

Siam and the Great War

World War I, the Great War in Europe, posed a peculiar problem for Siam. Britain and France, the same European powers that had menaced Siam's sovereignty and robbed it of its suzerainty over portions of what would become Cambodia and Laos, were now allies fighting against Germany, Austria, and Turkey. Siam had to move carefully to avoid being pulled into the hostilities on one side or the other. Complicating matters was Siam's reliance on members of the warring countries as advisors in all its government ministries. What side should Siam take in this war? Britain had been Siam's de facto defender, even if it had not always done as much as Siam's rulers had wanted. More worrisome was France as any move against France carried the risk of Siam losing its sovereignty and becoming another colony within French Indochina. Like Vajiravudh, several of his brothers had studied in England, others had studied in France. All were mindful of the dangers of crossing either power and leaned toward siding with the British-French Alliance.

The choice was not that simple, however. There were many Germans in Bangkok advising the government. More importantly, German engineers were essential to the ongoing expansion of Siam's rail network, which could link physically the far-flung corners of the kingdom Vajiravudh sought to unite with his rhetoric, symbols, and administration. German ships carried the bulk of Siam's shipping. Many educated Thais admired Germany for its material wealth and technological expertise. All the best imported products on sale in Bangkok – optical devices, scientific instruments, weapons, and musical instruments – were German made. Most importantly, Germany had never threatened Siam. Unlike Britain and France, Germany had never engaged in imperialism in Southeast Asia. Thai popular sentiment was most likely with the Germans at the war's outbreak.

Vajiravudh had his officials study all possible courses of action and, after reviewing their conclusions, chose to remain neutral in the conflict. The Siamese government asked the German military instructors holding honorary commissions in Siam's armed forces to resign. Beyond that, Vajiravudh did little to alter this neutrality. Throughout most of the war's duration, Vajiravudh resisted external and internal pressure to commit to one side or the other. It was not until 1917, after the war had dragged on for nearly four destructive years, that Siam moved to abandon its neutral stance and join a side. The causes were related to the growing horror at the war's human cost and the rise in German U-boat attacks on all shipping, military and civilian, in the Atlantic. (A U-boat attack on a passenger liner in 1917 would kill two Thai princes homeward bound from Europe.) Another critical factor was the United States. America had served as a model of neutrality for Siam. With German submarines sinking American merchant ships in the northern Atlantic, the United States pursued a moral argument for abandoning neutrality for war. Vajiravudh pursued a similar argument for Siam to abandon its impartiality.

Siam declared war on Germany and the Austro-Hungarian powers in July 1917. The Royal Siamese Navy seized all German ships in Bangkok's harbor and quickly took into custody those Germans working on the Thai railway to prevent acts of sabotage. In entering the war, Siamese leaders saw the opportunity to raise Siam's status in Western leaders' eyes. They hoped that by sending Thai soldiers to fight alongside European armies in Europe, Siam would appear as more "civilized" than the colonized Southeast Asian countries surrounding them. They sought to present their professional military units as a contrast to the "coolie" laborers from China, Vietnam, and other Asian countries working in France. They also hoped that their alliance with Britain and France would lessen the likelihood that either nation would someday seize Siam as its colony. In his study *Siam and World War I: An International History*, the historian Stefan Hell illustrates how far Siamese leaders went to demonstrate parity with their European allies. The Siamese refused to allow their soldiers to travel on ships transporting Chinese and Vietnamese laborers to Europe because they feared being associated in Western eyes with Asians whose lands were under colonial control. In their correspondence, they repeatedly stressed the dangers of allowing Europeans to equate them with these subjugated peoples. Such was their vehemence for distancing themselves from their Asian brethren that they seem to echo Western racist notions, perhaps unintentionally.

The Thai contingent turned out to be quite small. Siam contributed about thirteen hundred men. It did not send infantry, artillery, cavalry, or other conventional combat units. Instead, it sent aviation units and logistical teams that included ambulance corps, drivers, and automotive mechanics. The highly technical nature of the units was meant to highlight Siam's technological sophistication. They arrived in Europe during the final summer of the war and served until the armistice was signed in November 1918. Many of the Thai soldiers suffered terribly in the unfamiliar cold of France's autumn and winter. They also felt the sting of French bigotry while training and working with their *far-ang* allies. These Thai veterans of the Great War returned home with personal confirmation of the French people's disdain for the Siamese, a sentiment that had hitherto been merely theoretical.

Some scholars not familiar with Thailand's history portray the kingdom's leaders as mercurial opportunists who do not honor their friends by standing with them in war. In the case of World War I, they dangle the suggestion that Siam joined at the last minute so that the Thais could be counted on the winning side. Siam's shift away from neutrality just as Germany's forces faltered and the small size of its mostly non-combat contingent have encouraged some observers to point to this episode as an example the Thai people's tendency to be "fence-sitters," indecisive and uncommitted to an alliance until an opportunity comes along that they can then exploit for their gain. This same accusation would be leveled at them in World War II, the Cold War, and the Vietnam War. But the process was more deliberate, thoughtful, and humane than these detractors suggest. Furthermore, what some people see as opportunism can be more accurately labeled as pragmatism. The Thais had no stake in the Great War. Siam's leaders saw the conflict as less of a world war than a European war. The major European combatants had menaced, bullied, or attacked Siam in the previous decades. Moreover, the European powers themselves had generally favored Siamese neutrality because it prevented the possibility of the Great War expanding into Southeast Asia. These critics of Siam's neutrality apply a different standard to Siam than they would to their own self-serving countries.

Mistrust of Chinese Immigrants

At the time of Vajiravudh's great push toward nationalism, Bangkok was a largely Chinese city. It owed its energy to the influx of Chinese males who had fled the poverty and chaos of their homeland, especially in the wake of the Taiping Rebellion's bloody conclusion in 1864, to seek jobs as laborers and traders in Siam's expanding agricultural, commercial, and industrial enterprises. They worked in the ports and shipyards, on the farms and plantations, and the increasingly diverse merchant quarters of Bangkok and the provincial capitals. Many Chinese had come intending to work abroad for seven years before returning to China with their savings. But as the social and economic circumstances in China deteriorated during the Qing Empire's collapse, many of these temporary laborers settled down in Siam. They married local women and began a process of partial assimilation into Thai society.

Along with their increasing assimilation, these Chinese men became aware of the value of their labor to the Siamese economy and of their exploitation. Under the leadership of secret societies – self-help organizations set up along clan and native-place lines – they protested against what they perceived, probably with justification, as their mistreatment. They organized and went on strike. They shut down work in the capital and thus robbed the state of its revenue from commercial taxes.

Vajiravudh reacted bitterly toward the Chinese strikers, writing an infamous essay about the Chinese in Southeast Asia called "The Jews of the Orient." His target was the recently arrived Chinese who stirred up labor trouble and may have harbored communist sympathies. He seems to have been bothered also by the lack of cultural uniformity that unassimilated Chinese represented to his nationalism program. His essay compared the itinerant and diasporic Chinese in Southeast Asia with Jewish people in the West. Vajiravudh's depiction of Jews invoked the bigoted and stereotyped views of many Europeans and Americans. He was not the first writer to make this comparison. Vajiravudh's education in England had probably instilled in him the antisemitic anxieties of the British upper class. His essay said the Chinese of Siam were like the Jews of Europe in that they differed from the natives not only in matters of religion – most Chinese were not originally Theravada Buddhists – but also in race. The Chinese and the Jews viewed themselves as racially superior to the people in whose country they settled, claimed the king. He stressed both groups' reputations for being adept at making money out of any circumstance they encountered. He argued that the Chinese in Siam would never be fully loyal to their adopted country. Stressing their "parasitic" practices, he compared them to blood-sucking vampires. Vajiravudh was part Chinese himself. Like his Siamese monarch predecessors, he was the descendent of some Chinese parentage. He did not see his anti-Chinese diatribe as hypocritical or evidence of unconscious self-loathing. He was a prodigious writer who could be glib in his proclamations, even when they promoted bigotry and racism.

A Flirtation with Democracy

Vajiravudh's one flirtation with democracy was one of his stranger experiments. In 1918, he built a miniature city called Dusit Thani, originally in a park behind one of his palaces. It was like a theme park consisting of a miniature modern city with houses, temples, theaters, meeting halls, and an independent electrical company. It had a course for boat races and grassy lawns for other sporting contests. The residents were about two hundred of his courtiers who, unlike the residents of Bangkok, could elect their own mayor according to a constitution granted by the king. The pretend political parties presented and defended their platforms in debates. Dusit Thani was Vajiravudh's experiment in building a Western-style political society in Siam, albeit on a tiny scale. Because he created and controlled it, the political play-acting never threatened his absolute powers. This expensive experiment in building a democratic society turned out to be only a temporary diversion designed for his amusement. He did not mean it to be a model for possible future change. If anything, the costly indulgence probably antagonized the growing number of Thais who had come to resent the absolute monarchy during Vajiravudh's reign. Dusit Thani did not lead directly to any further democratic institutions in Siam, but its profligacy certainly encouraged antimonarchists to imagine a Siam without a king.

Improving Women's Rights

Vajiravudh could be progressive when it came to women's rights. He, more than any of his predecessors, pushed for women to be educated. He saw their education as necessary for a strong and modern nation. Thai men already possessed a relatively high rate of literacy, even by Western standards of the day. Many Thai boys had studied in Buddhist *wat* within a broad curriculum of religious and secular subjects. But the patriarchal nature of Buddhism meant that girls and young women did not get the same formal education as their male counterparts. Even when government schools were established throughout the kingdom, many parents did not see any reason to send their daughters to be educated. This concerned Vajiravudh, so he issued an act that made education compulsory for all, no matter their sex. Within a few years, the numbers of girls attending schools nationwide went from 7 percent to 38 percent, a huge leap that made a difference in many women's lives and changed the social dynamics of families.

Vajiravudh was also bothered by Thai women's dress and hairstyles. He wanted them to be more ladylike in the Western mode of the day. His time in Great Britain had exposed him to the opinions that Westerners harbored about Thai culture. He had read British writers who described Thai women in unflattering terms, finding their extremely short hair to be unfeminine. They were equally critical of the *pha nung* and *kraben*, rectangular bolts of cloth wrapped around the lower body, as ugly and inelegant dress. Worse still, the women's vermillion teeth, the result of chewing betel nut, disgusted them. These Western condemnations troubled Vajiravudh to the point that he encouraged court women to grow out their hair. He also promoted an idea of Thai femininity that would be both indigenous and compatible with Western tastes. He had them adopt the *phasin* (tube skirt), popular in the northern areas of Siam and in Laos, because it looked more like the Western idea of a skirt. The *phasin* caught on and became the national costume for women of this age. It is still worn by Thai women, often on Fridays, when many companies, schools, and government offices adopt traditional Thai dress in the workplace.

Vajiravudh's other concern about women had to do with polygyny. He was keenly aware that Westerners saw harems as marks of an uncivilized country. He was said to have favored monogamy like that practiced in the West, but he did not want to outlaw polygyny. He said it would be hypocritical for the Siamese court to outlaw a practice that was still pursued by so many of its members. The princes and nobles of this day had concubines and "lesser wives." To outlaw such an arrangement would stir resentment and perhaps even rebellion within the princely class. The other reason, he stated, was that such a law would cause a backlash in the Muslim areas of Siam's south where it was still common under Islamic custom to have up to four wives if the man could afford to support them. Instead, he favored the registration of these polygynous relationships so that the wives and the children had legal recourse for material support from men who had abandoned them.

Vajiravudh himself favored monogamy. But historical and perhaps personal circumstances conspired to make him go through at least four marriages and annulments in the final years of his relatively short life. Although he was a bachelor until nearly forty, he did see it as his obligation to produce an heir. True to his preference for monogamy, he got married and he made it a point to announce that his first bride would be his only one. He had his first marriage annulled after a short period, however, citing differences in temperament. More significantly, though, for his advancing age and poor health, he and his first wife failed to produce an offspring. He went through three other wives in rapid succession in the last few years of his life, with none carrying a child to term. Finally, surprisingly, his last wife, Suwadana, became pregnant with Vajiravudh's potential heir.

The question of an heir was pressing because so many of the Chakri princes who were Vajiravudh's brothers had died young, including the three who were next in line for the throne at ages 37, 31, and 33, respectively. Vajiravudh's own health had been precarious throughout his life. When he became ill with an intestinal infection in August 1925, there was considerable concern. The worst fears were confirmed when he did not recover in the months that followed, growing sicker as the year progressed. A few months later, on November 23, his wife gave birth to his only child. Alas, it was a girl, and thus would not be able to inherit the crown and rule Siam as a queen. When Vajiravudh was informed that the infant was a daughter, he reportedly accepted the news with weary resignation. He died thirty-six hours later.

Vajiravudh had greatly advanced the modernization projects started by his grandfather and father. He also brought Siam to the edge of financial ruin in his reign. He spent lavishly and recklessly, indulging in self-aggrandizing pomp and fanciful projects while disregarding his advisors, who cautioned him toward fiscal responsibility. Beginning with his elaborate coronation ceremony, he drained the kingdom's wealth with dangerous abandon. So profligate was his spending that one contemporary British diplomat described Vajiravudh's death as the late king's greatest service to Siam. His spendthrift reign helped set the stage for the absolute monarchy's demise.

CHAPTER 5

KING PRAJADHIPOK AND THE OVERTHROW OF THE ABSOLUTE MONARCHY

Siam's absolute monarchy ended on June 24, 1932. Siam's rulers had been exercising a form of highly concentrated power for decades, even centuries. The absolutism of the previous three monarchs was forceful, expansive, and uncompromising. Amazingly, it ended quickly, peacefully, and with certainty. The absolute monarchy vanished one morning at dawn with minimum effort from those who launched the coup that destroyed it and little resistance from those who had the most to lose.

At the center of this story is King Prajadhipok (Rama VII, r. 1925–35). He is not studied as extensively as many other Chakri monarchs, but he is as fascinating and admirable a historical figure as any Siam has produced in the modern era. Curiously, he is presented in Thai nationalist histories as the humblest of their Chakri kings, perhaps because he presided over the diminishment of the monarchy. An institute dedicated to promoting his legacy has become influential in Thailand over the last couple of decades. The museum it operates hosts special events designed to celebrate his accomplishments and burnish his image. The assembled photographs, texts, costumes, and artifacts on display argue that Prajadhipok was a wise and prudent ruler who guided the kingdom through a tumultuous time. Few foreigners visit the museum. But the evocative visual statements regarding the courage and resourcefulness of this king make the museum a worthwhile destination for even casual students of history.

Prajadhipok also has his critics. They point out that he is not "the father of Thai democracy," as some nationalist histories suggest. He resisted introducing democratic processes despite the growing sentiment among many influential Thai people for such changes. His failure to add even modest democratic elements helped bring about the downfall of absolutism. Further tarnishing his image is what he did after the coup of 1932. Rather than work with civil servants and military men to create a stable constitutional monarchy, he somewhat petulantly resisted measures for a smooth transition from one government system to another. His critics cite his obstruction of Thailand's democratic launch as a contributing factor in its historical weakness. They say his meddling and resistance condemned Thailand to autocratic rule that lasted long after he had left Siam and died in exile. His detractors could argue that he was neither a capable absolute monarch nor a good constitutional one. He failed at both.

A Reluctant King

Prajadhipok never prepared to reign, nor did he want to. He was the second youngest of Chulalongkorn's seventy-seven children and grew up believing that someone else would be king. Because his father had made it clear that he wanted succession to pass through the line of sons he had with Queen Saowabha, Prajadhipok grew up thinking that it would most likely be one of his older full brothers. Like many of his princely siblings, he went abroad for his education. He studied at Eton College and the Royal Military Academy at Woolwich in England. He pursued military sciences to become a career soldier who would play a leading part in developing the rapidly modernizing Royal Siamese Army. He spent more of his formative years abroad than many of his siblings and understood Western ways thoroughly. He held commissions in the Siamese and British armies, giving up the latter only when Siam declared its neutrality in the Great War. He cut short his military education and training in Europe to return to Siam in 1924 when his brother, King Vajiravudh, died. In all of those years abroad, he did not study state administration and diplomatic affairs as many of his older brothers had as they prepared themselves for government positions. Mild in his temperament and sensible in his habits, he was among the least assuming and least colorful of King Chulalongkorn's offspring. He was comfortable in fatigues and looked forward to training and leading soldiers.

All of his plans changed quickly as the 1920s got underway. With his brothers dying at unnaturally young ages, the ranks of princes born to full queens rapidly diminished. Two took themselves out of contention for the throne by marrying Europeans they met while studying abroad. Within a few years, the Chakri court found itself turning to this unassuming military man to be its next king. He was named heir apparent less than a year before he wore the crown. He did not welcome the abrupt about-face in his life plans but accepted the weighty responsibility as his duty.

Prajadhipok faced problems that were as perilous as those confronting his predecessors, but they seem less heroic in their abstractness. His challenges concerned international economics and national finances. He pulled his kingdom back from economic ruin early in his reign but failed when more dire problems emerged a couple of years later. During his time on the throne, he faced dangers that were immediate, unexpected, and personal. But because the monarchy emerged diminished after his curtailed reign, historical opinion has been less kind to him than to Mongkut, Chulalongkorn, and even Vajiravudh. This harsh judgment is probably not fair to the reluctant king, the self-described "dark horse" candidate for power, who displayed more tenacity and guile than any had expected from him. His military training had prepared him well for the challenges of kingship. He had learned the importance of gathering critical information (intelligence) before making significant decisions. Like many good military leaders, he listened to various and often conflicting opinions before issuing a judgment. He moved swiftly when he had to. He maintained a strict hierarchical structure but accepted blame for his faults and missteps. He had discipline, stamina, and courage, and was calm under pressure. He was also frugal and careful. He was a sportsman with a passion for golf. He came across as a devoted husband to his sole wife (and cousin), Queen Rambai Barni. All of these qualities helped him pass the earliest tests of his reign.

Growing Political Consciousness

Prajadhipok faced severe problems right from the beginning. Siam was virtually bankrupt at the time of his coronation. Vajiravudh's extravagances had left the royal coffers nearly empty, the princely ruling class nervous, and ordinary people, at least those Bangkokians who paid attention to political affairs, wondering if an absolute monarchy was the best form of government for Siam. Further roiling the waters was the growing influence of newspapers and novels. In his landmark study of the era, historian Benjamin A. Batson describes the often-unsympathetic attitude that the press had for Prajadhipok's court. In *The End of the Absolute Monarchy in Siam*, the principal source for this chapter, Batson illustrates how Siam's expanding journalism industry raised the literate urban population's political consciousness in the 1920s and 1930s. These newly established newspapers generated something akin to public opinion where none had existed before. The proliferation of politically themed editorials, essays, and stories could collectively challenge the wisdom of the Siamese government's policies and actions. Literary fiction also contributed to this new voice of public opinion. Novelists who specialized in translating foreign literature added to the Siamese population's growing understanding of social circumstances and political systems of the Western liberal democracies. Readers became more aware of popular political participation in the same foreign societies that the Thai aristocratic and royal households embraced for their material and educational cultures.

Perhaps because he never imagined himself as being the king one day, Prajadhipok may have been open to reform. His defenders argue that he considered introducing some form of democratic participation to Siam twice in his reign. In 1926 and 1932, he consulted with foreign political advisors about possible alterations to the royal system that guided state affairs. He asked whether Siam would be best served by some day having a parliamentary system like Great Britain's. He explored whether this Western form of government was suitable in an Asian country whose leaders, never mind its subjects, had only just started to think of their realm as a nation. As political scientist Federico Ferrara has pointed out in "The Legend of King Prajadhipok," the proposals that Prajadhipok considered were hardly democratic. Among the ideas floated was the addition of a prime minister who would guide his cabinet's administrative affairs. More tellingly, the king's advisors made no provision for an elected legislature while allowing the king to retain legislative, executive, and judicial powers. The proposed reforms were half-hearted considerations that went nowhere. Both Prajadhipok's foreign and Thai advisors opposed democratization as a potentially destabilizing force. They saw acquiescence to democratic appeals as the first step in a process that might ultimately remove the king from the throne. Prajadhipok and many of the Thai elite also worried that democracy would strengthen the power of ethnic Chinese. Like Vajiravudh, Prajadhipok and his advisors mistrusted Chinese immigrants and their leaders as a foreign presence that already wielded significant but undue unofficial power in Siam. Chinese made up about 10 percent of Siam's population at this point. Their high numbers in Bangkok almost ensured that a Chinese would win elections in Bangkok. The king was unlikely to make any changes that would legitimate Chinese influence in national affairs.

Siam in this period had become a base for anticolonial revolutionaries from other Southeast Asian countries who were organizing themselves into political, military, and intellectual groups. Their goal was to drive the French, Dutch, and other Western powers out of their homelands. Siam also saw an influx of Chinese revolutionaries who were inspired by Sun Yat-sen. Many were socialists and communists. They sought to spark Marxist-inspired revolutions in China and amongst the Chinese diaspora in Southeast Asia. By the end of the 1920s, they had formed the Communist Party of Siam. Although some Thais joined the group, the party concentrated on revolutionary activity in China, French Indochina, Singapore, and other surrounding lands. Its lack of a direct threat, however, did not stop the Thai leadership from fearing it. Thai elites were inclined to invoke a communist bogeyman to advance their agendas or undermine their rivals. These were heady political times in which any misstep could have serious consequences. A conservative at heart, Prajadhipok did little to introduce change.

Prajadhipok judged the Siamese people unready for democracy. While disinclined toward democratic innovations, the king oversaw some political reforms at the highest levels meant to stabilize the anxious bureaucracy and give him access to more viewpoints. He created a Supreme Council of State that would advise him in state matters. It was a five-man advisory board composed of princes, all of them Prajadhipok's older half-brothers or uncles, and all well-known figures who had held important positions in previous reigns. Most were favorites of Chulalongkorn who had fallen out with Vajirvudh. Several had returned from exile after Rama VI's death. The group did not have any official power. Instead, its members would offer the king different opinions to help him better solve the kingdom's pressing problems.

Financial Challenges

Prajadhipok's main challenge concerned national economics. Siam's finances were in a mess. With the Supreme Council's help, Prajadhipok cut Siam's budget nearly in half during his first year on the throne. To do this, he shrank the budgets of all ministries and departments. Predictably, the state ministers were intent on protecting their own ministries from efforts to rein in spending. They fought openly with each for greater portions of a shrinking national budget. In going after the Ministry of War, Prajadhipok faced particularly stiff opposition. Siamese leaders still feared further land grabs by the Western colonial powers. They had spent the decades since 1893 developing a national army that was better organized, trained, and equipped and that could resist the European colonial forces surrounding them. Complicating the matter, Siam's military contribution to the Great War in Europe had made the Royal Siamese Army a symbol of nationalist pride. Few wanted to see the military diminished in real or symbolic terms. But with the support of economic advisors, Prajadhipok pushed through cuts to the military budget. Many officers who had dreamed of well-paid service in a modern national army or navy found their salaries shrinking and their already outdated weapons aging. These soldiers grumbled about the state of Siam's leadership in this time of crisis. The minister of war, Prince Boworadet, clashed with the king and his financial advisors repeatedly over budgeting issues, such as military construction projects and salary increases for officers. But even this strong-willed prince could not protect the armed forces from budget cuts. Disgusted, Boworadet resigned as minister of war. His departure would have significant consequences for Thailand's history in the years to come.

To stem similar protests to his austerity measures, Prajadhipok appointed new ministers to most of the twelve ministries, nearly all of them royal princes. They were young, well-educated, and talented people whom he trusted to bring stability to the chaotic financial circumstances that Vajiravudh had left at his death. The Supreme Council also helped him bring the royal budget under control. The royal expenditures – the money paid to princes and other royals on the state payroll – were particularly opaque. No one knew precisely how much was being raised, how much was being spent, and who among the scores of princes was entitled to what funds. Prajadhipok stabilized the princely spending, but in doing so angered some royal figures who resented the belt-tightening.

The Supreme Council may have aided Prajadhipok in making sound decisions early on, but it probably caused him harm in the long run. The council introduced more elite advisors to Siam's absolutist government without giving the citizens any voice. To outside observers, the absolute monarchy had merely added a layer of autocracy to the top. Prajadhipok's reliance on his older siblings for advice made him look green and timid to foreign and domestic observers. He came across as indecisive and easily influenced. But this was a misperception. Prajadhipok was not a pushover. His humble nature belied a resolute spirit that few outside his immediate circle ever saw. He stood up to various members of the Supreme Council when he disagreed with their recommendations. He made his objections firmly but was not discouraging as Vajiravudh often was. Few appreciated how hard he worked. He was tireless in carrying out the affairs of the kingdom. Each day, he put in long hours reading and commenting on enormous volumes of official documents, including commoners' petitions. He traveled widely internationally and domestically, and was the first Siamese monarch to visit all areas of the kingdom. All of this work and travel gave him command of a vast body of knowledge about Siam's people and processes and furthered his ability to understand the complex problems facing Siam. It was an impressive feat for a king who had never planned to rule. But few saw this side of him.

For a few years, Siam looked like it was going to bounce back economically. But by 1930, the onset of a global depression sapped Siam's wealth. The price of Siam's most important foreign exchange earner, rice, plunged, dropping by two-thirds. Revenue on other export commodities, including rubber, teak, and tin, also fell. The situation worsened after Great Britain abandoned the gold standard. Siamese efforts to manage the resulting aftershocks failed to protect the baht's value. Prajadhipok and his advisors implemented policies to lessen the effects of the global depression, including cutting land taxes for rice farmers. But there was little that the king could do soften the blows caused by the global economic downturn. Hurt by the deteriorating economic conditions, more influential Siamese lost faith in Prajadhipok's leadership. In the deep shadows of Siam's officialdom, plans for revolution had started to come together.

Opponents of Absolutism

Who were the opponents of absolutism? They were the best young minds of Siam, commoners whose brains and hard work had earned them scholarships to study abroad in the early twentieth century. This overseas education gave the opponents of absolutism something in common with the royal princes. So how was a European education formative of both absolutist policies and the resistance to them in Siam? Since the reign of Chulalongkorn, the royal princes had been going to study in the West. They primarily went to European countries that still had royal houses, especially to Britain, and they did so with the idea that they would return to Siam to introduce innovations that would modernize Siam industrially, economically, militarily, and medically. In the mid-1880s, for example, Prince Chirapravati Voradej went to Great Britain to broaden his education before moving on to Denmark to study military sciences. Later, Chulalongkorn also sent some of his other princely sons, Vajiravudh, Abhakara Kiartivongse, Chakrabongse Bhuvanath, and Prajadhipok, to get military education and training in Europe. Another son, Prince Mahidol, the father of King Bhumibol Adulyadej (Rama IX), studied public health in Germany before going to the United States to study medicine at Harvard. Their elite educational sojourns gave cachet to the term "nakrian nok" (overseas student). These princes and others like them returned with plans to modernize Siam along the lines of European nations. But they did not advocate democracy. They were disinclined to weaken the system that ensured they remain privileged, pampered, and powerful.

The profile of the Siamese study-abroad student changed when commoners were allowed to compete for scholarships to study in these countries. In this new era, non-elite college graduates studied subjects such as law, political science, and military affairs in Western Europe and the United States. Unlike the princes and aristocrats who had been going abroad a generation ahead of them, these common-ers returned home to find that the avenues of power and influence had been blocked to them. They were frustrated that they could not serve Siam in leadership positions. Despite their advanced education abroad, they were stymied professionally by the large pool of Siamese princes who dominated the government's critical positions, courts, and military.

Pridi Banomyong, the son of a merchant from Ayutthaya, was one such student. Like many people in the lower Chao Phraya valley, he was part Chinese as his paternal grandfather had emigrated from China. His father and mother came from entrepreneurial families working chiefly in the rice industry. Pridi went to Bangkok as an ado-lescent to continue his education. He studied law at a school attached to the Ministry of Justice that was designed, in part, to generate new officials to serve in the rapidly expanding Siamese national judicial system. Pridi scored the highest in his graduating class and won a scholarship to study law at the Sorbonne in Paris.

Pridi arrived in Paris at an electrifying moment in European his-tory. After the Great War, Paris was the center of Western political thought. Many would-be reformers and revolutionaries imbibed the intoxicating and volatile mix of Marxist, socialist, and democratic ideas debated in the wake of the Russian revolution. The Thai stu-dents studying in Paris, more so than those studying in any of Eu-rope's other great cities, got caught up in this atmosphere of bold new political ideas. At one of the earliest meetings that Pridi attended in Paris in 1921, he met the young Ho Chi Minh, who was then using the name Nguyen Ai Quoc (Nguyen the Patriot). Ho was then just starting to work out the earliest planks of the political framework by which he would combat the French colonial domination of his Vietnamese homeland. The interaction between these two important Southeast Asian revolutionary figures was probably not profound. But Ho's presence at some of these meetings would later provide another weapon for Pridi's detractors when they accused him of being a com-munist and a secret agent of Moscow. Pridi met mostly with other Thai scholarship students in their dormitory in Paris's Latin Quarter. They frequently met to discuss their home country's seemingly backward political system and the limited opportunities that awaited them upon return. They talked about ideas, about revolution, and about a future in which the Siamese king might no longer wield absolutist powers. Their long-term goal was to promote change.

Pridi did not wait to return before stirring things up. In 1926, he made a name for himself as a leader in Paris by organizing a petition that demanded higher stipends for his fellow students. The France-based students resented receiving lower stipends than Thais studying in other European countries. Pridi delivered the petition to the Siamese minister in Paris. The minister threatened to withdraw Pridi's scholarship and send him back to Bangkok. Pridi's father intervened, pleading for his son to be allowed to finish his degree. The elder Banomyong won a reprieve for his son by arguing that Pridi would cool down when he returned to Siam and entered the royally directed bureaucratic ranks. The father's prediction would prove to be wrong.

Planning a Coup

Pridi emerged as the leader of those Siamese students who had gone beyond merely talking about a Siam without an absolute monarch to discussing how they would actively carry out that task. Pridi attracted similarly minded Siamese students from other European schools. One of the most important to join his group was a young army officer studying artillery at the French military school at Fontainebleau. He was born Plaek Kittasangkha in rural Nonthaburi, a commoner whose Chinese-Thai family raised durians, the large yellow fruit prized by Thai people for its powerful fragrance and exquisite taste (and despised by most foreigners for its odor). His family was not wealthy, but he was fortunate to have his education supported by a well-off patron who sent him to military school. His parents named him Plaek, which means "strange" in Thai, because of his odd facial features (his ears were lower than his eyes), but he was bright and capable and rose swiftly through the ranks of the Thai military, earning a spot studying advanced artillery tactics in France in the 1920s. Following a promotion to the senior officer corps, he received the noble title Luang Phibunsongkhram from the king. Later, he would drop the first part of the royally sponsored title to become Plaek Phibunsongkhram. In the West, he would be known primarily as Phibun or Phibun Songkhram.

Pridi also brought in other Siamese law students and military cadets, including naval officers, studying in Europe. The group came to be known in English as the Promoters because they promoted change in Siam's political system and, more directly, would promote the coup d'état that overthrew the absolute monarchy. While in Europe, they met in utter secrecy. The previous king had dealt harshly with the highborn coup-plotters around him. To get caught discussing these matters, never mind plotting a revolution, was dangerous. They risked more than the loss of their European scholarships. They could have been jailed for long periods or even executed.

Pridi, the law student, returned to Siam in 1927. He and his fellow Promoters won junior positions in government ministries. They observed close up the intricacies of the royal-heavy power systems. They also continued to meet in secret to discuss a possible future of constitutionalism in Siam. During this delicate early stage, they would sound out their military and civilian colleagues regarding political sympathies, especially their support for a constitutional monarchy. Military support was key. Phibun, the military man, managed to find about twenty mid-level officers who supported the aim to end the absolute monarchy. Their group was bolstered by the inclusion of some influential colonels who had studied in Germany and Denmark.

As the plot moved forward, the Promoters continued to operate in utmost secrecy. They were obsessed with caution, knowing what would befall them if discovered. They never committed anything to paper. They met in small groups only and always kept a deck of playing cards in front of them to simulate an unfolding card game lest any suspicious party come upon one of their secret meetings. Despite their extremely cautious measures, word circulated about the group. To set up an information smokescreen, they talked openly about other people's alleged disaffection with the king and the princely ruling class that dominated the army. Prince Boworadet, the European-educated prince who had served as the minister of war before resigning over budget cuts to the military, was indeed grumbling about his ill-treatment and dissatisfaction. But he was not part of the Promoters group. They threw out these stories as disinformation, what we might now call static, to obscure their own plotting. The plan worked well. It kept attention away from them.

Their big concern was how to capture the king. The Promoters spent a long time fretting over how to seize Prajadhipok. They knew they had to hold the king to prevent the possibility of him rallying troops to his side. They also had to avoid hurting him. The king's safety worried them for historical reasons. Ever since the Bolsheviks had killed the Russian czar, Siam's ruling circles had been anxious about losing their monarch to revolutionary action. The Promoters believed that their putsch would fail if the king remained at liberty or, worse still, was killed in any fighting that might erupt.

In the midst of their plotting, they got a lucky break. Prajadhipok left Bangkok the week they had planned to launch their attack. The king had gone south by train to Wang Klai Kangwon ("Far from Worry Palace"), his seaside residence at Hua Hin, a few hours south of Bangkok. He was out of the picture, and would not be a factor in their plan. Communication systems were still so primitive at Hua Hin that the king would have had difficulty communicating with loyalists in Bangkok when the coup unfolded. Just as they were going forward with the plan, the Promoters nearly got nabbed. They came within hours of being arrested and subject to punishment. But it did not happen. On the night before they launched their coup d'état, the interior minister, Prince Boriphat, received a list of people believed to be plotting against Prajadhipok. Many of the Promoters were on the list. But Boriphat delayed police action. He was reluctant to question educated and well-connected men at such a late hour. He thought it would be unseemly to go knocking on doors in the middle of the night. He told his staff that the investigation could wait until the next morning. Had it not been for this act of royal civility, the king of Siam might have held onto his absolute power, and princes like the minister of the interior would have kept their old jobs and authority. But the delay in police action meant that the plot could go ahead.

Sweeping Aside Absolute Monarchy

The Promoters launched their coup in the early hours of June 24, 1932. The pair tasked with neutralizing military defenses and capturing the princely leadership were two senior officers who had studied

Thai nationalist histories trace the beginning of Thailand's history to the rise of the Sukhothai kingdom as a regional power. Here a monumental Buddha rises among the ruins of Sukhothai. *(Photo: S-F @ Shutterstock.com)*

Today, Sukhothai's monumental ruins draw tourists to north-central Thailand. The remaining icons, temples, and palaces host cultural exhibitions, photo-shoots, and educational trips throughout the year. *(Photo: Inoprasom @ Shutterstock.com)*

Ayutthaya dominated mainland Southeast Asia for four centuries and established the Thais as a political and cultural force. Today, the wrecked buildings of the great city-state are a tourist draw. The magnificent ruins are a testament to the kingdom's glorious past. *(Photo: Avigator Fortuner @ Shutterstock.com)*

An enigmatic creation of man and nature: a Bodhi tree grows around the head of a decapitated Buddha icon at Ayutthaya National Park. The blending of tree and Buddha can symbolize Thailand's tradition of combining indigenous spiritual beliefs with Theravada Buddhism. *(Photo: SantiPhotoSS @ Shutterstock.com)*

Adorning the walls of many Buddhist temples are scenes depicting the Indian epic *Ramayana*. The landscapes, clothes, and villages of the Thai version, known as the *Ramakien*, are distinctly Thai in appearance. *(Photo: Renjeit1974 @ Wikimedia Commons)*

After World War II, several OSS agents chose to remain in Thailand. Among the most famous was Jim Thompson, a former architect who developed Thailand's silk industry into a globally recognized brand. The house he assembled out of Thai farmhouses is now a museum of art. *(Photo: cowardlion @ Shutterstock.com)*

Wat Phra Kaeo, the religious center of Thai Buddhism, houses the enigmatic image known as the Emerald Buddha. Located beside the Grand Palace, the temple and its famous icon host royally sponsored religious ceremonies and other official observances. *(Photo: Kittiwat Junbunjong @ Wikimedia Commons)*

Murals depicting elephant duels like those waged by Ayutthaya's King Naresuan against his Burmese rivals have remained popular in the modern era. The images provide a visual feast for those hungry for details about

premodern warfare. They are also a source of chauvinistic inspiration for
Thai nationalists concerned about the threat posed by regional rivals.
(Photo: Tris T7 @ Wikimedia Commons)

King Taksin established his resurgent Thai kingdom at Thonburi on the western bank of the Chao Phraya River. The new location had strategic advantages over Ayutthaya, especially its relative proximity to the sea. Although subsequent monarchs built up Bangkok on the opposite side of the river, Wat Arun

still stands as a visual reminder of Taksin's time. The gorgeous "temple of dawn" is a focal point for those who revere the audacious Taksin.

(Photo: Pattiveth.M @ Wikimedia Commons)

In a series of regional military campaigns and domestic construction programs, the first three Chakri monarchs (Rama I, Rama II and Rama III) laid the foundation for a Thai renaissance in mainland Southeast Asia.

As one of the most consequential Thai monarchs in the modern era, King Mongkut reformed the Buddhist sangha, renegotiated trade agreements with Western imperial powers, promoted historical studies of the premodern Thai kingdoms, and introduced Western curricula into the palace schools. Outside of Thailand, he is more famous as the basis for the waltzing monarch depicted in the musical *The King and I*.

Before government schools came into being, Thai communities relied on Buddhist monks to serve as educators. While their role as schools has faded, Buddhist wat remain as social and religious centers.

Bangkok was long connected to the rest of the kingdom mainly by rivers and other waterways. Today, the monsoon-fed rivers remain essential transportation lines.

For many Thais, the day starts with the merit-making ritual of offering food to passing monks. The act improves the karmic stores of the giver while sustaining the monk who collects the donated meal. *(Photo: Mai111 @ Shutterstock.com)*

Wat Pho, a temple located beside the old Royal Palace, houses a monumental reclining Buddha. The site remains a pilgrimage destination for Buddhists and a must-see spot for tourists. *(Photo: chocobluesky19 @ Shutterstock.com)*

The Grand Palace's ceremonial guards evince the cultural influence of Western militaries on Siam's armed forces.

Nicknamed "the Venice of the East" for its extensive networks of canals, Bangkok was a city of boat-borne commerce for much of its history.
(Photo: S-F @ Shutterstock.com)

King Chulalongkorn built Phra Thinang Chakri Maha Prasat at the heart of the Grand Palace. Its intriguing combination of a French Beaux-Arts main structure topped with a traditional Thai roof has inspired commentators to

describe the ornate structure as looking like "a European man wearing a Thai hat." *(Photot: Andy Marchand @ Wikimedia Commons)*

As the first Thai monarch to receive a Western-style education, King Chulalongkorn the Great grew up understanding the recent advances made by the Western powers in science and technology. He also recognized the dangers posed by the European imperial powers in Southeast Asia. The king worked throughout his reign to strengthen Siam's government, economic, and military institutions and present his court as "civilized" according to Western notions. His success in these endeavors – while not flawless – helped preserve the kingdom's independence.

King Chulalongkorn sought to maintain his modernization program into subsequent reigns by sending many of his sons abroad for their secondary and university educations. These princes returned to Siam with global perspectives.

together in Germany. Both carried the palace-awarded noble rank of *phraya*, indicating their high and trusted status. Colonel *Phraya* Songsuradet (Song), a military engineer who had served as director of education at the Military Academy, and Colonel *Phraya* Phahonphonphayuhasena (Phahon), deputy director of artillery, had been in on the plot from the beginning. In the months leading up to the coup, they had sounded out their fellow officers for antiroyalist sentiment while trying to reveal as little as possible about the Promoters' membership. Song was admired for his brilliant military mind and counted many former students as his acolytes. He took the lead in drawing up the rebels' military plans. They started by neutralizing the 1st Cavalry Regiment of the Royal Guards with a simple deception. The military members of the Promoters burst into the regiment's barracks shouting that a Chinese labor strike was under way on Yaowarat Road. The head of the Promoters' military faction discovered the guards on watch to be asleep when he arrived and he used their dereliction as a pretext for putting them under arrest. In the confusion generated by the false report of a Chinese riot and the arrest of the guards, one of the conspirators broke into the cavalry regiment's arsenal and seized weapons. The Promoters took control of these troops and ordered them to march to the grounds of the 1st Infantry Regiment's barracks in Bangkok.

Other Promoters had scheduled demonstrations of military maneuvers in the open fields around the palace that morning. By the time dawn broke over Bangkok, there were thousands of sleepy and slightly dazed troops gathered at the king's main residence awaiting instructions. The Promoters from the Royal Siamese Army ordered them to block the entrance of the palace and take it under their control. One Promoter from the Royal Siamese Navy took a gunboat within firing range of key princely homes. From there, he prepared for the possibility of shelling Prince Boriphat's palace in case the interior minister tried to use it as a staging ground for police action. Another renegade navy officer seized the weapons and ammunition from a navy arsenal and prepared to rush them to wherever they were needed. Quite suddenly, the officers at these various gathering points announced to the waiting troops that the absolute monarchy had been swept aside. The sleepy soldiers accepted the news without dissent. Some even cheered the news. The coup d'état had succeeded and no one had been hurt. The entire operation had taken barely three hours.

The main targets remaining were the princely leadership of the Supreme Council. The princes who made up the advisory body could act in the king's defense to order troops or police into action. To stop this, the Promoters dispatched units to capture all five of them and bring them to a central meeting place within the palace. They also grabbed other high-ranking princes whose positions would have put them in leadership positions capable of rallying support against the coup-makers. They were particularly worried about Prince Boriphat. Not only was he minister of the interior, the capable and crafty prince had previously been chief of the army and the navy. He held sway over the armed forces and might have been able to rally army and navy units against the rebels. The Promoters sent well-armed troops to grab these princes because many of the royal families had security guards to protect them. As it turned out, they got nearly all of them without incident. The Promoters held about forty of these princes together, without their servants, in chambers of the royal palace. Their royal hostages gave them a measure of protection while they awaited Prajadhipok's response. The Promoters, in announcing their treasonous action, threatened to kill these highborn princes if any military resistance was directed at them.

The Promoters were never concerned with any area of Siam outside Bangkok. They made no move to secure the many towns and military garrisons that lay beyond Bangkok. Much of the country had only recently come under Siamese sovereignty. There were upcountry princes and provincial military figures who could have created problems for the rebels. They could have challenged the Promoters' move by marching on Bangkok or they could have done something like secede from Siam and declare independence. But they did nothing. Bangkok was more than the capital of the political state at the time, it was its soul. The Promoters, like the royals, had always believed that the rural areas were too unsophisticated to understand the political concepts of constitutionalism and democracy that they studied, debated, and embraced. They had the urban superiority complex that compels city people to look down their noses at rural people, especially those living beyond the Chao Phraya valley, and see them as inconsequential rubes and bumpkins.

A New Party and a Manifesto

How do you tell the Siamese people, or at least the Bangkokians, that their king has been overthrown? The civilian wing of the Promoters swung into action. First, they gave themselves a name they hoped would garner support from the common people, Khana Ratsadon, meaning "the People's Party." They issued something called the Manifesto of the People's Party, displaying it around Bangkok and having it read over the radio. It was a severe indictment of King Prajadhipok. It said they had removed the king because his blundering regime was staffed through nepotism. It accused the king of exploiting his subjects by treating them as if they were slaves. The statement also laid out their plan for Siam's future. They promised to maintain Siam's independence, especially in matters of law, administration, and economics; develop the economy to ensure full employment for all adults; ensure the equality of all citizens; protect Siam's security from foreign attacks and internal disorder; guarantee freedom and liberty for all; and provide universal elementary education.

The Promoters also sent a note directly to the king. It too was harsh, but not as threatening as the Manifesto of the People's Party being read out in Bangkok. The military members of the group, the three full colonels, drafted and signed the note. It summoned the king back to Bangkok so that he could become a constitutional monarch. Any resistance on the king's part, the Promoters suggested, would force them to replace him with a more cooperative Chakri prince. The king, who was playing golf down the coast in Hua Hin when all this was unfolding, had the option of escaping, perhaps by sea to a British territory. He could have also unleashed a counterattack with forces loyal to him. In the end, he decided to cede to the demands of the People's Party. Prajadhipok sent word pledging his cooperation. He maintained his dignity, and perhaps his mistrust, when he refused to climb aboard the navy warship that the Promoters sent to retrieve him. He made it clear he would return to Bangkok as he had come: on the royal locomotive.

Prajadhipok returned to his palace and prepared his next move. When he was ready, he arranged for the Promoters to come and meet him. As delegates from the People's Party walked into the Ananta Samakhom Throne Hall, Prajadhipok leapt from his throne and greeted them. "I rise in honor of the Khana Ratsadon, the People's Party," he called out to them. Such a gesture, rising and welcoming commoners, would have been an unthinkable diminution of royal power in his father's or grandfather's time. To do so for commoners who had attacked him as they did would have been truly unimaginable. But Prajadhipok signaled that he was going to do what he could to work with these revolutionaries. He would find out in the coming weeks and months that it would not be an easy task. The Promoters released the captured princes but sent the most capable, Prince Boriphat, into exile. Although they initially considered seizing all of the princes' properties, they dropped the plan after some internal debate.

Frequently, coups rely more on perceptions than genuine circumstances. They often succeed with only a small percentage of military figures on their side. Sometimes only 10 percent of the military officers support the aims of a coup d'état while another 10 percent oppose it. The 80 percent in the middle decides who wins, waiting to see which side, the coup-makers or the loyalists, is bolder and better organized before making up their minds about who to support. Siam was no different. The coup plotters were a tiny and loosely structured group of no more than a hundred people. Yet, they captured two military regiments, a palace, and a bunch of princes. They made it look easy. Perhaps this was the start of a problem for Thai political history that would continue to plague the nation from this point all the way up to the present: coups could be made to look easy. They could be pulled off with a minimum of bloodshed, with a minimum of fuss. The winner who captured the king or secured his blessing could claim everything. It would be a tempting option for scores of generals who grew up on tales of this first and most important of coups. The sudden appearance of tanks and milling soldiers outside government and military installations became a depressingly regular sight in Bangkok in the following decades. This coup d'état fixation that started on June 24, 1932 would be a burden for Thailand and its people for a long time. By 2014, Thailand would hold the world record with twelve successful coups and another seven unsuccessful attempts over a hundred-year span.

CHAPTER 6

DIMINISHING DEMOCRACY IN POSTABSOLUTIST SIAM

Ending the absolute monarchy seemed surprisingly easy at the time. Constructing a new governmental system that satisfied the competing factions turned out to be all but impossible. The hundred or so civil servants and military officers who overthrew King Prajadhipok's regime in late June 1932 found this out the hard way as they stumbled and argued through the various phases of transforming Siam from an absolute to a constitutional monarchy. Despite the careful planning by the civilian faction led by the brilliant Pridi Banomyong, the Promoters were underprepared for the monumental task of bringing into being the government they so fervently sought. They made several major mistakes in the months that followed their "revolution." Likewise, the royalist faction, including Prajadhipok, was incapable of abiding by a constitutional monarchy despite the political realities confronting them. Their efforts to preserve royal power frustrated the reform processes and stymied democratic development. Having lost their official support, the princes found avenues to prominence through business, sports, and the arts.

Putting Together a Transitional Government

Two days after the Promoters met with the king, the first assembly convened to create a government. It was a heady and confusing time for both those in the ascendant and those on the way down. The Promoters had a loose plan to guide them through the early phase. They would pass a temporary constitution that would serve them until they could promulgate a permanent one. Then they would create a seventy-member People's Assembly that included members of the People's Party and sympathetic outsiders. The People's Assembly membership would select a leader. The Promoters drew members from the People's Assembly to create a smaller People's Committee that would carry out much of the necessary work in remaking the government. The People's Committee was accountable to the Assembly and reported to them. The second stage called for the creation of a permanent constitution that would be ratified within six months. The new government would consist of a National Assembly of which half the members would be appointed and half indirectly elected. The body's reliance on appointed members undermined the democratic claims of the Promoters. In response, the Promoters explained that they would phase in democracy over time, but only after critical changes in Siam had taken place. They planned to improve the country's education standard over the coming decade by building schools, training teachers, and promoting learning. Only then, after all of the farming folk, laborers, and traders had been adequately educated, could the Siamese people participate in the political system. Even the people who carried out the coup against absolutism had little faith in the intelligence and good sense of the rural folk who made up 80 percent of Siam's population. The Promoters, like King Prajadhipok and the princes, were guilty of the same urban chauvinism that many educated city dwellers harbored.

Two days after seizing power, the Promoters presented a constitution to Prajadhipok for him to sign. Prajadhipok himself wrote "interim" on the document to assert some control over the tumultuous events. This charter would serve until a new one could be drafted and approved by representatives of a yet-to-be-formed government. Pridi had written the constitution while planning to overthrow the king. Prajadhipok, after making a few other minor suggestions, all of which were accepted, signed it. The temporary charter removed nearly all of the king's power. In its place, it turned over the administration of Siam to the People's Committee, which acted as an executive council. The larger body, the People's Assembly, was dominated by the civilian and military factions of the Promoters, but it also included some members of the previous regime who were known to be honest and competent.

In retrospect, these moves proved to be the first of many mistakes the Promoters would make in those early months. By giving Prajadhipok a role in the process, they opened the door for more resistance from the royal class they had overthrown. As the leader of the swept-aside princes, Prajadhipok would do what he could to preserve royal prerogatives at the cost of genuine democracy. Another mistake was to include officials from the previous regime in their new government. The Promoters brought back old guard members to ensure a smooth transition to a new form of government. Their inclusion was vital because it reassured anxious observers – the princes, public, and foreign community – that the new government would not be a wrenching change from the previous regime. But it also made the Promoters appear unready to lead on their own. This apparent reluctance to run the state emboldened their enemies from the old regime to resist. Finally, the Promoters failed to mobilize the people to their cause. They never seemed to know where they stood with the common people. They appeared unprepared to rally them to their side despite having studied in Western countries in which public relations had already been an effective weapon in politics.

The Promoters selected *Phraya* Manopakon Nitithada (Manopakon) as the People's Committee head. Manopakon came from outside the Promoters' group. He was a lawyer who had been educated in England. The Promoters nominated him because they believed his time living and studying law in a constitutional monarchy would make him ideal for setting up this new government. Moreover, he had famously clashed with the princes on Prajadhipok's Supreme Council. Manopakon had pushed for cuts in the royal privy purse to help lower official expenditure as the worst of the global depression hit. The incensed princes fired back by blocking his appointment as minister of justice. The Promoters assumed that his bad blood with the princes would guarantee his support for their venture. Manopakon seemed surprised that the Promoters had selected him, but he took the job. It would soon become apparent to the Promoters that their selection of an outsider, especially one who came from the old establishment's ranks, was a bad idea. Manopakon's values were more in line with the princes than with those of the Promoters.

As the Promoters put together a transitional government, Siam grew increasingly chaotic. The press, long subdued by royal restrictions, took the opportunity to print increasingly wild stories of princely corruption and incredible wealth. Outrage spread among the reading public. Egged on by the liberalization of the press, petitions describing corruption by princes, government officials, and employers flooded the new government. The Chakri princes braced for a seizure of their wealth. One of the first things Manopakon did as leader of the People's Committee was to warn the press against rumor-mongering and inciting unrest. His chastisement fed rumors that the Promoters were not the liberal democrats they claimed to be but autocrats intent on supplanting the king's absolute power with their own. Disorder flared throughout the kingdom as laborers walked out on strike, citizens stopped paying taxes, and rumors of regicide circulated. Leaflets appeared in Siam's major cities denouncing the Promoters and calling for the creation of a Soviet-style state. All these developments contributed to fears that Siam was edging toward a bloody revolution. It was a tense time.

Phraya Songsuradet, the army colonel who had organized the military action for the coup, took control of the army. He retired most of the army's and navy's senior leadership and gave those positions to the military members of the Promoters. He also tried to concentrate military power within the Bangkok garrisons to reduce the likelihood of intrigues, rebellious plots, or even civil war. Songsuradet moved all ammunition in the provincial garrisons to Bangkok, ostensibly for inspection. He reorganized the all-important Bangkok garrison so that no one would be able to stage a countercoup. Songsuradet claimed to have built a republican-style army to replace the monarchical one. But in doing so, he arranged the army's structure around himself, and thus became more powerful along the way.

The king's lack of cooperation was another problem. Initially, he had played along with the Promoters, but within weeks of losing power, he withdrew. He stopped appearing at official functions. Rumors spread about his whereabouts. Some said he was under house arrest. Some believed a worse fate had befallen him. Even as the Promoters were drafting their new constitution, they saw that the king would not step aside. It is impossible to say whether many people outside Bangkok would have cared. Some probably still considered a king to be a necessary element of a Siamese state. Many still would have believed he possessed the same divine essence all the Chakri kings harbored even if a coup had erased his absolutism. But in the early 1930s, the king was still a remote presence in most subjects' lives. A British Foreign Office report suggested that Siam's foreign minister had convinced the Promoters to keep the king by warning of intervention by a foreign power if continuity was disrupted. King Prajadhipok, merely by doing nothing, was starting to see how much leverage and bargaining strength he had in this new arrangement. Manopakon took the trouble to consult him on the constitution's progress, partly to quell grave rumors about the fate of the king. A little later, he led a group of Promoters to the palace to pay their respects to Prajadhipok. Pridi Banomyong even apologized for his harsh judgment of the king in the People's Party's Manifesto. He also acknowledged that the Chakri dynasty's leadership had benefited Siam. Pridi's rhetorical backtracking hurt his immediate cause by emboldening the royalists to resist. His generous words also aided the Chakri court's later claims that its monarchs had been a force for democracy throughout the modern era, even though such claims are exaggerated or even absurd.

Attempts at Economic Transformation

The initial economic plan that Pridi created was idealistic and ambitious. He had developed a national economic program along the six principles outlined in his People's Party Manifesto, and he hoped this program would protect Siam from further turbulence during the global economic depression. But it was a highly controversial scheme. Although the rural people played no role in overthrowing the absolute monarchy, the People's Party's economic plan was primarily concerned with transforming Siam's agricultural sector. Pridi wanted to improve the living standards of Siam's poorest citizens. He proposed nationalizing agricultural production, making the state the owner of all farmland and agricultural machinery. The government would pay farmers as employees for their labor. Pridi reasoned that since farmers often only worked half a year planting and harvesting, they could give their labor to government enterprises in the fallow season. Such control of labor would keep workers productive while helping Siam to develop economically. His manifesto argued that this increased economic output would enable Siam to cut its dependency on imports, especially from those nations threatening Siam's independence. Pridi stressed that this was not a French Revolution-style attack on the aristocratic and wealthy classes as no one would forcefully have their land or businesses taken from them. Instead, the government would issue bonds to the landowners as payment for their property. A follow-up plan also proposed provisions for the state management of some industries, a move that would bring nearly the whole economy under state control. The principal target here was urban industries such as rice milling and manufacturing that were dominated by the Chinese.

The old guard, including Prajadhipok, exploited worries about the plan's socialist elements to brand Pridi a communist. Pridi fought back by pointing out that he had woven in many mechanisms to facilitate capitalist enterprises. His explanations did not allay public fear and uncertainty. His opponents attacked him in the press, publishing wildly exaggerated claims about his ambitions. The fear-mongering seemed to work. The cabinet finally voted on Pridi's economic plan in late March 1933. The plan was defeated with seventeen votes against and only four votes in favor. Opposition to the proposal was so vehement that Pridi announced that he would go into voluntary exile to let tensions abate.

The turmoil took its toll on the People's Party's government. A few days after it voted down Pridi's plan for the economic transformation of Siam, the Assembly tried to pass an annual budget. Manopakon opposed a lengthy debate on the topic. He proposed instead that a representative from the Finance Ministry come over and read out the budget, and then the Assembly would pass it immediately without debate. The civilian members, many of them Pridi's supporters, objected to this proposal as authoritarian and undemocratic. Why had the economic plan they had supported been rejected outright, they asked, while Manopakon's budget was to be passed without discussion? These young civil servants demanded debate on every line of the budget as it was read aloud. The Assembly was bogged down in a morass of arguments and parliamentary procedure. On April 3, 1933,

Manopakon, in disgust at the tactics, prorogued the government, even though the government had not been defeated. Manopakon's proclamation ending the session implied that Pridi's economic plan had been the problem, not his bungled presentation of the annual budget. He suggested that he acted to defend the king from hostile elements and to spare Siamese families from financial ruin. A State Council would run the kingdom in place of the Assembly. Many of the military members of the Assembly supported Manopakon's move. Siam had made its first attempts at representative government, and when things had become difficult, a powerful member of the ruling class took it upon himself to scuttle the government rather than try to work through the dissension to arrive at a consensus. It was the first bad example of how easily someone could brush aside a government, almost without consequence, when he did not get his way.

In the aftermath of the first government, Manopakon and his allies tried to prevent Pridi from reclaiming his leadership role in the Promoters. Pridi's control of its civilian wing, and the intellectual force he brought to the group, meant that neither the titled bureaucrats nor the military men could ever fully control the People's Party. Pridi would always be an internal opposition figure who could challenge their dominance. To further harm Pridi, the State Council issued an anticommunist law that carried draconian punishments for those who violated it. The new act punished anyone who advocated nationalizing Siam's industries and agriculture with the death penalty. Those found to be promoting similarly "communist" ideas faced a prison sentence of ten years. The act seemed excessive in light of Siam's current political circumstances. At the time, there was no indigenous communist movement. The Communist Party of Thailand would not come into being for another ten years. There were communists in Siam in the late 1920s, but they were mostly those Chinese and Vietnamese who were using Siam as a base for their anticolonial operations. In some cases, Siam's royalist governments had knowingly harbored these anticolonial revolutionaries because they supported, albeit tacitly, resistance to the French in Indochina. Few of the Chinese and Vietnamese anticolonial radicals put any effort into making Siam a communist country. The Act Concerning Communism of April 2, 1933 seemed designed to keep Pridi out of Siam while the career bureaucrats, many with lingering royalist sympathies, consolidated their gains in the new administration. On top of the accusation that Pridi was a communist working to transform Siam into a Soviet-style state, they published newspaper articles suggesting that Pridi planned to kill the king. This regicidal smear campaign would haunt Pridi for the remainder of his life.

After Manopakon had gotten rid of Pridi, he sought to press his advantage by squeezing out the powerful military members of the State Council. He shared his plans with King Prajadhipok via written correspondence. The king seemed to support and even encourage the move. But before Manopakon could get rid of the State Council's four most influential military members, a group known as the "four tigers," they resigned. They said that the government was stable enough to continue without them. After they left, Manopakon delayed replacing them. The departed members assumed that other military men would get their spots. When this did not happen, they suspected rightly that Manopakon was shoving them aside, just as he had done with Pridi, to concentrate power in his hands. Worse still, they started to worry that his plan might be to restore Prajadhipok as an absolute monarch. To prevent this, they staged another coup.

The Military Seizes Power

In this next coup, barely a year after the first one, the military seized power. On June 10, 1933, *Phraya* Phahonphonphayuhasena (Phahon), an army colonel, carried out a similar troop deployment to take critical offices. Using tanks, he captured the Ministry of Defense, key military barracks, and the throne hall. Overthrowing a wobbly constitutional government was less dangerous than toppling a king because the rebels had fewer potential adversaries who might resist and because the new leaders lacked the aura of authority possessed by the Chakris. Prajadhipok was not a significant factor in the second coup. As with the first, the king was away at his beachside palace in Hua Hin. While Colonel Phahon's more senior military faction led the coup effort, it was the junior army officers, led by Phibun Songkhram, who had lobbied hardest to seize power. An artillery specialist, Phibun rallied the faction of junior military officers who had begun to resent their assignments after the coup. They saw their paths to power thwarted by

Manopakon's maneuverings. Phibun was also a friend of Pridi, their association dating to their student days in Paris. Phahon made himself the prime minister. But while the coup was simpler the second time around, creating a new government proved to be just as challenging.

The Boworadet Rebellion

Phahon was better at staging coups than organizing governments. As the new government struggled to find its way, its opponents were emboldened. The biggest challenge came from Prince Boworadet. He was the prince whose removal as minister of defense the Promoters had used as a smokescreen while plotting their coup. Under the old regime, he had seethed about how Prajadhipok and the Supreme Council treated him. So intense was his dissatisfaction with Prajadhipok's court that many observers had assumed Boworadet was the Promoters' secret mastermind. Many still believed that he was pulling the Promoters' strings from somewhere in hiding even in the postabsolutist phase. But those people had it all backward. As a prince whose father was born to a king and a queen, Boworadet had a stake in the old system's continuation. He had never been with the Promoters. Boworadet had faded into the background while trying to figure out a countermove to the new regime. He had taken leave of his duties in Bangkok to go upcountry to Nakhon Ratchasima (Korat). There he met with the military leaders of upcountry garrisons who felt slighted by the consolidation of military power in Bangkok that Songsuradet had carried out. Throughout August and September 1933, Prince Boworadet gathered them together and set out his own plot to stage a countercoup. He planned to overthrow the new government and restore King Prajadhipok to some form of his previous power. With Korat as his base, he brought in the Ayutthaya garrison that was vitally important because of its location just above Bangkok on the Chao Phraya River. He also needed the units surrounding Bangkok, so he made overtures to the Ratchaburi and Petchaburi garrisons located south and southwest of the capital. But before he could get together a strong coalition, and before the monsoon rains had petered out sufficiently to secure a viable military campaign, word of his planned rebellion reached Phahon, the new head of the government. The leak forced Prince Boworadet to launch his uprising earlier than he wanted to, and before he could bring in the overwhelming force he needed to ensure success.

Despite losing the element of surprise, Boworadet had some early success. On October 11, 1933, he launched his first attacks. He rushed his troops down the rail lines toward Bangkok. They teamed up with the Ayutthaya soldiers and moved toward Bangkok, fighting their way into the northern suburbs of the capital. Boworadet told his troops that they were fighting to rescue the king from the faction of "communists" who had come to power.

Prince Boworadet nearly succeeded in his aim. His men captured their biggest prize when they took Don Mueang airfield, the airport used for international flights that was also a base for some military aircraft. With this air base and its resources, he had the potential to destroy the forces defending the city. But he made a significant mistake when he had his troops delay their assault on the city center. He used the time to issue his demands and to wait for negotiations. The army colonel sent against him was Phibun Songkhram. Phibun and the junior military officer faction had a lot to lose if Boworadet successfully restored the monarchy. Phibun deployed his artillery units to the capital's north, where they pounded Boworadet's forces mercilessly. Some Boy Scouts, college students, and other civilians helped Phibun's forces in non-combat duties. Artillery shells from both sides rained down on the surrounding areas, killing many civilians. In the campaign, Boworadet sent crewless railway cars down the tracks that collided with trains rushing north to meet them. The loss of life, especially the deaths of civilians, infuriated Phibun, and he struck back with increased ferocity. Prince Boworadet summoned troops from other provincial garrisons, especially from Ubon Ratchathani, and tried to hold on until they could arrive. Fighting raged along Bangkok's rail lines as the two sides tried to push back each other's troops.

In the middle of all this, King Prajadhipok was summoned to Bangkok by the People's Party from his seaside palace at Hua Hin. He refused to comply, saying he felt safer outside Bangkok. The People's Party did not trust him. They suspected that he was complicit in the rebellion. Moreover, he was not far from some of Prince Boworadet's rebellious garrisons that may have appeared to be protecting him. Instead of waiting to be taken by either side, Prajadhipok got in a small yacht and headed south toward Songkhla. His vessel ran out of fuel along the way, and the royal escape party bobbed helplessly in the Gulf of Siam before being rescued by a passing foreign ship.

By then, Prince Boworadet's units were starting to fall apart. Phibun's artillery barrages had driven them back and scattered some of them. Troops loyal to the government had attacked Korat. In response, Boworadat divided his forces to send some back to Korat to help those remaining forces now under attack. The troops coming from Ubon mutinied rather than join the rebel forces, and turned around and went home. Sensing defeat, Prince Boworadet fled. He escaped by airplane into French Indochina as other rebel officers scrambled to make similar getaways.

According to Thai records, the official casualty figures were fourteen government troops and two policemen dead, with another fifty-eight wounded. There is no mention of the apparently high number of civilian casualties, nor do they offer any figures for rebel dead or injured. The assumption is that the government tried to play down the extent of the fighting to minimize the discontent's scope and hide how closely they had come to being swept away by the rebellious prince. In 1936, the government constructed a monument to the police and soldiers killed defending the new postabsolutist government. The Constitutional Defense Monument stood in northern Bangkok for more than eighty years as a reminder of Thai democracy's uncertain early days. Over the decades, civil rights activists cherished it for commemorating an early victory for democratic forces. Late in 2018, the pro-royalist government of Prayuth Chan-ocha removed it to make way for a new elevated train line. They said they were moving it some forty kilometers outside Bangkok. Likewise, another monument, a small bronze plaque marking the spot where Phahon announced the creation of the constitution in 1932, was removed in 2014 by the same administration. The government never revealed the fate of the vanished plaque, and it remains lost to this day.

Prelude to Abdication

Political repression worsened in the aftermath of the Boworadet Rebellion. The government arrested many of its detractors and accused them of siding with the rebels. It passed laws criminalizing anyone who challenged the constitution. The crime carried a twenty-year prison sentence, although it did not define what was meant by "challenging the constitution." They arrested and tried members of the royal family who had been sympathetic to Boworadet's rebellion. They even imprisoned one Chakri prince, the younger brother of Boworadet himself, breaking a taboo on incarcerating royalty. The government shut down newspapers that it deemed antagonistic or unfairly critical. King Prajadhipok's father-in-law owned one of the targeted newspapers. The censorship incident set off a series of conflicts that culminated in Prajadhipok's abandonment of his crown.

The People's Party was not really a political party, nor was it about the people. Its members saw their role as guiding the government. They wanted the power to appoint members of the National Assembly but they did not think it necessary to run for their positions. When a group tried to organize a political party to challenge them, the People's Party announced that political parties would be banned. The challengers called their would-be party the Khana Chat, a name that translates to "the Nationalists." The government ordered the Nationalists to disband and investigated its members for seditious motives. Although the People's Party overthrew the absolute monarchy in the name of democracy, they were reluctant to introduce democratic institutions.

When the new Assembly met, it tried to pass several bills that antagonized the royal family, including some that especially angered Prajadhipok. The Assembly proposed a law levying an estate tax on royal property transfers at death. Another law was designed to bypass the king in death penalty cases. Typically, the king signed all death penalties. This responsibility is one reason that Thai kings require enormous karmic merit (*barami*). They must spend that moral power by taking the lives of criminals. Prajadhipok was upset about both laws, and he threatened abdication rather than sign either.

Prajadhipok's efforts to get along with the People's Party had largely failed. Both sides were still too suspicious of the other. Boworadet's failed rebellion had likewise discouraged the king. Reverence for the monarchy among military units, like in the general population, seemed shallow. After three years of this, Prajadhipok had had enough. He announced that he was going overseas, something the People's leadership feared because, for one thing, they could neither monitor nor control him when he was abroad, and that he would return at an as yet undetermined date. He said it would be a private visit, no state functions. He would visit continental Europe, the United Kingdom, and the United States. The primary purpose was, he said, to see doctors about his various ailments, especially his failing eyes. Phahon, fearing for what Prajadhipok might do or say in Europe, offered to bring in at government expense any doctor in the world that he required. The king left anyway.

He defied the government almost as soon as he was gone. He left Siam with members of his former Supreme Council. They met with exiled princes staying in Singapore. In Italy, his non-state visit included meeting King Victor Emanuel, Benito Mussolini, and Pope Pius XI. He was in Paris, Berlin, Copenhagen, London, Budapest, and Prague. He went back to London for surgery in September 1934. The procedure did not improve the condition of his eyes. Doctors warned him against further operations until he was stronger. Rather than return home, he took a six-month lease on a home in Surrey and settled down to stay. There he laid out the terms by which he would return to Siam. He wanted greater control over royal expenditures. Despite his frugal ways, he resented commoners controlling the palace's purse strings. He also demanded that the government free the rebels captured and imprisoned after the Boworadet Rebellion. With some of them facing death sentences for their actions, he sought a return of the king's right to be the ultimate arbiter of capital offenses. He pursued other constitutional powers, including the power to appoint half of the National Assembly and veto power that would require a 75 percent majority to override. The Promoters gave no ground on any of these demands.

The man who never thought he would be king no longer wanted to be king. Exhausted and dispirited, Prajadhipok chose to exit the Siamese political drama from his position offstage. On March 4, 1935, he abdicated. In a note he sent to *The Times* of London, he said he had wanted to play a role in the new constitutional monarchy but had been thwarted and lied to by a regime that was more concerned with authoritarianism than with democracy. His concern for democracy seems disingenuous considering that he had resisted democratization both before and after the June 1932 coup d'état. It may have been more sour grapes from a figure who could not reimpose more of the royal powers he had lost, especially from abroad. Prajadhipok did not inform the government of his abdication plans ahead of time. He ended his announcement with an apology to the Siamese people for not serving until death as had his predecessors. It was his own little coup, a surprising defiant final act from a one-time absolute monarch demoted to figurehead in a short and rocky reign. He did not name a successor.

Choosing a Successor

The People's Party kept the abdication a secret from the Siamese people while they met to determine what to do. After a meeting of the Assembly, they chose Prince Ananda Mahidol, a grandson of King Chulalongkorn and son of one of the Chakri's most progressive princes who had died a few years earlier. The new king was nine years old and living in Switzerland. His father, Prince Mahidol Adulyadej, was the 69th son of King Chulalongkorn and Queen, Sawang Vadhana. Mahidol was of the first generation of Chulalongkorn's children to study abroad. He had studied at Harrow in England before going to Germany for military studies. After returning to Siam to serve in the Royal Siamese Navy, Mahidol chose to dedicate himself to public health. In 1917, he enrolled in Harvard University's medical school, intending to become a doctor. While in the United States, he courted and married a Thai commoner named Sangwan Talaphat, who was in Boston to study nursing. As newlyweds, Mahidol and Sangwan traveled widely throughout the West. While staying in London in 1923, Sangwan gave birth to the couple's first child, a daughter named Galyani Vadhana. Mahidol suffered from ill health. In 1925, while in Germany for Mahdiol's medical treatment, Sangwan gave birth to their second child, a boy they named Ananda. Their third child, Bhumibol, was born in Brookline, Massachusetts, as Mahidol was finishing his medical degree. After becoming a doctor, Prince Mahidol moved the family to Siam so that he could practice medicine in Bangkok. But his status as a prince, as a son of King Chulalongkorn and half-brother of Kings Vajiravudh and Prajadhipok, made it impossible for him to examine patients who recoiled in abeyance at his royal touch, some of them falling to the floor. To escape the obstacle of royalty awe, Prince Mahidol went north to Chiang Mai to work in a hospital set up by American Presbyterian missionaries. He was more anonymous there and could work without inspiring fear or excessive deference in his patients. His short time working in the north took a toll on his already fragile health. He returned to his family in Bangkok in 1929 after some months away and died suddenly from a liver abscess.

The Promoters chose Mahidol's eldest son Ananda to be king because the nine-year-old would not assume the throne until he was twenty. As long as he was studying in Switzerland, he would also be far away from the royalist intrigues roiling Siam's government. In the meantime, they would appoint a Council of Regents from among their political allies to carry out the boy king's duties while he was away. They would not have to worry about royal opposition now or maybe ever if they could establish a system of diminished royal power. For members of the royal family who had hoped for a counterbalance against the increasingly powerful People's Party, these developments seemed to signal the end of the Chakri dynasty in all but name. But those fears turned out to be premature.

CHAPTER 7

THE DIFFICULT TIME OF PHIBUN SONGKHRAM

After King Prajadhipok abdicated in 1936, the surviving royalists – the princes and officials of the old regime – lost much of their remaining power. Ananda, the newly crowned boy king studying in Switzerland, did not provide a good symbolic figure around which to organize themselves politically. They could not present themselves to Siamese society as defenders of the country and its traditions when the figure they sought to champion was studying French and mathematics in Europe. The senior bureaucratic elites who had enjoyed some power when the Promoters made Manopakon Nititada the first prime minister quickly faded when the Siamese military brushed Manopakon aside. The civilian factions of the People's Party led by Pridi Banomyong also lost much of their stature when Pridi was made the scapegoat for every ill-conceived economic or educational policy to surface, as well as the bogeyman for all the collective fears of communism and the social upheaval with which it was associated. Pridi's forced exile and trips abroad weakened them. The senior military figures in the People's Party, of which Phraya Phahon was the most visible, proved that they were not up to the task of ruling. They lacked the charisma, support, and vision that Siam needed in the vacuum created by the loss of the monarchy. Only one faction remained vital and organized: the junior military officers led by Phibun Songkhram.

Phibun's Rise to Power

Phibun's rise to power is a story of ambition and foresight. He used the unstable political and economic circumstances of the mid-1930s to advance the role of the military in Siamese society. He elevated himself to the position of supreme leader at a time when similar strong leaders were emerging in Italy, Germany, and Japan. But he does not fit the caricature of a thuggish fascist that some of his detractors have applied to him. He possessed a complex combination of personal ambition, nationalist fervor, and Thai chauvinism. His gift was that he managed to harness the existing sentiments of his time and attach them to his ambitions. Phibun was a striver who emerged from near obscurity to become the dominant figure in Thai politics for more than two decades. He remained the central figure amid rapidly changing political circumstances, including those brought on by World War II and the Cold War. Hungry for power and fame rather than wealth and comfort, Phibun acted always with an eye fixed on his historical legacy.

Phibun rose to power on the shoulders of the Royal Thai Army. Since the reign of King Chulalongkorn, Siam had spent ever greater amounts on the military. At one point in the early twentieth century, the country was spending 30 percent of the national budget on defense. The first move Phibun made was to affirm this elevation of the military in Thai society. He began by recasting the formula for Siamese nationalism that King Vajiravudh had put forward a few decades earlier. Instead of the monarchy, Buddhism, and the country, Phibun gave speeches arguing that the formula necessary for Thai nationalism should be the monarchy, the Assembly, the government, and the military. He removed Buddhism, substituted the National Assembly and government for the country, and placed the military as the most important. He likened it to a table with four legs, saying that the first three were the least stable elements in this table-like base. All were subject to change because of the changing personalities of the people who filled those positions. The military was critical, he suggested, because it was the only one that could safeguard all the others. Phibun laid out a plan by which the military would guide political affairs while the country underwent a period of political transformation. The army would guide government affairs while the rest of the country learned about modern political systems and the duties of a civil society. Only after the people had acquired sufficient political knowledge would the government grant a constitution guaranteeing popular participation. During this period, Phibun oversaw the construction of the Democracy Monument, an imposing sculpture complex commemorating the overthrow of the absolute monarchy. The centerpiece of Bangkok's Ratchadamnoen Avenue, it was built in imitation of Paris's Champs-Elysees. The monument shows the constitution resting upon two golden ritual presentation bowls (*phan*) guarded by four wings that represent the branches of the military.

To reach young people, Phibun formed a military training organization for high school-aged males called Yuwachon. Although some suggest it had parallels to the Nazi's Hitler Youth program, its actual inspiration was the high school military training programs that existed in Britain and the United States. Phibun used the organization to bring the military into the daily lives of young people and their parents. He had military displays set up at schools to encourage enrollment and to bring regular people into contact with the military. Soldiers would put tanks and artillery pieces in public parks and invite the people to tour them. He encouraged shooting contests as public competitions. Members of Yuwachon trained in military tactics for a few hours each week. The group attracted about six thousand adolescent males.

Creating Thai Nationalism

Luang Wichit Wathakan (Wichit) provided the Phibun era with a specifically nationalist Thai history that helped to define Phibun's heavily militaristic and chauvinistically Thai nationalism. He wove together history, drama, literature, fine arts, and politics to construct an idealized past for the Thai people. In the process, he composed something akin to a Thai cultural character that most Thais still embrace. His propagandistic literary initiatives earned him the trust of both Phibun and Pridi, who made him director of the newly established Department of Fine Arts in 1934. He used the post to develop traditional Thai arts, but always according to his political and aesthetic ideals. To ensure the growth of this initiative, Wichit created a drama and dance school at the National Museum, which developed its own acting troupe to perform plays for the public that would popularize his vision of Thais in history.

At the Department of Fine Arts, Wichit took traditional Thai stories, many of them old dance-dramas that had entertained Thai people for centuries, and rewrote them in order to advance the post-absolutist government's political, social, and cultural agendas. He directed the Department of Fine Arts to publish and disseminate these updated classics to schools and theaters around the country. Wichit also wrote several historical plays to promote the postabsolutist government's idea of Thai-ness. In plays like *Luat Suphan* (1936), *Ratchamanu* (1937), *Phrachao Krung Thon* (1937), and *Chaoying Saenwi* (1938), he conjured a Southeast Asian past in which Thai historical actors won the admiration of neighboring peoples through their martial valor, kindness, and Buddhist piety. They were deeply romantic plays in which the lead rivals progress from mistrust and hatred to affection and love for each other. The heroes of the plays were not Chakri kings or princes but nobles, soldiers, and commoners who demonstrate loyalty to their premodern "nations." The one exception, King Taksin in *Phrachao Krung Thon*, was a savior figure who was destroyed by the Chakri's supporters. Wichit set these dramas in wars that pitted Thais against Burmese and Cambodians, whetting the national appetite for the recovery of Siam's "lost territories" in Laos, Cambodia, Burma, and Malaya that Phibun promoted in his speeches. Phibun and Wichit described Siam and Laos as separated siblings who longed to be reunited as the core of a powerful Tai national family, along the lines of Hitler's program aimed at uniting the greater German peoples into a single state.

Wichit borrowed other political or propaganda elements from the Nazis. He revived King Vajiravudh's characterizations of Siam's ethnic Chinese as "the Jews of the Orient" who enjoyed parasitic prosperity in Siam, Laos, and other Southeast Asian countries by exploiting the so-called native peoples. Wichit himself was of Chinese heritage, but coming from a family that was largely assimilated, and having invested himself intellectually and emotionally in a specifically Thai-centric cultural mythology, Wichit went after the Chinese as an enemy "other," launching verbal and literary attacks with little impunity. In one notorious speech in which he quoted King Vajriavudh's essay, he cited the vast sums of money that Chinese remitted to their families in China from Siam. Some of the willingness to embrace Wichit's anti-Chinese propaganda was a result of Chinese labor action in Siam. Many Chinese enterprises had organized anti-Japanese boycotts and protests after Japan invaded China in 1937 and began its bloody military campaigns in Shanghai and Nanjing. The anti-Japan activities intensified when Japan invaded southern China, including Shantou in Guangdong Province, the area from which many of Siam's Chinese population had originated.

Siam's leaders reacted strongly to the anti-Japanese sentiment for several reasons. While not being overtly pro-Japanese, they admired Japan for its dramatic industrialization and militarization in the first decades of the twentieth century. They also appreciated that Britain and France were wary of Japan's economic and diplomatic advances into Southeast Asia. France was afraid that Siam would form a partnership with Japan that would allow Japanese forces to use Siam as a base for attacks on Indochina. Britain was afraid that Siam would allow Japan to use Siamese territory to invade Malaya, and on to Singapore, in the event of a war. To a certain extent, that is exactly what happened a few years later.

Thailand for Thais

Wichit was the principal agent in changing Siam's name during this period. Siam had never, in fact, called itself Siam. Wichit believed the story common in his time that Siam as a term came from Cambodia. It was said that "Sa-yam" was a Sanskrit term meaning "dark-skinned" people that the Khmer had used for the Tai peoples living to the west of Cambodia. Linguists have never confirmed this and, as many people have pointed out, Thai people are generally lighter complexioned than their Cambodian neighbors. It is more likely that the term came from Chinese. This theory, developed by Thai scholars, is that Siam is derived from the two Chinese characters (for Xi and An) assigned to the ancient kingdoms of Sukhothai and Ayutthaya. The name was adopted by other countries who came in contact with the Chinese, especially Chinese mariners who sailed to Southeast Asia. Either way, the Thais never used it to refer to themselves. They always called themselves Thai, and called their *mueang* (city-states or polities) by the name of their city (Sukhothai, Ayutthaya, Lopburi, and so on). During the Bangkok period, Thai leaders called their kingdom Rattanakosin. Over time, they accepted Siam as the foreign rendering of their name, and even incorporated this foreign term into their language and official correspondence, but many leaders never felt at ease with the foreign appellation.

Wichit tapped into this concern to argue for a change in the country's name. He wanted a name that would provide a core for the "lost territory" claims he was promoting when he wrote and performed plays celebrating the greater Tai universe that included Laos and parts of Burma, Vietnam, and southern China. He argued that a fiercely independent nation as great as his should not be saddled with a foreign-derived name. The problem was the name itself. The Thais called their country Mueang Thai or Prathet Thai, both difficult for foreigners to pronounce. Others protested that a name change would create confusion. But the leadership went ahead and changed the name in June 1939 to Prathet Thai. The English translation was Thailand. The new name also made it clear that Thailand was the Thais' land. It did not belong, according to the rhetoric of the day, to the Chinese, Khmer, Malay, Vietnamese, Hmong or any other cultural grouping living within it. It also meant that all people, no matter their ethnicity, were "Thai" (*chao thai*) as long as they lived in Thailand. But as much as Phibun and Wichit wanted to coin a name that owed nothing to foreign influence, the new name's arrangement of ethnicity linked to a homeland displayed obvious parallels to such European states as England, Scotland, and Deutschland.

Cultural Mandates

Phibun launched a cultural movement to advance his political aims. Starting in 1939, he issued a series of cultural mandates (or "state conventions") called *rathaniyom*. His goal was to transform the Siamese into a "civilized" people by promoting behavior and habits similar to those found in Europe and the United States. He created a National Council on Culture to lead this effort. Wichit helped him draft the policies. The mandates encouraged Thai men to be more like Westerners by dressing in shirts, shoes, slacks, and especially hats. At the time, most Thai men and women still covered their lower body with a length of cloth called a *phanung* or a pair of loose trousers.

They covered their tops with a light tunic, a short vest, or nothing at all. The government asked prominent women from the world of fashion and high society to set an example by wearing Western-style hats. Many obliged, happy to explore the various bonnets, cloches, tams, and caps required for all social interactions and occasions. But not all were enthusiastic. When asked to promote the mandates by wearing a hat, one royal woman replied acidly, "If you want me to wear a hat, cut off my head and put a hat on it."

Phibun's regime also sought to promote exercise and sports, especially gymnastics and hiking. The government recommended that people divide their day into three equal parts: one for work, one for personal obligations, and one for sleep. The mandates encouraged new dietary habits such as eating more meat and vegetables. The *rathaniyom* are one likely origin of the popular noodle dish *kuay thiao pad thai* or *pad thai*, as it is known around the world. According to one popular story, Phibun was said to have been particularly fond of noodles, so the mandates prodded the Thais to eat more noodles in greater varieties and dishes. Working with his household cook Phibun and his wife, La-iad Bhandhukravi, concocted the recipe by combining rice noodles with several other popular ingredients such as tofu, eggs, dried shrimp, bean sprouts, red chilis, peanuts, chives, fish sauce, and tamarind paste, to make a stir-fried "national dish" that was unique, tasty, and filling. Satisfied with their creation, Phibun had the government issue the recipe to Thai street chefs who could whip up the dish at any time for breakfast, lunch, dinner, or a late-night snack. Phibun's son, the diplomat Nit Phibulsongkhram, said later that his father had designed the recipe around numerous ingredients because he was trying to spur economic growth. True or not, these stories endure as the historical source of what has become one of the most popular Thai dishes for people around the world.

The mandates also promoted literacy (in central Thai) and patriotism. Phibun made it compulsory for all to stand and remain at attention when raising or lowering the national flag or whenever the national anthem was played. Even today, all Thais stop their regular activities in spaces such as schools, train stations, and government offices at 8:00 am and 6:00 pm to stand and face the flag while the national anthem is played.

The mandates had a secondary, less obvious purpose. Phibun pushed for the cultural changes because he wanted to create a homogenous "Thai" culture that would mark non-adherents as outsiders. He needed to convince the other Tai peoples, such as the Lao of the northeast, that they were now simply "Thai." Those who did not follow the modern Thai cultural mandates would appear as opponents to the new Thai nation. More pointedly, he tried to delineate Sino-Thai identity as being "un-Thai," and thus at odds with the state. His attempt to label Bangkok's Chinese as a threatening alien presence was ironic for a couple of reasons. First, Chinese had been living in the area of Bangkok even before Rama I built his city there. Second, ethnic Chinese had played a vital role in the rapid development of the new capital city. And, third, many Bangkokians, as well as many Thais in the lower Chao Phraya valley, had Chinese heritage. Some of Phibun's hostility to the Chinese arose from fear of the ethnic Chinese growing domination of labor, trade, banking, and other business enterprises. More specifically, he targeted the Chinese for undermining his efforts to draw Thailand into a closer strategic relationship with Japan. In mid-1939, he issued directives that barred Thais from expressing opinions about international circumstances if such statements hurt Thailand's security. Prominent Chinese leaders led boycotts of Japanese goods during this period to protest Japan's invasion of China. Phibun saw an alliance with Japan as a possible safeguard against further territorial losses to the Western powers. But he also realized that stronger ties to Japan came with their own dangers.

Reclaiming "Lost Territories"

The looming war in Asia provided Phibun with great opportunities and great risks. The historical grievances that Thais had nursed against France and, to a lesser extent, Britain, could be addressed or even rectified under the right circumstances. The risks were that Thailand could be sucked into a destructive war and, quite possibly, transformed into a colony or protectorate of Japan as was the case in China. But they could gain a lot, too. The historian Shane Strate has examined how the "never been colonized" discourse popular in nationalist histories was turned on its head in the late 1930s and early 1940s. During that period, a subtheme emphasizing the "lost territories" was exploited by Thailand's leadership by promoting what Strate identifies as "national humiliation discourse" – linking the rise of Western imperialism in Southeast Asia to the gradual loss of Thai prestige in the region. It argues that Siam's former regional dominance could be regained if Thailand were to reclaim its so-called "lost territories" in Laos, Cambodia, Burma, and Malaya.

By 1940, Phibun saw his chance to make a move on the "lost territories" in the French colonial possessions of Laos and Cambodia. He also wanted to remake the border with British Burma and British Malaya. Phibun saw that France and Britain were preoccupied with the intensifying conflict in Europe. Just as importantly, Japan wanted an access point into southern China to facilitate its war there. France, feeling bruised and vulnerable as Hitler's forces smashed their way across Europe, did not want to allow Japan any deeper influence into its Southeast Asian territory. Phibun recognized this as his best chance at playing off the European powers against Japan. But his plan held risks for Thailand.

What Phibun wanted in 1940 was what might be called a rationalization of the Thai-Lao border. The northern border between Thailand and Laos deviates from the Mekong River to put a lot of territory into Laos's possession. The areas opposite the Thai province of Nan are the Laotian provinces of Sainyabuli and Luang Prabang. The French, in claiming Laos in 1893, took the territory owned by the Lao king on the west bank of the Mekong River. It was fertile land that was also the site of the palaces and temples that so obsessed the French colonialists. Their claim put the northern part of the Mekong River far from the Thai-Lao border. There is a similar deviation from the Mekong River in the southern part of Laos in Champasak. As in the north, the border swerves west away from the river to put more of that west bank into French Indochina. This area has great Angkor-era Khmer ruins, including a magnificent site called Wat Phu, and it has the royal palaces of the former king of Champasak. Phibun also wanted to claim large parts of Cambodian territory, mostly from the areas of Battambang, Sisophon, and Siem Reap, in this first land-grab campaign. In some ways, the Cambodian claims were even more audacious because they would have put huge sections of northern Cambodia, the heart of the former Angkor empire, into Thailand. Phibun saw the circumstances of 1940 as his chance to remake the border and ameliorate Thai "humiliation" by Western powers. More than just the gain of land, the reclamation would provide Phibun with a conflict. He would have diplomatic confrontations and perhaps even real military engagements to further expand and intensify the political rhetoric on which he and his administration made their claim of legitimacy. Phibun needed a war, but he knew Siam was not strong enough to defeat French or British armies. He sought instead a small war against greatly weakened and distracted European colonial forces that would give him a better chance at victory.

Urged on by his Japanese counterparts who wanted to use French territory against China, Phibun ratcheted up the rhetoric, mobilized his forces, and by October 1940, the end of the rainy season in mainland Southeast Asia, he moved troops into a border area that Thailand had formerly kept demilitarized out of fear of sparking another confrontation with France. At this point, though, he wanted a provocation for war. The United States was struggling to maintain the status quo amongst its allies, rivals, and potential enemies in that corner of Asia. In November 1940, Washington, alarmed by the potential for an outbreak of war, canceled delivery of ten American aerial bombers it had sold to Thailand earlier that year. Phibun seized on this American about-face and launched a sharp anti-American propaganda campaign that furthered his drift into the Japan-Germany-Italy grouping. Phibun's fit of anti-American pique would have consequences for Thailand and the United States during the war and long after.

With the rains over by November 1940, sporadic fighting broke out along the Laos-Thailand border. The Thais put in about sixty thousand troops. They sent motorized cavalry, artillery, and aircraft. The French were less well armed. They rushed about fifty thousand troops into the area. Most of the French units were poorly trained and haphazardly equipped colonial troops. The Thais fired artillery across the Mekong River at different points and occasionally sent up small military aircraft to bomb French positions. Periodically, the Thais launched aerial bombardments of French sites in major towns, including Vientiane and Phnom Penh, which proved to be skillful and accurate. On the ground, both sides pursued cautious and half-hearted skirmishes. One interesting account of this shooting war of 1940–41 was written by

Pierre Boulle, author of the novels *Bridge Over the River Kwai* (1952) and *Planet of the Apes* (1963). Boulle had joined the ragtag French Indochinese colonial army when Germany attacked France, and was sent with a group of poorly armed and barely trained Vietnamese and French soldiers up into Laos from Vietnam. In his memoir of the period, Boulle describes almost sleepy exchanges of fire between Thai and French positions that were sporadically broken up by the appearance of Thai aircraft overhead. It was not much of a war, nor was it anything like the glorious historical campaigns conjured by Wichit in his chauvinistic dramas. But it was enough for Phibun's purposes.

In January 1941, Thailand's armed forces moved into French Indochina. Their infantry and armored units fought well against the French colonial troops. They drove the French from their positions, and hit their retreating forces in the open. The Thai navy, however, fared poorly. In mid-January, the French sought to win at sea what they could not win on land by striking Thai navy vessels in the Gulf of Thailand around Koh Chang. In the surprise attack, the French sank two Thai torpedo boats and damaged a cruiser before retreating. The Thais caused only minor damage to the French flotilla. The Japanese, anxious to take advantage of the situation, rushed in and offered to negotiate an end to the conflict. They pushed through an agreement that gave Thailand territory in Laos and a new border along the lines established by the Mekong River. Thailand also got territory in Cambodia. The French, although they lost territory, gained an assurance from Japan that they would not lose any more. Japan was the big winner. It got a treaty with both Thailand and France promising that neither would form an alliance with a third power against Japan. This would prohibit Thailand or France from forming an alliance with Britain against Japan if Japan attacked Singapore, Burma, and Malaya.

As thrilled as Thai leaders were to "regain," as they termed it, large swaths of territories in Laos and Cambodia, they remained uneasy about a closer relationship with Japan. They also felt increasingly nervous about their deteriorating relationship with the United States. As war loomed, Thai diplomats and military leaders feared being dragged into an alliance that would expose them to the kind of destruction that China was enduring. So Phibun tried to put on the brakes.

War Comes to Thailand

Thailand's stance on the eve of World War II is often described as an example of its "bamboo diplomacy." The term refers to the Thai leadership's ability to remain flexible and independent, to move closer to the dominant regional power while maintaining relationships with weaker powers without fully committing itself to any one side. Like bamboo stalks blown by a strong wind, Thailand will bend in the direction of least resistance while not being figuratively uprooted, pushed to the ground, or broken. The beauty of the term "bamboo diplomacy" is that it is either a positive or negative, a compliment or an insult, depending on the user's view of Thailand. The meaning it imparts is as flexible as the phenomenon it describes. Scholars and commentators would continue to apply the term to Thailand throughout the latter half of the twentieth century, especially in the Cold War. The Thai phrase describing this tendency is different, though, but it reflects a similar pragmatism. In Thai they call it "placing both feet on a rocking boat."

Phibun regretted his rash outburst against the Americans. As war in Southeast Asia loomed, he scrambled to repair Thailand's relationship with the United States for several related reasons. First, he needed weapons. Demonstrations of Japan's and Germany's military might had reminded him how vulnerable Thailand was against nations with modern armed forces. If the Japanese could intimidate the British, French, and Americans, the Thais were unlikely to fare well if they stood up to the East Asian power. Second, Phibun apparently decided that he did not want to be embraced by the Japanese. He wanted to remain neutral if war broke out. As Siamese leaders did during the Great War a generation before, Phibun's regime looked to the United States as a guide for neutrality. The United States had not fully committed itself to the growing war in Europe despite its sympathies for Germany's victims and opponents. Thai leaders worked to maintain a similar neutrality while still signaling support for Japan's aggression in eastern Asia. In August 1941, Phibun announced that Thailand would remain neutral.

Japan sought to better define its ambiguous relationship with Thailand as its military plans for Southeast Asia moved forward. It gave the Thai leadership three options by which they could dispel some of that ambiguity. In the first, Japan sought permission from Thailand to move its soldiers and equipment through Thai territory in an attack on the British in Malaya and Burma. Accessing Thai territory meant the Japanese would not have to land their forces under fire but could get them into the area safely before launching an attack. Thailand would not be obliged to aid Japan or fight alongside it; it merely had to let them pass through. This option presented Thailand with the least close relationship with Japan. The second option was a supportive agreement between Japan and Thailand. Japan wanted Thailand to provide military and logistical assistance to Japan's Southeast Asian forces while they were in the region. In return, Japan would protect Thailand in the event that Britain or the United States took military action against Thailand. The third choice was a clear military alliance in which Thailand would actively join Japan in its conquest of Southeast Asia. The Thai military would move with the Japanese Imperial Army as it fought its way across Asia. Japan offered as an enticement the rest of Thailand's so-called "lost territories," specifically, the areas of northern Malaya that Siam ceded to Britain in 1909.

These options were pressed on Phibun in early December 1941 as Japan was preparing to attack British forces in Malaya and Singapore and attack the United States in Hawaii, the Philippines, and across the Pacific. The pressure on Phibun was enormous. While the Thai leader was willing to allow the Japanese to move through southern Thailand to hit the British, he did not want Japanese forces to occupy Thailand, and he especially opposed their presence in central Thailand. He felt trapped by circumstances. He wanted to hold onto those "lost territories" as the crowning achievement of his irredentist campaign. But he could not announce a change in geopolitical alliances to the Thai public or to his political and military rivals without causing a lot of worry. In fact, Phibun seems to have been overcome with anxiety and ambivalence about a Thailand-Japan alliance just as war was erupting in Southeast Asia and at Pearl Harbor. Phibun was in the Cambodian territories that Thailand had recently acquired when news of the attack reached Bangkok. Mysteriously, he did not rush back to the capital by plane despite the urgency of the circumstances. While his ministers and Japanese officials waited impatiently, Phibun made his way back slowly by car.

The war unfolded without him. Japanese landed its forces in southern Thailand on December 8. Thailand's military forces in the southern province of Songkhla did not know how to react. Local leaders wondered if they should shoot at the Japanese as an alien force attempting to land huge amounts of weapons and men in Thailand without a formal treaty. The Thai army officers on the scene requested guidance from Bangkok but, while everyone was waiting for Phibun to reemerge, got no instructions. In the absence of clear orders, some Thai forces resisted. Local police and units of the Yuwachon, the military youth movement, shot at the Japanese as they tried to land. For several hours, these provincial police units did a respectable job holding back the Japanese from landing on the beach. Eventually, the Thais were instructed by their superiors to stand down and let the Japanese come ashore. About 150 Thais, including some civilians, died fighting the Japanese landing.

Phibun eventually returned. Still not decisive despite the erupting war across the Pacific, he opted to bring Thailand into a Japanese alliance in stages. The Thai cabinet allowed, albeit somewhat retroactively, to allow the Japanese to use Thai territory. Then Phibun declared martial law throughout the country. He gave a speech informing the country that he was doing so because Britain had taken Thai territory some three decades earlier. In late December, he formalized an alliance between Thailand and Japan. The last step, a declaration of war against the Allies, was a more complicated matter.

Thailand Declares War

Thailand declared war on Britain and the United States on January 25, 1942. It came at a terrible time militarily for the Allied Powers. The British were buckling in their defense of Singapore, and the American defenders in the Philippines were about to be crushed. Thailand's expression of hostility was another blow during an abysmal month. The differing reactions of these two countries to Thailand's declaration of war is important. The British were furious at Thailand. They believed they had been betrayed, stabbed in the geographical back, as it were, by a former friend. Thailand exacerbated this British ill will by invading the Shan States of the former British Burma in May 1942 and claiming the territory as part of the new expanded Thai state. Despite treating Thailand as a de facto colony in much of its dealings with Siam over the previous decades, the British leadership in Thailand believed they had a special relationship with the kingdom that would prevent the Thais from going to war against London. The Americans took a more sympathetic view. Thailand's minister in Washington, M. R. Seni Pramoj (Seni), helped maintain this mutual benevolence. In doing so, he may have spared Thailand the miseries of war suffered by other Asian countries.

Seni was a young Oxford-educated lawyer who had served in the Ministry of Justice before his posting to the United States. A great-grandson of Rama II, he nonetheless cooperated with the People's Party leadership that had toppled the absolute monarchy. Seni and Pridi shared many political ideals for Thailand in the postabsolutist age, views that differed from the military faction led by Phibun. Their relationship was not without its own tensions, but their mutual trust would prove critical for Thailand during the war. Thanks in part to Seni's actions in Washington, the United States chose not to recognize Thailand's declaration of war. The oft-told story is that Seni never delivered the declaration of war sent to him by Bangkok. He was said to have locked the cabled message in his desk for the duration of the war. The more likely explanation was that Seni successfully convinced the US leadership that Thailand was acting under duress when it formally declared war on the Allies. Seni wanted the United States to treat Thailand not as an enemy nation but as an occupied country. He did not cling to neutrality, rather, he committed himself and his staff to helping the Allies in Southeast Asia. He wanted the United States to recognize a Thai government in exile, something Washington was not committed to doing. Seni's arguments resonated with US intelligence regarding Thailand. Many sources suggested that while Phibun may have been enthusiastic about Tokyo's aims in Southeast Asia, most Thais were ambivalent about the Japanese presence. Seni pressed the American officials to continue recognizing him as the legitimate representative of Thailand and to cultivate methods to bring other anti-Japanese Thais into an alliance with the Allies. Seni actions had long-ranging effects on Thai history.

With Seni's cooperation, the Americans organized an anti-Japanese resistance unit from within the United States. They called their group the Free Thai Movement and set it up along lines similar to that followed by Polish and other European anti-Nazi exile organizations formed in Britain. With Seni's guidance, the Americans recruited Thai graduate students studying in the United States for this organization. Having studied in America for several years, many of these students opposed the Japanese and were dismayed at Phibun's decision to ally Thailand with Japan. Rather than be repatriated at the outbreak of hostilities, they opted to stay in the States and help the Americans in their anti-Japanese war effort. The United States' wartime intelligence service, the Office of Strategic Services (OSS), trained several dozen Thai graduate students in intelligence gathering and guerrilla warfare. The OSS described Thailand as a blank spot on their intelligence maps, a kind of information dead zone in which they had no spies or sources. The idea was that the OSS would train these Thais to send back information and perhaps even carry out sabotage operations against Japanese positions in Thailand. The Allies urgently needed the Free Thai Movement because it was beginning to bomb Japanese positions in Burma, Siam, Malaya, and, later, French Indochina, from bases in eastern India and Ceylon. Seni was able to use Thai assets that the United States had frozen in American banks to set up the America-based Free Thai effort. This financial independence meant that the Thais were paying their way, at least partly, in the war against Japan.

At the same time that the United States was setting up a Free Thai Movement in America, the British were putting together their own Free Thai force in the United Kingdom, albeit more cautiously than the Americans. Britain's Special Operations Executive (SOE) constructed their Free Thai scheme around royal figures living in Britain as exiles, a group that included even Prajadhipok's widow, Queen Rambhai Barni, and her brother, Prince Suphasawatwongsanit Sawadiwat (known as Prince Suphasawat). Suphasawat became the nucleus of the British Free Thai Movement, and kept the effort alive in the face of British wariness and indifference. He helped British intelligence draft their earliest strategic studies of wartime Thailand, including political profiles of its leadership, and made maps of important areas. He played a role in recruiting Thai students within the United Kingdom for intelligence gathering and guerrilla operations. In an extension of lingering royalist-civilian tension extant in Thailand's People's Party, the British-based Free Thai Movement faced internal frictions over the role of Thai royalty in the leadership. More problematic, British suspicion of Thais as harboring anticolonial sentiments hampered cooperation between the groups.

Initially, many Thais welcomed the Japanese. As a response to the decades of unequal treaties, bullying, and land seizures on the part of the Western imperialists in Thailand and throughout Southeast Asia, some citizens hailed the defeat of the British as a victory for Asians. Japanese victories over the British, especially its sinking of the British battlecruiser HMS *Repulse* and battleship HMS *Prince of Wales* in the Gulf of Siam on December 10, 1941, encouraged these Thais to reassess their opinion of the Western powers, Western culture, and even Western civilization as a whole. But, as in other Southeast Asian lands, it was not long before many Thais grew disillusioned with the Japanese. The arrogance and viciousness that many Japanese displayed toward the local people disgusted many Thais. Thais endured public embarrassment when Japanese soldiers slapped them for real or imagined slights. Thai civilians bristled at this abuse, while Thai soldiers occasionally struck back. Several times, fights broke out, including exchanges of gunfire, between Thai and Japanese troops. The war's disruption of the economy and the failure of the Japanese to provide many of the commodities that had been supplied by the Western countries alienated some Thai people, especially those living in cities. Rural people saw fewer disruptions. Farm folk lost some income from the collapse of international trade networks, but Japan made up for some of this loss by buying Thai agricultural products for its war effort. As the war dragged on, Japan increasingly relied on Thai paper currency it had borrowed from Thailand to pay for these foodstuffs. Inflation skyrocketed. The Allies' later bombing of strategic communications sites, including Bangkok's Hualamphong train station, killed some Thais.

The Burma-Siam Railway, the notorious rail line built to link Bangkok and Singapore with Rangoon, brought much suffering to Thailand in 1942–43. Better known as the Death Railway, it is today the site of one of the most popular day trips for tourists staying in Bangkok. Visitors take the narrow-gauge rail line west to Kanchanaburi to explore the history made famous by David Lean's 1957 antiwar film, *The*

Bridge on the River Kwai. The steel bridge that most tourists have their photograph taken on is not actually over the Khawae Noi River of the story's title, but is a postwar bridge built to span the Mae Klong River. During the war, two parallel bridges, one wooden and one steel, sat in the present bridge's location. Japan needed the railway to convey supplies to its forces in Burma because it lacked adequate shipping to move material by sea. The Japanese Imperial Army used a plan drafted at the turn of the century by British colonial engineers who then abandoned the scheme as too difficult, expensive, and politically sensitive. Japan's 263-mile line passed through the Three Pagoda Pass, the strategic mountain corridor separating Burma from Thailand that various armies had used while on campaign against a neighboring kingdom. The terrain is among the most treacherous in Southeast Asia, with knots of dense jungle surrounded by jagged mountains. Adding to the misery are disease-carrying insects, poisonous snakes, leeches, and other noxious pests. Japan forced some 60,000 POWs from Britain, the Netherlands, Australia, and New Zealand to work on the line. Most had been captured in the fighting for Malaya, Singapore, and the Dutch East Indies, and held at Singapore's Changi Prison before being sent north. They were joined by American POWs captured on Java and from the sinking of the USS *Houston*. More than 13,000 Allied prisoners died while working on the line. The Kanchanaburi War Cemetery located near the bridge is the burial site of 6,982 of these victims. Tourists and war veterans from Thailand and abroad visit the cemetery when in Kanchanaburi, with many lingering there to read the moving tributes on the tombstones and to consider the relative youth of these wartime casualties. It is a somber and affecting site. Although these Allied prisoners get most of the historical attention in books, films, and even in the Kanchanaburi museums, it was the 250,000 Asian laborers pressed into service or recruited under false pretenses who completed the bulk of this deadly engineering feat. Tamils, Javanese, Chinese, Malays, Burmese, Thais, and others worked under slave-like conditions. Cholera and starvation took away many, as did Japanese mistreatment and executions during railway construction in 1942–43. It is estimated that some 100,000 of these Asian workers died in the fifteen months it took to complete it. Thai laborers were more successful than others in slipping away from the deadly enterprise, aided in their flight by their countrymen in the surrounding villages. The escapees spread word of the horrific work conditions and of the deaths. The stories of the sick and dying were another factor in the changing attitudes of many Thais toward the Japanese Imperial Army's presence. Within a year, many had grown hostile to Japanese military endeavors and found themselves hoping for the return of the prewar status quo. They quietly questioned Phibun's decision to ally Thailand with Japan as they waited to see who would win the war.

CHAPTER 8

THAILAND IN WORLD WAR II

As in London and Washington, an anti-Japanese Free Thai effort came together in Bangkok. The homegrown version of the Free Thai developed around those leaders, bureaucrats, journalists, academics, and even some members of the military, who opposed their country's alliance with the Japanese. Several groups were formed in the first months of the war, each with different organizational structures and ambitions. Eventually, the groups got wind of each other and coalesced into one more or less coherent indigenous Free Thai Movement. The nominal leader of this movement was none other than Pridi Banomyong, the civilian leader of the People's Party and the Promoters who helped overthrow the absolute monarchy. He was Thailand's finance minister at the war's outbreak, and was still getting along with his fellow Promoter Phibun Songkhram. Unable to stomach Thailand's cooperation with Japan, Pridi resigned from Phibun's government. Phibun gave Pridi the position of royal regent, the representative for the young king Ananda who remained in Switzerland for the war's duration. Pridi's promotion to regent was more than a little ironic. In less than a decade, Pridi had gone from being viewed as the most prominent antimonarchist in Thailand to being the principal caretaker of the king's interests. Pridi used the prestigious but largely powerless position of royal regent to coordinate various Free Thai factions into a united movement. He was joined by the civilian members of the People's Party who disliked Thailand's sharp shift into military authoritarianism. Also joining his group were representatives of the Royal Thai Navy who chafed at the power and influence that the Royal Thai Army gained in teaming up with the Japanese. Ethnic Chinese played an important role in the anti-Japanese underground. These Sino-Thais had opposed Japan since its invasion of southern China in the late 1930s. They had their own underground network that smuggled people, information, and rare commodities, including opium, in and out of Thailand during the war. Finally, another important group in the Free Thai Movement included influential political figures from Thailand's northeast. These ethnic Lao politicians sought to use the war to liberate those areas of Laos that had fallen under French control. The Free Thai would claim nearly a hundred influential figures working inside Thailand to undermine the Japanese, but its numbers swelled as the war drew to an end.

Free Thai Operations

Pridi's first task was to establish contact with the Allies. He sent out Free Thai representatives who crossed the frontier of occupied Southeast Asia into southern China with the goal of teaming up with the British and American intelligence units operating out of Kunming and Chongqing. The first two groups Pridi sent out vanished en route to China, never to be heard from again. But in 1943 Pridi sent out a politician-turned-journalist named Chamkad Balankura, who traveled by bus, boat, and foot through northeastern Thailand, Laos, northern Vietnam, and into China. His mission was to contact the Allies and to inform them that a Thailand-based anti-Japanese underground was already in existence and at their disposal. He also sought to convince the Allies that they need not think of Thailand as an enemy. Pridi's underground movement was especially worried about the harsh attitude that Britain had taken toward the kingdom. Chamkad carried a proposal from Pridi's group asking that the Allies smuggle Pridi out of Thailand and spirit him off to the United States or Britain where he could set up a Free Thai government in exile. Chamkad's fate as he attempted to carry out this mission tells us a lot about the obstacles faced by the Thais in trying to liberate themselves from the Japanese and maintaining good relations with the Allies during the war.

Chamkad was arrested by the Nationalist Chinese almost as soon as he entered China. Despite their shared goal of defeating Japan, the

Chinese, British, and Americans did not trust each other. In the besieged and claustrophobic atmosphere of occupied China, the three sides spent a shockingly unproductive amount of time spying on each other and confounding each other's schemes for opposing the Japanese. Chiang Kai-shek's intelligence service arrested Chamkad because they did not want him to join the Americans or the British. The Chinese wanted Chamkad to work for them exclusively. The Chinese intelligence service, under the direction of the enigmatic Dai Li, had its own network of spies and black marketeers across Southeast Asia and it wanted Chamkad to become part of that network. The Nationalist Chinese may have harbored plans to occupy Southeast Asia at the war's conclusion, and perhaps even to annex parts of northern Thailand for China. Chamkad struggled to get messages out to the Americans and British from his Chinese prison cell. Around the same time the Allies became aware of his existence, the Free Thai agent Chamkad fell ill under mysterious circumstances. He died in a Canadian mission hospital in Chongqing. He was only thirty-two years old. Many have assumed that the Chinese intelligence service killed him rather than let him work for the British or the Americans. It is unlikely we will ever know the truth about what killed the Free Thai "exfiltrator."

Thailand's leadership in World War II provides a vivid example of this so-called "bamboo diplomacy." The term, in fact, might be only a mild description of what Thailand was doing. The most influential figures seemed to be serving both sides throughout the conflict. The head of the government, Phibun Songkhram, was cooperating with the Japanese in their war effort against the Allies. At the same time, his erstwhile friend and political partner, Pridi Banomyong, one-time foreign minister and finance minister who was now the king's regent, was working to aid the Allies in their war against the Japanese. Both were practically working side by side to assist their favored party in the war. Phibun, as head of the government, almost certainly knew of Pridi's involvement in these anti-Japanese activities as they were being carried out by high-ranking former government officials, several of them Phibun's friends from their Promoters days. If he had wanted to put a stop to Pridi's Free Thai Movement, Phibun probably could have exposed it to the Japanese and used their military and his own forces to root out their agents and wreck their plans. Instead, he let them fight for their cause while he pursued his own.

That the Thai leadership was hedging its bets in the war became abundantly clear by 1943 when it was obvious that Japan would not score the swift victory it had banked on. Phibun must have welcomed Pridi's secret missions as a card up his sleeve to be played if the Japanese started to falter and the Allies gained the upper hand. The Thais were not exactly fence-sitters waiting out the war to see who was going to win. They were active participants on both sides: one powerful faction operating openly with the Axis powers while one less powerful faction worked covertly with the Allies.

The United States had trouble getting its Free Thai guerrillas into Thailand. The problem was not the Japanese but the Chinese. Just as the Nationalist Chinese intelligence service stopped Chamkad from reaching the allies, they tried to stop the American-trained Thai guerrillas from getting into Thailand. The Nationalist Chinese did not want their American allies to have underground network in place as a rival to its own. While waiting in southwest China to be infiltrated into Thailand, Dai Li's agents threw multiple obstacles in the Thai guerrillas' way. They sent prostitutes to spy in their ranks; they blocked them from acquiring pack horses for transport; they withheld military cooperation at the China-Indochina border; and they may have even killed one of their American pilots assigned to fly them in. Chinese disruption left the American-run operation in tatters. When the first group of four guerrillas finally did go out in mid-1944, they did not make it into Thailand. Thai police arrested them at what had been the Lao-Thai border and, according to one source, executed them.

After months of intrigue and quarreling amongst the Americans, British, and Chinese, the Allies got their Free Thai guerrillas into place. The American-trained group teamed up with the indigenous Free Thai movement. Working well together, the two groups built secret bases in rural areas for use in a future attack against Japanese forces. They sent out intelligence on Japanese positions and troop movements, which helped the Allies bomb Japanese installations in Thailand. The Free Thai guerrillas also helped rescue downed American fliers before the Japanese could capture them. They built clandestine airfields to facilitate an Allied invasion. Toward the end of the war, the United States was parachuting their own OSS agents into Thailand from airdrops launched from eastern India. The American OSS agent Nicol Smith is one of a small group of participants to publish an account of their experiences with the Free Thai movement. His thrill-filled memoir of the war years, *Into Siam: Underground Kingdom*, includes descriptions of the sometimes-absurd circumstances of the divided Thai leadership. After Smith infiltrated Thailand, the Thais hid him and the other American guerrillas in the same buildings that the Japanese and Thai intelligence operatives worked out of. He hid, literally, under the noses of the people searching for him. Smith also described the lavish feasts of Thai and Western food – multicourse dinners concluded with ice cream – that the Free Thai fed the OSS agents. He does not say it in his memoir, but Smith's account shows the Thais pointedly manipulating the emotions and opinions of the Americans who might speak up for them when Japan was finally defeated. They were using rich food and friendliness to win the Americans to their side in a postwar period as a hedge against the British.

Thailand Distances Itself from Japan

The Americans and British cooperated uneasily with each other regarding Thailand during the war. Their differing views of Thailand's culpability survived the war. The British continued to view Thailand as an enemy country, even after Pridi and his faction were aiding the Allies. Like the Nationalist Chinese, the British indicated their desire to occupy Thailand at the conclusion of the war, and to punish it for what it saw as betrayal. British wartime leader Winston Churchill announced toward the end of the war that all of the former European colonies in Southeast Asia should be put into a trusteeship for thirty years or so until they had matured politically to the point at which they could be allowed to govern themselves. In announcing this intended policy, Churchill included Thailand in the list of former European colonies, something that worried the Thai leadership. The Americans, for their part, maintained their position that Thailand was an occupied country that acted under duress. This differing view became even more critical when it became apparent that Japan would lose the war. By 1944, it was obvious to all in Thailand that Japan's once mighty military machine was crumbling. Thais who listened to the Japanese-controlled news each night after dinner knew it. Some

Thais, especially young boys, kept maps of Japan's victories across Asia and the Pacific Ocean. They marked the sites of these battles as they listened to the radio each evening. By 1944, all map watchers could see that Japan's "victories" in the Pacific theater were occurring on islands ever closer to Japan. Even children could see that Japan's proclamations of success were desperate propaganda incapable of hiding the truth. Phibun knew Japan would lose the war as well as anyone else in Thailand. The former Japan-admirer scrambled in 1944 to find an exit strategy for Thailand. He had grown increasingly disillusioned with the Japanese, especially after they had started losing the war. The Japanese heavy handedness toward Thailand further strained the relationship. Japan took so much food and raw materials that the Thai people had begun to be affected, even the relatively self-sufficient farm folk in the countryside. Japan's "borrowing" of huge sums of gold from Thailand to fund its losing effort also crushed the already weakened Thai economy. Phibun bore the strain of the war badly. He seemed overwhelmed by the stresses placed upon him by the Japanese and his Thai colleagues, including those working against the Japanese. He suffered from flights of fancy. He floated plans to move the capital north to the city of Phetchabun, ostensibly to give the Royal Thai Army a better position from which to fight the Japanese. His propagandist Wichit had repeatedly compared him to the great warrior kings of Sukhothai. To some, it appeared that Phibun was intent on establishing a new royal house with himself as the first king. Earlier in the war, he had ordered the construction of a Buddhist temple, as the Chakri kings had done, and awarded it a sacred status despite the absence of any relics housed in it. He seemed to be edging toward delusions of grandeur.

Khuang Replaces Phibun

In August 1944, Phibun resigned from his post as Thai premier. He seemed intent on restructuring his government and then reemerging as the nation's leader. To maintain some power, he held onto the position of supreme commander of the armed forces. He wanted a second act as Thailand's savior. But Pridi and his faction outmaneuvered Phibun. They blocked his return by having their own candidate elected. They picked Khuang Aphaiwong that same August. He was one of the

Promoters who actively participated in the overthrow of the absolute monarchy. He was born in Battambang while his father was serving as what would be the last Siamese governor of Siam's Cambodian territories before they lost them to the French. His family had retained the land it owned in Cambodia. He was someone who had benefitted from the territorial campaigns of Phibun while managing to stay on good terms with Pridi and the people he had around him. Known for his straight-talking ways, as well as his ability to joke his way through uncomfortable situations, Khaung acquired the nickname "the Comedian."

Khuang's masterful wit is what Thailand needed at the time. The Japanese had become aware of the Free Thai movement's existence, and they were desperate to root out those supporting it. They knew the group was led and aided by high-ranking members of the Thai government. They also knew that the bombing of Japanese positions was being guided by Thais and their British and American allies hidden throughout the country. Their ruthless and dogged intelligence apparatus was pressing the Thais hard to neutralize these operatives. The Japanese were under pressure throughout Southeast Asia. On March 9, 1945, they turned on their nominal French allies in Indochina and arrested them all. They may have been planning a similar turn in Thailand. Khuang's job was to use his social and political gifts to keep the Japanese off-balance while maintaining peace between the pro-Japanese and anti-Japanese factions around him. It is not that the Japanese found Khuang any more agreeable than Phibun, but his reputation for being direct and engaging was a welcome change from Phibun who, despite his fascist leanings, was never fully trusted by the Japanese.

Further Threats of Colonization

The war's sudden conclusion in August 1945 stunned all the parties focused on Thailand. After Hitler's defeat in early May 1945, many of the OSS people, its agents and planners, were rushed from Europe to Southeast Asia to carry on the war against Japan. From India and Ceylon, they prepared for operations within Thailand. They accelerated the construction of Free Thai military camps throughout the country and prepared to strike against the Japanese. More Thais joined the anti-Japanese resistance and prepared to fight alongside the American and British forces. But the atomic bomb changed all those plans. It appeared so suddenly and unexpectedly that many of the warring sides in Thailand had to scramble to assume whatever position of authority that they could find. All sides aimed to look as strong as possible in the days and weeks after news of Japan's surrender reached Thailand.

Thai leaders favored a strong American presence in Thailand after the war. They were fearful of potential British plans to occupy Thailand and run its affairs. They sought to placate the British by immediately offering to give back the areas of northern Malaya – the former tribute states of Siam – that they had taken during the war. This offer to return territory was not, incidentally, something they offered to the French. For the time being, Thai leadership worked to keep the areas of Laos and Cambodia that Thailand acquired at the start of the war. The Thais exploited the goodwill generated by the close working relationships that the Free Thai agents had formed with the OSS and other members of the US military at the end of the war to protect them from British reprisals. At the forefront of this worry were rumors about London's plans to make Thailand a British protectorate. So proud are the Thais of having never been colonized by a European power that the threat of British conquest stirred more than the mere dread of foreign subjugation: it would rob the Thais of their one enduring claim of cultural and historical superiority over their Southeast Asian neighboring states.

The British wanted Thailand to pay for its supposed treachery. London demanded the right to station British troops in Thailand indefinitely. It also sought an indemnity of sorts to be paid in 1.5 million tons of rice. Britain needed the rice to feed its troops, many of them colonial forces from British India, as they reoccupied war-ravaged Southeast Asia. They also wanted all their former territories that the Thais had taken, including the Shan States in Burma, to be returned, The Thais gave back the territory, but did not want to give Britain this rice indemnity. Years of deprivation caused by Japanese wartime demands for food and natural resources put parts of Thailand on the verge of famine. The Americans, as the Thais had hoped, intervened on their behalf and persuaded the British to back down. In the end, Britain bought the rice from Thailand.

As for France and its former territories, the Thais were in a less accommodating mood. They believed, and many still do today, that France stole Thai territory when it took the Lao principalities, and they did not want to give them back to France. Pridi even sought to buy the territories back by paying France for them. But the European powers, backed by a triumphant Britain, pushed hard for a return to the prewar status quo. The Western powers, their prestige badly damaged by their initial poor showing against Japan, sought to recoup their vanished fortunes by reclaiming their industries, properties, and resources in the region. These European nations planned to exploit their erstwhile colonies to help rebuild the home economies in the postwar period. France vowed to block Thailand's entry into the United Nations and, in effect, leave it a pariah state if it did not return the Lao and Cambodian territories. Thailand, threatened with a loss of sovereignty and a ruined economy, had little room to negotiate. Under intense diplomatic pressure from the Allies, Thailand ceded all of its so-called "lost territories" to the French and the British.

Reestablishing Democracy

The immediate post-war period was marked by the entry of Free Thai-connected figures into the political scene. Seni Pramoj, the head of the Thai mission in Washington, returned home to become prime minister in September 1945. Seni lacked a political powerbase like those of Pridi or Khuang. He had never built the same kind of coalition of supporters that his rivals had assembled. He also lacked manipulation skills and political calluses acquired by more seasoned Thai politicians. But most Thai politicians saw good reasons for making him the first postwar premier. His close relationship with the Americans during the war was deemed by Pridi and his circle as the best way to ensure American support and protection. Seni had friends in Washington and London who could smooth over the potentially harsh reckoning that Thailand would face after the war. Pridi set aside their mutual antipathy to let Seni become prime minister. But the diplomat Seni was really not suited for the rough and tumble of Thai politics, especially in the aftermath of the war. He was tolerated by all as Thai leaders sought to look as pro-American, or as anti-Japanese, as possible at this crucial juncture.

Several of the OSS agents who came to Thailand at the war's conclusion ended up leaving their mark on Thai history. Alexander MacDonald stayed around and founded the *Bangkok Post* newspaper. He, along with Free Thai member Prasit Lulitanond, obtained a rotary press that the Japanese had imported to publish a Japanese-language daily during the war. Their first general news editor was a German journalist who had covered Asia for a Nazi-subsidized press service during the war. MacDonald remained in Thailand for a decade, and left only when the paper was on solid footing and capable of being run by his Thai editorial staff. The paper survives to this day as the leading English-language daily in Thailand. Its roots as the brainchild of an American wartime intelligence officer, however, leads to the occasional but enduring accusation that the *Post* is secretly a press organ for the CIA.

Jim Thompson was an architect from Delaware who was sent by the OSS to Thailand. He stayed around and played an instrumental role in reviving the Thai silk trade. His Jim Thompson Silk Company sparked a multimillion-dollar silk industry that has helped make the lustrous cloth nearly synonymous with Thailand today. Thompson built a striking house in Bangkok out of six traditional wooden Thai farmhouses he brought from Ayutthaya, and filled it with fabulous examples of Southeast Asian religious art. For a couple of decades, anyone who was anyone in the Western arts world came to see his stunning house and art collection while visiting Bangkok. Thompson disappeared in 1967 while walking in the Cameron Highlands of Malaysia. The cause of his disappearance remains unsolved to this day. His house was transformed into a museum and has become one of the main tourist draws of Bangkok today. The estate of Jim Thompson has since built similar buildings around his inspired architectural masterpiece as shopping outlets and performance centers. These recent imitations, created to cater to the many tourists who visit each day, diminish the former arresting beauty of the original building. But they have not utterly obliterated it. The site is still worth a visit by anyone interested in Southeast Asian history, art, architecture, and industry.

The acute political and diplomatic anxiety gripping Bangkok eased a bit after six months or so. Thailand entered a rare phase of constitutional democracy in which political parties of various leanings, including communists, could operate openly. Pridi's political faction emerged as the winner in the first postwar elections in January 1946. Although Pridi had stepped down as regent the previous month to devote more time to politics, he made Khuang the prime minister once again. This time, "the Comedian" lasted only a couple months as premier. He suffered a vote of no confidence and dissolved his short-lived government. This development is noteworthy, despite the government's instability, because of the landmark it represented. Fourteen years after these same men had overthrown Thailand's absolute monarchy, the nation finally had a premier who was elected. The others had either come to power in coups or had been appointed by the National Assembly. In the next election of March 1946, Pridi's group once again came out on top. This time, Pridi assumed the premiership himself. One of Pridi's first acts as prime minister was to draft a new constitution. While still maintaining Thailand as a constitutional monarchy with a parliamentary system, the new charter contained elements familiar to the governmental structure of the United States and other strongly democratic systems. It introduced a bicameral structure of legislators with an elected lower house, called the House of Representatives, and an upper house, called the Senate, whose members were elected by the lower house. Although he had always been close to the center of politics since 1932, Pridi had never been allowed to fully lead the country. Events had always conspired to keep this brilliant and progressive figure out of the government's highest position. But backed by the politicians, officials, and intellectuals who had made up his Free Thai Movement, Pridi seemed poised to finally lead Thailand on the course he had charted decades earlier while still a student in Paris. Only now he was wiser, tougher, and more practical.

Thai politics seemed unusually harmonious during the first months of the postwar period. With Phibun and his associates in jail and the Free Thai-connected politicians in ascendancy, the kingdom's leadership was temporarily stable. Pridi, Seni, and Khuang had all worked in concert from their various positions to help the Allies defeat the Japanese. In the immediate postwar period, these leaders cooperated to maintain American and British trust so that Thailand would not suffer any loss of sovereignty or pay too high a price for its alliance with Tokyo. Their cooperative spirit concealed faint but rapidly expanding fissures. By the time they set about creating their first postwar government, the former Free Thai leaders had begun splitting into factions. On the surface, their differences seemed slight, but underneath lay deep divisions about the ideal structure of the constitutional monarchy.

Thailand had escaped the war largely unscathed while every other country in East and Southeast Asia had been shattered by the fighting. Throughout the first months of 1946, there was a sense in Thailand that the kingdom had skillfully, and maybe opportunistically, sidestepped the horrors of World War II. Although its commercial and transportation infrastructure had been badly damaged by Allied bombing, it had maintained some semblance of normalcy while its neighbors, and indeed much of the world, were devastated. Almost as if to rectify this injustice, fate landed a terrible blow on Thailand, just as its subjects were becoming optimistic about their collective postwar future. For some, it seemed as if destiny was obliged to deliver a dose of karmic retribution to balance the cosmic scales. In doing so, Thailand suffered a tragedy that has haunted its people up to the present.

A Palace Tragedy

King Ananda came from Switzerland to Thailand in December 1945 after an absence of six years. With the war over, and now twenty years old, Ananda was brought from Switzerland as another measure to reassure the Thai people and the foreign powers that all was well and stable with the kingdom. All along the route from the airport to the palace, crowds cheered the arrival of their young king. Neither Phibun's anti-Chakri rhetoric nor the long vacancy of the palace had dampened enthusiasm for the young monarch. Many embraced his return as a hopeful sign that the horrors and uncertainty of World War II were behind them. Thin and fresh-faced, the young expatriate king who wore stylish Western suits could easily have been the physical embodiment of the nation's optimism for better times ahead. Ananda, born and raised, for the most part, in Europe, returned to Thailand to begin learning how to become king. In his childhood, he had been sickly and delicate, and his mother sheltered him from threats to his health and from those who would draw him into political intrigues. He was bright and friendly, but he lacked drive and did not apply himself to his studies. Now on the verge of adulthood, he would have to do the hard work necessary to transform a sheltered and foreign-thinking schoolboy into a Thai king worthy of the Chakri monarchs who had preceded him. He was described in several foreign accounts written by people who had contact with him as a shy and nervous young man. Louis Mountbatten, uncle of Britain's Prince Philip and, later, a mentor to Prince Charles, knew Ananda when he met him in his capacity as supreme allied commander of the Southeast Asian theater after World War II. Mountbatten described Ananda as miserable. He got the impression that the Thai young man did not want to be king.

Alexander MacDonald, who met Ananda shortly before founding the *Bangkok Post*, paints a portrait of a neurotic and uncertain young king in his memoir of that period called *Bangkok Editor*. MacDonald describes an awkward day spent together in which he, as a representative of the OSS, escorted Ananda and his retinue to visit a Free Thai-OSS guerrilla base outside Bangkok. MacDonald said Ananda seemed ill at ease, almost lost, in every setting that day. The one exception, he notes, is when they set up a firing range in the camp and invited King Ananda and Prince Bhumibol to come forward to try their hands at shooting weapons. The arsenal came from supplies brought in by the Americans for the Free Thai guerrillas at the end of the war. The United States had distributed small arms broadly to the various underground factions, adding to the surfeit of guns that many Thais acquired during wartime. According to MacDonald, the shooting event was the only part of the day in which Ananda seemed comfortable. He became animated when he was given the opportunity to fire a gun. The young king looked briefly happy as he shot the targets to pieces. It was a reassuring end to an otherwise uncomfortable day for all involved. Moved by Ananda's apparent affinity for weapons, MacDonald presented the king with the gift of a brand-new U.S. Army Colt .45 from the supply of unused pistols.

In the months that followed their return to Thailand, the two brothers, Ananda and Bhumibol, delighted in firearms. They acquired a small collection of automatic and semiautomatic weapons, carbines, and side arms. They stockpiled ammunition in their palace quarters, and practiced shooting from external balconies down into the courtyard and gardens of the palace. The guns were among the few happy diversions amidst days spent studying and carrying out official obligations. The other escape was a US Army Jeep that the two had acquired. In their free time, they roared around the palace grounds, and even took the vehicle into Bangkok to joyride incognito.

Ananda's life ended in a tragic incident that to this day has not been fully explained. On the morning of June 9, 1946, he died from a gunshot wound to the head. According to accounts given by his mother, Ananda awoke that day not feeling well. She checked his temperature, gave him a dose of castor oil, and sent him back to bed. A few minutes later, a gunshot sounded from the king's bedchamber. His mother and brother rushed in to find him in bed with a pool of blood spreading out from under his head, a gunshot wound on his forehead, and a Colt .45 pistol beside his hand in bed. Initially, everyone thought he had killed himself. Whether he had fired the shot intentionally or by accident, no one could determine. None of the people who knew him best seemed certain one way or the other. News of the death rattled MacDonald. The former OSS agent worried that his gift of a Colt .45 had led to the king's death, either by suicide or accident. Later, an investigation would determine that the pistol that fired the fatal shot did not come from the OSS supplies. But in the tangle of lies, evidence tampering, and mistakes that characterized the investigation of Ananda's death, it is impossible to say for certain.

Accusations of Regicide

Ananda's death shook Thailand to its core. It threw many Thais into a state of grief and worry unlike anything they had experienced during the war. A right-wing political faction compounded the tragedy through their exploitation of the young man's death. They seized on the shock and mystery surrounding Ananda's killing to assist their return to power. By now, Pridi was prime minister, and although he was no longer the regent for Ananda, he still maintained an unofficial relationship as advisor to the young king. Pridi was protective of Ananda and Bhumibol, and acted as almost a father figure to the young Mahidols when they were settling in. But Pridi's enemies, many of them Phibun's supporters in the Royal Thai Army, seized upon the event to undermine his leadership. They revived the public image of

Pridi as being an antimonarchist dating from his days as the civilian leader of the Promoters who overthrew the absolute monarchy. Ignoring his otherwise astute support of the young king and his throne during the war years, they spread rumors that Pridi not only failed to protect the king but that he was active in the plot to assassinate him. To advance this ludicrous theory, Pridi's opponents turned up at cinemas to shout "Pridi killed the king" in the dark as the feature films were about to begin.

Pridi did not help his own cause. He made things worse by failing to offer a clear explanation of what happened. To protect the dignity of the palace, Pridi blocked journalists from publishing speculative reports about what might have happened. He declared a brief state of emergency, and had newspaper editors and a couple of his political rivals arrested. Many Thais refused to believe the king could have died by accidental shooting; it was too horrible to contemplate. Wild theories thrived in the vacuum of plausible explanations. Pridi also resorted to repressive means to silence his accusers, reviving accusations that he was a regicidal radical working for the Kremlin. Many in Thailand were already disenchanted with Pridi after his government failed to slow the spiraling cost of food after the war, a by-product of British demands for Thai rice. In October 1946, while under enormous pressure, Pridi resigned as premier. In his place, Vice Admiral *Luang* Thawan Thamrongnawasawat (Thamrong) took over, while Pridi remained in the background. Thamrong's and Pridi's belated efforts at improved communication failed to silence their critics.

The new government's initial opponents were their erstwhile allies. Khuang, Seni, and Kukrit Pramoj (Seni's brother) banded together to form the Democrat Party. Despite its name, the party's principles did not include increasing popular participation in political life. Instead, the Democrats worked to reinstate the aristocratic privileges of old. They used the anxious national mood about the economy and Ananda's death to stoke hostility toward Thamrong's shaky government. They presented themselves as royalists dedicated to preserving the monarchy as a national institution and protecting Bhumibol from the threat of harm. Khuang and the Pramoj brothers worked with pro-army politicians to drive Thamrong and Pridi from power. To curry support with the military, they dropped hints to the press that they were willing to allow Phibun to return to politics. Having escaped a possible war crimes trial, and perhaps execution, Phibun had initially promised to keep a low profile in retirement. But, sensing the changing mood about the Thamrong-Pridi government, the disgraced military strongman tested the waters for a possible return. In two interviews with a Chinese- and an English-language newspaper, Phibun suggested that he was obliged to return to public life, even briefly, to clear his name with the Thai people.

Pridi tried to halt the return of the military to politics. He removed from power many of the pro-Phibun army leadership that had cooperated with the Japanese. In their place, he appointed former Free Thai military figures, some of whom had worked directly with the Americans at the end of the war. Pridi sought to raise morale in the army and navy by securing American aid for the Thai military. The armed forces wanted funds and equipment, especially weapons, to modernize Thailand's defense forces. But Pridi, who had been closer to the British than the Americans, could not secure enough aid from Washington to quell the restive army leadership. On November 8, 1947, after many months of increasingly poisonous rumors and worsening economic circumstances, a cabal of mostly junior officers overthrew the government in a coup d'état.

Democracy in Thailand was, and is, a seemingly peculiar system by Western standards. On the one hand, it had been introduced not by popular demand but by a military coup. The pro-democracy group that brought it into being acted nearly as authoritarian as the court it replaced. Thus, it is tempting to ridicule Thai democracy as a sham. On the other hand, it is a system that has its own rules and boundaries recognized by Thai political participants. It functions according to Thai political parameters that differ greatly from those of the United States, Great Britain, France, or any of the other Western democratic nations. What happened after the overthrow of the Pridi-Thamrong faction, however, ushered in a dark period for Thailand's democratic system that even its staunchest defenders would find hard to justify.

CHAPTER 9

TAKING SIDES IN
THE COLD WAR

Within a few years of the end of World War II, the disgraced Phibun Songkhram and a gang of army officers were back in power. How did they go from sitting in jail cells awaiting possible execution for potential war crimes to running the country? How did the military repair its tarnished reputation in the eyes of the Thai public? Why did so many Thais acquiesce to a return to unelected government when the nation seemed poised to become a legitimate democracy? Three main events in the four years following the war explain the military's stunning change in fortunes and the public's about-face.

The first, and a major factor, was the death of King Ananda. The young king's death was a far greater psychological blow than almost anyone could have anticipated. This is especially true of the People's Party leadership and those who supported their overthrow of the absolute monarchy in 1932. They failed to see that Ananda was more than a relic of a bygone age, that he embodied popular hope for a stable and prosperous future. He came to be associated with an idealized past that many Thais had remembered, or believed they had remembered, from the pre-1932 days. His youth itself offered the possibility of a fresh start after the terrible war years. The optimism that had greeted Ananda's return to Siam was replaced by a period of angry mourning that caused many to feel adrift and frightened. The mysterious circumstances surrounding Ananda's death encouraged many in the press to lose confidence in Pridi Banomyong and, by extension, the civilian-led democratic regime he represented. The inconclusive investigation Pridi oversaw left the public confused and suspicious. In trying to protect the royal family's privacy, Pridi could not offer a plausible account of exactly what had happened in that royal bedroom. Pridi had such little public support that his fall from power caused little concern outside Thai political circles. Only Free Thai figures and their American and British supporters lamented his departure from the national stage.

Secondly, massive shortages of food, especially rice, continued in the aftermath of the war. Corrupt officials entrusted with food distribution used their positions to accumulate graft. They profited by sending food staples needed in rural areas to cities and export markets. Rice commanded a significantly higher price in neighboring Malaya and in other regional markets, making smuggling inevitable. Thais had become accustomed to food shortages, but hunger after the war seemed at odds with the expected return to normalcy. Pridi's and Khuang's governments had not been responsive enough to these shortages. These urban elites were of touch with the problems faced by the many people who worried about finding food. Making matters worse, there was an appearance of government-sanctioned corruption surrounding its relief programs. For example, when members of parliament were given surplus farm equipment to donate to their constituents to help them get through this difficult period, many MPs sold the equipment to merchants and pocketed the profits. Moreover, inflation caused by Japan's wartime raiding of the Thai treasury for "loans" and the related overprinting and circulation of Thai currency continued to bedevil the national economy. Lawlessness in the form of piracy and banditry in rural areas compounded the people's misery.

A third factor was the Royal Thai Army's wounded pride. Although the number of people affected by this was far lower than those worried about hunger, corruption, crime, or the dead king, this may have been the most significant factor leading to the coup d'état of November 1947. The army had been the most important institution in Thailand for the first decade of the postabsolutist era. The government had celebrated the army's modest battlefield victories to the point of distortion. From the dizzying heights of its early, albeit small-scale successes in Laos, Cambodia, and the Shan States, the Royal Thai Army was made to suffer terribly at war's end. Its soldiers, many racked with malaria, were forced to find their own way back from the Shan States and other territories after the Allies seized their vehicles to remove Japanese forces. With little food, proper clothing, or footwear, many soldiers had to walk home. Villagers and bandits attacked some of the homeward-bound troops, adding to the soldiers' collective bitterness. Some of the officers who seized power in November 1947 were veterans of those disastrous withdrawals, including principal figures like Col. Phao Siyanon, Col. Sarit Thanarat, Col. Kat Katsongkhram, and Lt. Gen. Phin Choonhavan. Together, they would lead a faction of about three dozen army officers known as the Coup Group (Khana Ratthaprahan). Several had harbored political ambitions that were suddenly curtailed by the war's outcome and by Pridi's ascendency. They were antidemocratic in principle and inclined toward authoritarianism. They believed in the Royal Thai Army's prerogative to dominate the political, economic, and cultural spheres. They resented the military's de facto exclusion from politics. All except Sarit had been forcibly retired because of their connections to Phibun. They also resented Pridi's apparent favoritism for the Royal Thai Navy and the implication that the army had "lost" the war. Despite their retired status, they were still able to rally enough like-minded troops to seize power in a bloodless coup on November 7–8, 1947. Although they cited government corruption, public suffering, and the death of Ananda as the principal reasons, the group acted to restore power to the army. Their motive had obvious appeal to many, but not all, army units. Scattered efforts by troops loyal to the government failed to stop the insurgent troops, most of them from Bangkok's 1st Regiment of the 1st Division. Pridi's allies among the leadership in the Royal Thai Navy and the Royal Thai Marines did not commit forces capable of stopping the coup. Toppling the government was easy. Pridi evaded capture, however, slipping out of Thailand via the navy's facilities at Sattahip before making his way to Singapore and then China.

Phibun's Political Resurrection

The army strongmen who staged the coup needed a front man to represent them to Thailand and to the international community. None had the national stature and name recognition necessary to win support from the Thai people in this brief quasi-democratic period. Even more daunting, they lacked the ties to officials from the international community, namely Britain, the United States, and France, to bring about foreign recognition of their undemocratic regime. They required a high-profile and trusted figure as the public face of their group, partly to shield them while they enriched themselves on government funds and related opportunities. Initially, they turned to Phibun. The former premier seemed a good pick for several reasons. His name was synonymous with the army's heyday a few years earlier; he was still the handsome and charismatic figure who had dominated Thailand's public stage during its modernization drive in the late 1930s; he had formerly enjoyed a good working relationship with the senior coup organizer, Phin; and although he still bore the disgrace of his wartime support for the Japanese, enough time had passed to make such matters seem irrelevant. The recent public disillusionment with Pridi rendered his political opponent a potentially viable alternative. The international community would be harder to convince, though. Many officials in the British, American, and French governments saw Phibun as the Thai embodiment of the global fascism they had just defeated. They regarded him as a former enemy akin to Japan's wartime leader Hideki Tojo. Changing their impressions would require work from the Coup Group.

Phibun, however, was not eager to join their venture. Perhaps fearing for his life in the event of a countercoup, he initially turned down offers to head their unconstitutional regime. Having wielded considerable uncontested power as Thailand's sole leader for so many years, he may also have been uneasy about becoming a figurehead for a gang of ambitious and ruthless officers. Declining the premiership, Phibun instead took control of the army, a job he was more comfortable in while the national and international political landscapes remained uncertain.

Unable to bring in Phibun, the Coup Group approached Khuang Aphaiwong with an offer to return as premier. They found Khuang's leadership of the increasingly rightist Democrats made him a suitable civilian premier. They especially valued his strong dislike for Pridi and left-wing politics in general, which would be useful while the Coup Group targeted Pridi's allies. Khuang had maintained good relations with diplomats from Britain and the United States, which made recognition of the new regime more likely. His jokey demeanor made him seem potentially malleable to the cabal. But the coup plotters misjudged Khuang. The glib politician proved to be difficult to control or outmaneuver. Shortly after agreeing to work with these army officers, Khuang made it clear that he was not interested in being a puppet of the military. He insisted on creating his own government without interference from the Coup Group. With Pridi's allies jailed, exiled, or disenfranchised, Khuang's Democrats had no serious competitors for power. Even the pro-military party created by Phibun and his army faction failed to muster a challenge to the surging Democrats. In the first postcoup election held in early 1948, Khuang's Democrats took a substantial majority of the seats in the lower house. He quickly went about trying to mitigate friction between Thailand and the dominant Western powers. While much of the immediate ill will stemmed from the coup, there was also lingering friction from the war that had not fully abated in London, Washington, and Paris. Summoning his famously affable demeanor, Khuang masterfully patched up the thorny relations with the French, the Americans, and, prickliest of all, the British.

Domestically, Khuang's policies proved popular. He worked to ameliorate food shortages and stifle corruption, earning his administration strong support from the public. He also used his time in power to rebuild royal power, working to restore the palace's properties and financial assets that Phibun had taken for the government after Prajadhipok's abdication. He also raised the king's budget for royal expenditure. His leadership encouraged many at home and abroad to see Thailand as ready to move beyond the political dysfunction of the immediate postwar years.

Khuang's growing political confidence rankled the military men who had sought to use him. The civilian premier made it clear that he saw no role for the military in state and diplomatic affairs. During their short-lived alliance, Khuang and his political allies clashed with nearly all of the Coup Group leadership. Kat and Phin had used their positions in this regime to brazenly and ruthlessly enrich themselves, and they wanted even more opportunities for graft. The military men wanted Phibun placed in an important position, as head of the Supreme Council or even prime minister, so he could protect them while they carried out their schemes beyond the spotlight. Khuang strongly resisted their efforts to brush him aside. Summoning his famous tact, he sought to bring some of the Coup Group members into his cabinet as a way of controlling them. Tensions grew as both sides tried to find the means to pressure the other. When it appeared that Khuang was going to check some of the Coup Group's power by cutting military budgets, the officers acted. On April 6, 1948, the Coup Group turned up at Khuang's house with a demand: he had twenty-four hours to resign as premier and dissolve his government. Khuang used the time to try to outfox the military men. But with the threat of violence hanging over the Coup Group's ultimatum, he opted to step down just before the deadline. True to his sour-sweet sense of humor, Khuang let it be known to the world that his resignation had actually been a "mugging."

With Khuang out of the way, the Coup Group went about eliminating their rivals. Using corrupt law courts, violence, and intimidation, they sought to clear the political landscape of obstacles to unfettered power. They focused their attention on wiping out remnants of Pridi's supporters, especially those affiliated with the Free Thai. The effort succeeded. Trumped-up charges and mysterious deaths removed their most formidable political opponents while scaring off potential challengers. They even went after their own. Threatened by Kat's growing influence and embarrassed by his public braggadocio, the Coup Group drove him into exile before he could challenge Phin, Phao, or Sarit for their shared control of the Thai government and all the riches it provided.

In the midst of the bloodshed and internecine that marked the Coup Group's consolidation of power, Phibun began to appear like a welcome alternative as Thailand's next premier. Phibun did not have the reputation for graft and terror that surrounded Phin and Phao. He even looked good to those disappointed by Pridi's tolerance for corruption. Thailand had seen five civilian-led governments come and go in the two years after World War II. The fact that army interference had toppled them was less obvious to the public than that they were ineffectual and fragile. Phibun seemed to promise the stability of an earlier era. Enough time had passed that many in the press, and the public at large, could look beyond his checkered past as an antimonarchical, quasi-fascist, cultural-reforming military strongman who had backed the losing side in the war. The foreign diplomatic community was less forgiving.

Exploiting Cold War Fears

To win over foreign diplomats, Phibun went to work on the Americans. It was already clear to Thailand's leaders that Great Britain would no longer play the role of dominant Western power in Asia as it had in the prewar years. Among his earliest initiatives after retaking the premiership, Phibun approached the Americans with a proposal to restructure the Royal Thai Army along US military lines. More importantly for his supporters in the army, he also sought American weapons to modernize his forces' military hardware. At the time, Thailand's army was largely equipped with British weapons. Phibun wanted American guns and aircraft for a new force that would be trained by American advisors. He also sought their guidance in changing Thai officers' education to a curriculum modeled on that used by West Point. Phibun knew how to draw the Americans in. At the time, armed insurgencies in neighboring Burma, Malaya, and Indochina were sources of increasing worry for the US State Department. Many of these insurgent groups drew ideological and material support from Moscow or from Mao's communist movement. Mindful of the United States' growing anxieties about communist expansion in Asia, Phibun made it clear that Thailand would situate itself more solidly on the "Free World" side in the emerging Cold War. Phibun could present Thailand as a potential anticommunist bastion that would could use its location at the crossroads of Southeast Asia to help the United States contain communism.

Phibun tapped into that worry to advance his cause for military and economic aid, but, in truth, he did not share Washington's anxiety for communism. Thailand did not have a communist insurgency. It barely had any communists. It had some high-profile leftists and peace activists who irked Phibun and Phao, but Thai communists were mostly remote and unobtrusive. Thai leaders were not alarmed at the anticolonial insurgencies. If anything, anticolonial sentiment in Thailand led many to look favorably on the insurgents. At the time, Thailand's northeast had Vietnamese communities for whom Ho Chi Minh was a hero. American officials visiting Isan in the late 1940s were unsettled to find Ho's image displayed in shops and homes throughout the region. Washington wanted Phibun to disrupt the movement of arms through Thailand to the Indochinese guerrillas. World War II had spawned an extensive underground arms smuggling infrastructure that later equipped, among others, the communists fighting the American-backed French colonial forces. Phibun allowed the flow of arms to continue, and largely turned a blind eye to the insurgents moving through Thai territory. His own lingering anti-French sentiments were probably still stronger than any concerns he might have had about communism. Phibun did worry about China, though. The presence of ethnic Chinese in Thailand, especially in Bangkok, made events in China consequential for Thailand. The gains of Mao Zedong's People's Liberation Army (PLA) over Chiang Kai-shek's Kuomintang (KMT) forces in 1948 had emboldened the more radical leftists among Bangkok's ethnic Chinese factions. They sought to press their advantage over Chinese groups supporting Chiang's KMT. Their street fighting and labor actions posed more immediate public-order worries for Phibun than did any of the distant conflicts that worried Washington. In private, Phibun entertained the idea of recognizing Mao's regime if the PLA were to triumph. But for the sake of appearances, he let the Americans believe he was learning toward anticommunism.

Pridi was another problem blocking Phibun's rehabilitation. Although the Coup Group was busy harassing and persecuting Pridi's Thai allies, he still had many influential supporters in the US diplomatic corps and Thailand's expatriate community. Prominent Americans living in Thailand, many of whom had worked with Pridi at the end of the war and in the immediate postwar period, wanted Pridi restored as Thai premier. They were loath to see Washington help the fascist-inclined Phibun with his rehabilitation and return to power. These former OSS agents had become businessmen and entrepreneurs who exercised considerable influence over US representatives in Bangkok. Their wartime experience as spies and saboteurs caused some in Phibun's circles to see them as pro-Pridi interlopers and troublemakers. Compounding his effort was the State Department's reluctance to replace Great Britain as Thailand's main protector. Historically, Thailand had never had any economic or strategic importance to the United States, and Secretary of State Dean Acheson was wary of a costly commitment to a Southeast Asian country that could potentially pull the United States into a land war.

Pridi Strikes Back

Phibun and Pridi maintained their complex relationship as cooperative rivals into this period. The erstwhile friends had sustained a measure of mutual trust throughout the heady changes in their political fortunes over the previous two decades. They had shared the dangers of antimonarchical plotting leading up to their overthrow of the absolute monarchy in June 1932; neither sought to destroy the other while their respective factions were competing for power in the immediate postabsolutist phase; they had a cordial working relationship even while aiding opposing sides in World War II; and both had shown restraint while the other endured a perilous political crisis after the war. As Phibun worked to reassure the Americans that he deserved their support, he floated the idea in various political and diplomatic circles that he was open to allowing Pridi to return to Thailand to reclaim his place in the political arena. It is difficult to say how serious such a proposal was considering it came at a time when Phibun's cohorts Phao and Phin were imprisoning and killing Free Thai politicians and other Pridi supporters. It is unlikely that Phibun would have been able to protect his former friend from the murderous attentions of his political patrons. Phibun soon dropped the topic of allowing Pridi's homecoming.

A few months later, in February 1949, Pridi slipped back into Thailand clandestinely. He rushed about Bangkok finalizing plans for an operation designed to drive the army clique from power. He moved about in disguise. He wore a navy uniform and a mustache, and removed his dentures, giving his normally full-cheeked face a gaunt quality. Pridi built the plan around Royal Thai Navy units, including some marines, and caches of American weapons that the OSS had left for Free Thai forces at the end of the war. Pridi's team used the Thai military's joint services exercises to obscure their preparations. On February 26, while army and navy units were practicing live fire exercises outside the city, Pridi's group moved into Thammasat University as their operational base. At midnight, they grabbed the Publicity Department and Radio Thailand headquarters and announced that Phibun and his clique had been dismissed from their positions. They were to be replaced by senior naval officers who would run Thailand until elections could be held. The group named Direk Jayanama, a

Promoter and Free Thai figure, as prime minister. Shortly afterward, one Pridi loyalist, a navy captain, captured the Grand Palace, just below Thammasat University, and prepared to fight Phibun's army units from the palace and from ships in the Chao Phraya River. The plan called for pro-Pridi military units from throughout the kingdom to advance toward the capital. These anti-Coup Group units were supposed to join the rebellious navy and army units in Bangkok, using their combined forces to defeat forces loyal to Phao and Phin.

The Grand Palace Rebellion (Kabot Wang Luang), as it came to be known, failed almost before it began. From the outset, the plan relied on the actions of only a small number of Free Thai figures to rally supporters. Few of the anticipated antigovernment units mobilized fast enough. Delays in the provinces, especially in the northeast, allowed Phibun's group to arrest pro-Pridi military commanders before they could get their forces under way. One critical troop transportation vessel missed the high tide and got stuck in the Bang Pakong River west of Bangkok. By sunrise, the Coup Group assembled a force to quash Pridi's. Sarit Thanarat moved troops from the Royal Thai Army's 1st Division, the high-profile army unit that had played a critical role in launching and thwarting coups, into place outside the Grand Palace. The rebels' assembled forces were far smaller than planned, but they still hoped they had done enough to carry off their coup. There was a sense that because coups had largely been bloodless, the more dynamic side could win control of the armed forces and the government merely by seizing key positions, arresting their opponents, and presenting the move to the relevant parties and the public as a done deal. But Sarit made it clear that he was willing to fight it out with the rebels. He brought tanks and artillery pieces. Throughout the city, army units fought marines in heated battles. Fighting engulfed sections of Wireless Road, Prathunam, the Ratchaprasong Intersection, and the Democracy Monument. Some of these engagements went on for days. But the main action was quelled in a day. From inside the Grand Palace, Pridi's side had to decide whether they were willing to subject downtown Bangkok's population and architectural treasures to the horrific destruction of tank warfare in a crowded urban center. They chose to surrender instead. But police units were inclined to kill participants rather than take them into custody. In his account of the

Grand Palace Rebellion's aftermath, Prasit Lulitanond, a Free Thai radio operator and a cofounder of the *Bangkok Post*, describes how he and his accomplices had no opportunity to surrender when caught trying to escape via a fishing boat. With no warning, a police sergeant shot one of Prasit's friends repeatedly and would have shot Prasit had a police captain, who recognized the journalist, not intervened to spare him. Prasit went to jail for nine years before Phibun pardoned him in 1957. Confronted by this coldbloodeness, Pridi's rebellion crumbled.

Many US officials expressed disgust at the Coup Group's hard-hearted political violence and unwillingness to compromise. The outbreak of war on the Korean peninsula gave Phibun his best opportunity to mend relations with the United States and to demonstrate his commitment to their anticommunist effort. In July 1950, Bangkok heeded Washington's appeal for allied contributions by agreeing to send military units to Korea. Soon after, Thailand sent the 21st Combined Regiment (later nicknamed "the Little Tigers"), a unit of some 4,000 troops. The Thai forces fought in several major engagements, including the Battle of Pork Chop Hill. The Royal Thai Navy dispatched two corvettes and two frigates, as well as transport vessels and support craft. In return, the United States granted Thailand $10 million in military aid. With Thai troops fighting alongside American GIs in Korea, the United States had to give Thailand's armed forces the weapons, training, and aid Phibun had sought. Furthermore, Thai officers began traveling to US military bases and schools for training.

Throughout 1950, Phibun's regime made moves domestically that were designed to convince the Americans that Thailand was now a stalwart anticommunist ally. Their efforts, however, were often half-hearted and inconsequential. Thailand banned the importation of foreign-language books on Marxism and shut down some pro-communist newspapers and journals. Phibun rushed to draft a new anticommunist law to restore the 1933 act that Pridi had repealed.

The Manhattan Rebellion
Phibun's improved relationship with the Americans did not necessarily translate to increased control over government affairs. He struggled against his army allies Phin and Phao, who controlled most of the important aspects of the state's apparatus after the coup. The Coup

Group bound themselves together through business and family ties (Phin's daughter was married to Phao) that did not include Phibun. The Coup Group saw Phibun in utilitarian terms, and had little concern for his aspirations or well-being. Proof of this came in a bizarre episode known as the Manhattan Rebellion.

In the aftermath of the Grand Palace Rebellion, tension heightened between Royal Thai Navy personnel and Thailand's army-dominated leadership. With Pridi's failure to seize back power from the Coup Group, many navy officers and enlisted grew despondent about their future role in military and national affairs. The Coup Group's persecution and killing of navy officers made it clear that the Royal Thai Navy would be made to suffer for its support of Pridi and the Free Thai politicians. The army's ruling strongmen would make sure the navy occupied the bottom rungs of the armed forces ladder, lower than even Phao's police force. The navy's increasingly anxious collective mood fed plans for more rebellions. With few influential navy leaders free to organize another attempt at grabbing power, junior officers took it upon themselves to strike against the army. Their lack of experience and political savvy doomed their scheme from the start.

On June 29, 1951, Phibun had gone to a ceremony on Ratchapradit Pier just outside the Grand Palace on the Chao Phraya River to accept the transfer of the US Navy dredge *Manhattan*. The ceremony was a high-profile event, with members of the international diplomatic community, foreign military attachés, Thai officials, and the press there to witness the handover. In the middle of the program, junior officers of the Royal Thai Navy abducted Phibun in full view of the invited guests. Their intention was to use him as a hostage to force Phin, Phao, and their henchmen to accede to their demands. Principally, they wanted Pridi returned to power and the creation of a new constitution. The coup leader announced a new government and summoned all navy vessels to join them at the abduction site. They ordered all navy personnel to prepare to fight. In the middle of this, the coup leaders had Phibun transferred to their floating headquarters aboard the Royal Thai Navy's flagship, the *Si Ayutthaya*, and crossed to the Thonburi side of the river.

These junior officers made several mistakes that thwarted their effort. First, they failed to open the Memorial Bridge, the span just below the Grand Palace, thus blocking the naval reinforcements they needed to hold off a counterattack. Second, they failed to realize how little value the Coup Group put on Phibun's life. Sarit's army units hit naval forces and their installations in the areas surrounding the *Si Ayutthaya*, depriving the rebels of needed support. Royal Thai Air Force planes joined the counterattack to hit naval installations. The combatants showed little concern for the civilian population cowering in their homes alongside the river. In the midst of the fighting, the *Si Ayutthaya* was disabled, leaving the rebels trapped aboard. Their gamble of using Phibun as a human shield and bargaining chip had failed. In desperation, the rebels forced Phibun to record a message urging restraint while the two sides negotiated. Army units continued to hit the faltering navy units throughout the day.

Fighting died down in the night, but flared anew at dawn. Royal Air Force bombers hit the *Si Ayutthaya*. As the ship rapidly took on water, the navy rebels freed Phibun rather than let him die in the attack or drown. Phibun leapt overboard and swam to the Chao Phraya's embankment while the doomed ship went down. In their disregard for his life, Phao and Sarit had demonstrated how little they needed or cared for Phibun. They were the true powers, and they could continue their competition for ever more power and graft without him. Phibun emerged from the water alive but considerably less secure as premier. The Royal Thai Navy fared worse. In the months that followed, the Coup Group gutted the navy lest it threaten them again. They dismissed its leadership and rooted out suspected rebels. They seized facilities, weapons, vessels, and aircraft, and slashed its budget. Objections by senators came to nothing. The Coup Group left the Royal Thai Navy as a ghost of its former self.

While never as firmly in charge as he had been in the late 1930s, Phibun increasingly struggled to bring order to the government after the Manhattan Rebellion. Various political actors and their factions from parliament, the cabinet, the palace, and the military jostled for power according to different ideas about political legitimacy. Adding to this atmosphere of instability, university students emerged as another voice in the national political debate. One worrying source of dissent came from Thammasat University students. The students overwhelmingly supported Pridi, who had founded their school, and resented the presence of soldiers within the school's walls. Pridi's rebels had used Thammasat as a staging area for his uprisings, leaving the impression that the university was a bastion of anti-Coup Group sentiment. The army occupied Thammasat after the Grand Palace Rebellion and sought to acquire it as an army base.

In the midst of this growing political unrest, the Coup Group staged one of the strangest power grabs in Thailand's history. On November 29, 1951, the ruling clique took power from a government that it dominated but did not fully control. Citing the threat of communism, they announced via a radio broadcast that they were dissolving the government immediately and replacing the current constitution with the 1932 constitution. Because they seized power over the radio, this incident is known as the Radio Coup. The reversion to the 1932 constitution allowed active-duty military officers to serve in parliament or the cabinet. The change would make it easier for them to bring their military cohorts into key positions in the government. It would also help dissolve the power of various MPs whose parties and regional blocs were increasingly united in their opposition to Phibun. The new charter made all senators appointed. It helped bring about an anticommunist law that Phibun and Phao could use to persecute its political rivals and unsupportive journalists. With Thailand's foreign policy now formulated against Moscow and Beijing, the anticommunist law made leftists potentially guilty of treason. In November 1952, Phao's police arrested scores of writers, journalists, academics, politicians, and military officers in an episode known ironically as the Peace Revolt. Phao saw any effort promoting global disarmament or peaceful coexistence with the Communist Bloc as evidence of potential pro-Soviet sympathies. Some of those arrested in this phase, including the celebrated novelist Kulap Saipradit, spent several years in jail.

The new constitution also erased all the power the palace had acquired since the end of the war. The coup's timing was crucial as King Bhumibol was expected back in Thailand from Switzerland in a matter of days. When Bhumibol returned, police chief Phao pressured him repeatedly, hounding him at his Hua Hin palace and back in Bangkok, until he finally agreed to sign a constitution that would limit his royal power. In a hint of Bhumibol's growing political savvy, the young king made it clear that the 1932-style constitution would be provisional until a better charter could be drafted. Bhumibol had matured considerably since the death of his brother. In 1948, the monarch survived his own brush with mortality in Switzerland when he crashed his Fiat 500 into a logging truck outside Lausanne. The accident badly injured his back and cost him the sight of one eye. While convalescing from the near-fatal mishap in Europe, the king courted Sirikit Kitiyakara, the daughter of Thailand's ambassador to the United Kingdom. The royal-blooded Sirikit was beautiful and vivacious. Her marriage to Bhumibol a year later was an important factor in restoring public enthusiasm for the monarchy. Bhumibol got more than a queen in Sirikit, he gained a strong and clever partner in his burgeoning quest to restore luster to the Chakri throne. He would need all the power he could muster to stand up to the bullying of Phao and his cronies.

Phao's Police Terror

Phao took advantage of the navy's diminishment to expand the Royal Thai Police in size and authority. He set about transforming the police into a force capable of rivaling the army. He boosted police officers' morale by raising their profile in the nation's political discourse and by introducing schemes to make them recipients of more money, much of it illegally obtained. He created the Knights of the Diamond Order, an organization of the vicious elite who were responsible for carrying out his bidding. He rewarded this gang of cronies with specially designed diamond rings, who displayed these ostentatious symbols for intimidation. Below this circle of loyalists, Phao had some 43,000 police under his command, with many more affiliates willing to help. Within a few years, the police force was large and strong enough to take on the army. Phao himself became enormously wealthy during this period, with much of his riches coming from his domination of the opium trade. He ruthlessly destroyed anyone who stood in the way of his underground ventures. By targeting the navy so fiercely, he could control the coastal stretches that sent his opium out to the world. He was also notorious for eliminating police who did not join his criminal enterprises.

The United States government was another important factor in the rise of Phao and the police. With the memory of Phibun and the Royal Thai Army's collaboration with the Japanese in World War II still fresh in their minds, US officials in Thailand found the police a useful alternative to the army. More importantly, the police seemed more like a viable force for opposing the threat of an internal communist insurgency. Phao repeatedly exploited these American fears by playing up the threat posed by Thailand's then miniscule communist movement. He put forward himself and his police force as the best offense against communism in Thailand. The United States, in turn, showered a huge arsenal of weapons, money, and support on the police, including tanks and other armored vehicles, police aircraft, helicopters, and boats, modern weapons, and communications facilities. The only paratrooper training facility in Thailand at the time was one set up by the United States to train the police. The United States also set up a secretive business front called the Sea Supply Company, among whose many functions included training the Thai police in methods to counterguerrilla warfare. The CIA guided and funded a special forces unit called the Police Aerial Reconnaissance Unit (PARU). Its agents trained a few hundred Thai police recruits in antiguerrilla special warfare techniques for operations on both sides of Thailand's borders. Another CIA-sponsored police unit, the Border Patrol Police (BPP), operated along Thailand's borders with Cambodia and Laos. In his study of this geopolitical symbiosis, *A Special Relationship: The United States and Military Government in Thailand*, historian Daniel Fineman demonstrates how the CIA and the Thai police manipulated each other openly and clandestinely to advance their respective domestic and international agendas.

Phao held several powerful positions in the national government. Not only was he the police chief, he was also the deputy minister of defense, deputy minister of finance, and official spokesman for parliament. He also oversaw much of the investigation into King Ananda's death. He built a case against Pridi and his associates as the killers. He imprisoned the king's secretary and two pages for their alleged role as accomplices. The case was so flimsy that defense lawyers dismantled it with ease. Shortly after, two of the defense lawyers and some of the defense witnesses were killed. Their deaths kept the case against the three court figures alive in the upper courts. Eventually, the court convicted them. Phao attended the executions, watching as the men were pushed to their knees, tied to T-shaped frames, and, while holding a clutch of lotus flowers and incense sticks, shot in the torso near the heart. Phao was responsible also for the deaths of members of parliament who formed the closest thing to an opposition that the government had at this point. He had four politicians, all former Free Thai agents, executed while in police custody. They were shot while still in handcuffs by policemen with automatic weapons for allegedly attempting to overpower the heavy police escort transporting them. He killed several more high-profile Pridi supporters late in 1952. Two of the five victims had been MPs from Isan. Phao arrested them on trumped-up charges regarding an alleged communist-supported plot to overthrow the government. The men vanished while in police custody in Bangkok. A later investigation would reveal that Phao's men had strangled the five detainees and transported their bodies to Kanchanaburi where they were cremated and buried. After failing to gain the support of a leftist newspaper, Phao had the owner killed while the man was on his honeymoon. Like a mobster, Phao used killing to both eliminate his rivals and to cow any possible opposition. Among the more audacious examples, he orchestrated the killing of a member of parliament who dared challenge him publicly for his terror tactics. He also killed a police informant who had been sent to spy on that bold MP. Phao had them strangled and then thrown into the Chao Phraya River, their bodies weighted down by concrete. Phao awarded generous cash bonuses to police who carried out some of these notorious killings.

Other members of the Coup Group took advantage of Phibun's diminishment to advance their own agendas. In the early 1950s, Sarit Thanarat and Phibun had overcome their mutual dislike to protect each other from the increasingly aggressive Phao-Phon clique. Like Phibun, Sarit was a soldier's soldier who relished his time with the troops. During the Boworadet Rebellion, he saw combat in the fight for the Don Mueang airfield. In World War II, he led an infantry battalion into Burma, and fought along the Salween River. The Royal Thai Army was his passion, and he gave nearly all his energy to advancing the interests of the force. But unlike his patron, he seemed to have only minimal interest in politics until the late 1940s. His family's roots were in the northeast, a region whose Lao-based culture was distinct from that of the lower Chao Phraya River valley, birthplace of nearly all other leaders. Sarit's mother was Lao, and he was related to important figures in Laos's government at the time. He was a lifelong military man who, unlike Phibun and many of the other Promoters, had not studied abroad. He lacked the gloss of cosmopolitan sophistication that the previous generation of Thai military and political figures had acquired. He was not familiar with the capitals of Europe or Western higher education systems. His reference points were almost always limited to Thailand and Laos. The other military men, including Phibun, looked down on him. Despite this, Sarit found success in Washington. He deftly sized up his American counterparts, and found ways to extract ever more military aid and closer cooperation from the United States. He could be dour to the point of humorlessness, which enhanced the aura of menace that surrounded him. He was a heavy drinker and a philanderer, famous for his scores of *mia noi* ("minor wives" or mistresses) that wealthy and important men often accumulate. He was bigger than life in the true sense of that phrase. He was a rotund man at a time in Thailand when most people, especially army officers, remained trim. Like Phao, he trafficked in opium and pursued wealth from criminal and corrupt enterprises. He was vain and dapper, despite his size and dissolute ways. Because of his weight and frowning persona, there is a tendency to treat him as being cartoonish or unsophisticated. This is a mistake. Sarit was focused, driven, and clear. He was more than just another greedy military lout who used intimidation and brute force to enrich himself, but a clever tactician who could read situations and opponents keenly.

Phibun rewarded Sarit's trust by giving him increasingly powerful (and lucrative) positions in the military and the government. Sarit rose quickly, holding the highest ranks not only in the army but in the navy and air force as well. He became commander in chief of the army in 1954, and a year later got promoted to field marshal. Two years later, he became the supreme commander of the armed forces and minister of defense, positions that gave him enormous control over the country's internal security affairs as well as Thailand's international relations with the United States and other allies. Even after he moved on from commanding the Royal Thai Army's 1st Infantry Division, Sarit made sure that his army protégées obtained high positions within the RTA's 1st Army command that controlled it. He put Thanom Kittikachorn, Praphas Charusathien, and Krit Siwara into its various leadership billets. These three figures would dominate Thailand's military and political affairs for the next two and a half decades. By 1957, Sarit had moved squarely into the realm of politics and had become defense minister. But just as important as his military and political posts, Sarit's control of the National Lottery Bureau helped him toward his goal of challenging Phibun, Phin, and Phao for power. Over the years, the Lottery Bureau gave Sarit access to huge amounts of money that could be diverted from Thailand's legal lottery and used for constructing his political and military networks and for supporting his ever-increasing number of mistresses for which he was to become notorious.

Phibun Challenges the Palace

While the other military men of the Coup Group sought to scare off civilian political competitors, Phibun maintained some of his youthful commitment to governing from within a legitimate parliamentary system. He appeared inclined toward a more liberal constitutional system even when such moves put him at odds with Phao and his supporters. But his tendency toward heavy-handedness and unlawful treatment of his opponents flashed intermittently, undermining his efforts at restoring a participatory political system.

Part of Phibun's plan for ruling with a popular mandate was to cultivate his image as a kind of father figure to the nation. He attempted to further steer the course of national culture by building Thai monuments and by presenting himself as the protector and patron of Thailand's Buddhist institutions. He had the government restore and rededicate many historic temples, monuments, and shrines while he presided over their reopening. He used Buddhism's twenty-fifth centennial celebration – the 2,500th anniversary of the Buddha's birth – to place himself at the center of Thai Buddhism and, by extension, world Buddhism. He was behind such celebrations as the ordaining of 2,500 new monks and the casting of 2,500 new Buddha statues. He presented his regime as the protector of Buddhism. He did not, as was pointedly observed, give King Bhumibol a big role in these celebrations. In the decades following his participation in the overthrow of the absolute monarchy in 1932, Phibun had not changed his opinion of royalty. He saw little value in maintaining the monarch, and had begun to see the threat to his authority posed by the growing popularity of the king and his photogenic queen. He sought to claim the paternalistic role as the father of the nation like that played by the Chakri kings, especially Rama V and VI. To make his position on the monarchy clear, Phibun had statues of King Taksin and *Phraya* Phahon cast and dedicated. The celebration of these two figures was meant to be a slight to the palace. King Taksin was not of the Chakri line, and was put to death rather cruelly by Rama I's supporters, but emerged as a favorite of the Thai people. Phibun's elevation of King Taksin was a reminder that the savior of Thai civilization from Burmese was hated by the Chakri's champions. The *Phraya* Phahon statue was a more direct swipe at the palace. The Promoter and People's Party leader had played a key role in diminishing the Chakri dynasty by overthrowing King Prajadhipok and driving him into exile.

Phibun's mistrust of the Chinese also survived and even intensified in the 1950s. Many ethnic Chinese entrepreneurs prospered in the postwar period. Numerous wealthy Chinese businessmen had fled China after Mao Zedong's People's Liberation Army defeated Chiang Kai-shek's Kuomintang in 1949, and many settled in Southeast Asia by joining existing family networks in Thailand. Phibun sought to counter their influence by promoting a kind of ethnic nationalism in business and industry that favored Thai firms. He established several state enterprises, almost all of which failed. He tried to restrict Chinese-owned ventures by passing laws unfavorable to alien-owned firms. The Chinese got around this by appointing influential Thai political figures to their boards who would protect their interests in the Thai parliament. Likewise, Mao's communist revolution in China had inspired political confidence among ethnic Chinese throughout Southeast Asia, who resented the mistrust and poor treatment they received from their adoptive countries' governments. The Chinese-language press became increasingly outspoken against the mistreatment of these Sino-Thais. The Communist Party of Thailand (CPT) developed into an entity whose leadership was largely ethnic Chinese while drawing its followers more and more from a largely urban population. Phibun sought to limit Mao's appeal to these Thai-Chinese by placing restrictions on Chinese-language schools and native-place associations in Thailand. Somewhat incongruently, Phibun conjured a Chinese bogeyman who was both a capitalist and a communist. Phibun's regime largely ended Chinese immigration to Thailand, bringing to a halt a movement of people from China to Thailand that had endured with vigor for a few hundred years.

Phibun's chauvinist policies had serious repercussions for Thailand's Muslim minorities, especially in the areas of southern Thailand where several of the provinces have an ethnic Malay and Muslim majority. These were areas that only a few generations ago had belonged to the Patani Sultanate before being integrated into Siam. In his first period of rule, Phibun had sought to ban Islamic dress and surviving elements of Sharia law. He also pressed these Malay-speaking minorities into mandatory attendance at Thai government schools. Phibun did not ban the Malay language in Thai schools, but his return to power in the late 1940s antagonized Muslim activists who sought to preserve a separate cultural and religious identity. His policies sparked riotous antigovernment demonstrations. In response, Phibun sent gunboats and army troops to put down the protesters. He clamped down on their political activities and arrested and imprisoned many of their leaders. His harshness transformed a political problem into a military one by driving these Muslim Thai citizens to become insurgents committed to autonomy and even separatism. He arrested one of their leaders, Haji Sulong, and sent him to jail for three years. Shortly after this Muslim leader was released from jail, he and his son vanished. It is believed that the Thai police drowned them and hid their corpses.

Phibun also had to contend with a small but worrying ethnic Lao separatist movement in Thailand's northeastern provinces led by several of Pridi's former Free Thai allies. Isan remained the poorest of Thailand's five regions. Its sandy soil and unpredictable rain gave its farming families meager crop yields. Bangkok had long afforded Isan the lowest priority in development and assistance. Many central Thais harbored bigoted attitudes toward the farming folk of Isan, further antagonizing the separatists. An Isan secession movement was met with both ridicule and overreaction. As in the south, Phibun's response involved violence. He was complicit in the assassination and extrajudicial killing of these political leaders by the police and those acting on police orders. Bangkok labeled the Lao separatists "communists" when they killed them. Phibun's brutal treatment of dissenters scared political figures from challenging him, but those military men closest to him were unafraid.

By the mid-1950s, Phibun faced direct challenges to his premiership from Phao and, less directly but just as worryingly, from Sarit. To shore up foreign support, in 1955 Phibun went on a long overseas tour of Europe and the United States that was designed to improve Thailand's international reputation as more than just another military-dominated authoritarian state. He concluded the trip by assuring the US Congress that he would implement fully representative democracy, and that Thailand would remain a staunch US ally. Some have suggested that this trip influenced Phibun by encouraging him to experiment with a more open form of democracy than anything Thailand had seen before. Others say he was just trying to hoodwink American lawmakers and outmaneuver his political rivals by beating them at the ballot box. His plan was to try to curtail the growing power of both the police chief Phao and the former army commander in chief Phin by getting rid of the members of the government's legislative committee who were in Phao's and Phin's pockets. Achieving "true democracy" became the most common theme for his public speeches that year and the next, no matter what the event or venue.

Toward this end, Phibun proffered outlets for free speech by holding press conferences and by allowing the creation of a free speech zone in Sanam Luang, the expansive lawn beside the Grand Place that was based on the model of London's Hyde Park. In theory, it was meant to give Thai people a venue to speak their mind on any issue. The problem was that Phibun's rivals, especially Phao, hired agents to use the venue to denounce Phibun and accuse him of corruption and other crimes. On several occasions, Phibun found himself having to answer some spurious charge or another that had originated in the free speech forum he himself had organized. If he was going to get rid of Phao and his clique, he realized, he had to do it soon or they would reduce his stature and power to irrelevancy.

Phibun's solution was to lurch toward democracy, to proffer a taste of the democracy he had crushed quite effectively up to that point. Desperate for a clever solution to his imminent showdown with Phao, he offered the country an election. Those elections marked the beginning of the end for Phibun.

CHAPTER 10

SARIT THANARAT'S REGIME

The elections that Phibun Songkhram oversaw in February 1957 were his undoing. Ambitious influence-seekers from across the political and social spectrums formed some twenty-five parties that each fielded multiple candidates. The most important party was the Seri Manangkhasila, which was formed from the government's legislative committee. Prime Minister Phibun was its party leader, Field Marshal Sarit Thanarat was deputy leader, and Police Chief Phao Siyanon was secretary general. Their biggest rival was the royalist Democrat Party still under the leadership of Khuang Aphaiwong. In addition to his jocularity, Khuang possessed strong chameleon-like qualities that allowed him to adapt easily to changing political situations. Khuang and his Democrats had endured despite the Coup Group's sustained assault on constitutional democracy throughout the 1950s. Khuang, the Pramoj brothers, and other Democrats astutely read the public's growing support for the monarchy that Bhumibol and his young family elicited. The election was a lively, albeit farcical, affair. The government's Seri Manangkhasila Party won the most seats ultimately, but the election was tainted. Observers saw that Phibun had been losing to Khuang throughout the vote counting for Bangkok until last-minute manipulations and vote-stealing chicanery rescued a victory for the military men. Phibun's democratic experiment had been a sham and, even worse for him, had made him look insecure and inept.

Protesters led by the Democrat Party came out to challenge the election results. The ruling triumvirate responded by sending out thugs to rough up the demonstrators. In desperation, Phibun declared martial law and tried to clamp down on the newspapers carrying stories about election fraud. Phibun put his trusted ally Sarit in charge of the clampdown, which proved to be the biggest mistake of his political life. The dutiful Sarit had learned much about political theater in the previous decade. His burgeoning public relations talents identified opportunities to make himself look good, or at least look better than his political boss. Phibun's grandiose rhetoric about the importance of democracy and all of the press coverage dedicated to the forming of rival parties had set up the Thai public for profound disappointment at the results. Students at Chulalongkorn University, the ruling elite's principal postsecondary school, flew their flag at half-mast. Newspapers wrote dispirited editorials decrying the dirty results. People felt let down. Even Phibun's foreign backers were hard-pressed to say anything positive about the election. Protestors took to the streets and clashed briefly with troops sent to quell them. Sarit ordered the troops to avoid bloodshed. When Sarit went to meet with the demonstrators, he became an unlikely hero by telling the assembled crowd, many of whom were students, that they were right about the election being stolen. He said it was the dirtiest election he had ever seen. His trick was to appear to the students as an honest figure who was brave enough to speak the truth and to challenge the sinister forces that had corrupted the electoral process. That he himself was one of the corrupt figures who stole the election was mostly lost on the students. The demonstrators were thrilled to have such a prominent figure as Sarit confirm their accusations. Sarit found himself, probably to his surprise, hailed as a champion of transparency and good government.

Getting Rid of Phibun

But how was it possible to get rid of Phibun? The answer came in a couple of national scandals. A severe drought in the northeast had devastated Isan's crop yields. Many farmers came to Bangkok as economic refugees looking for work, far more than otherwise would have come during the lull in the yearly planting-to-harvesting cycle. Newspapers carried stories of near catastrophic famine in the region.

Phibun sought to silence the increasingly strident criticism from Isan's representatives by paying them off. Predictably, MPs who had not been bought off complained loudly. The press excoriated Phibun for his policy failings and the payoffs. Phibun's administration made things worse when the inspection team it had sent to Isan returned with a report characterizing the lack of rain as merely behind schedule. Shortly afterward, another scandal came to light in which logging businesses associated with Phibun's political party benefitted from timber deals at the site of a hydroelectric dam under construction in the north. Things grew worse for the government during a general debate in parliament when Phao was accused of supporting newspapers hostile to the king. The accusers went as far as to suggest Phao's involvement in a plot to assassinate the king.

Sarit saw his chance in this time of roiling discontent. Rather than be brought down with Phibun and Phao, he removed himself from the ruling triumvirate by resigning as minister of defense, taking with him his closest subordinate allies. Generals Thanom Kittikachorn, Praphas Charusathien, and Krit Siwara all resigned their posts as deputy ministers and abandoned the government to go with Sarit. With so many senior military officers fleeing their government posts to join him, Sarit felt confident enough to issue an ultimatum demanding that Phibun dissolve his newly formed government and hold new elections. Phibun refused. Police chief Phao and former army commander in chief Phin scrambled to distance themselves from Phibun by resigning from the government. But Phao and Phin had not been Sarit's allies for years, and they found themselves caught somewhere in the growing battle lines between Sarit and Phibun.

Sarit's stance brought the corruption-weary public to his side. On September 15, 1957, a large crowd of students gathered on Sanam Luang to denounce Phibun's government and, especially, the police under the control of Phao. The students hailed Sarit as an exemplary leader for Thailand despite his professional ruthlessness and personal dissolution. The crowd marched to Sarit's house to chant their support for him. When they found him not home, they marched to Government House, smashed down its gates, and made increasingly volatile speeches denouncing the government and celebrating Sarit. When word spread among the students that the field marshal had returned home, they marched back to his house to hear him speak. Sarit told them they had confirmed his belief that in pressuring the government he was carrying out the will of the people. The next morning, he overthrew the government in as swift and efficient a coup d'état as Bangkok had ever seen. The city braced for a counterattack from Phao's police force that never materialized. Sarit had taken the city, the government, and the country in a matter of hours. Not a single shot was fired. Phibun fled to Cambodia, and then to the land of his World War II ally, Japan. Phao departed for Switzerland, reportedly taking a lot of money with him. Both men died in exile a few years later without ever returning to Thailand.

A Cold War Warrior-Ruler

Sarit was a new kind of leader for Thailand. He was embraced as a popular ruler and a much-needed antidote to the dictatorial-democratic muddle of the Phibun years. He presented himself as a savior figure who possessed the power to transform Thailand, and many chose to see him that way. Sarit used American development aid to not only modernize his armed forces but to develop Thailand's logistical infrastructure and its industries. He also presided over a period that saw the first developments of Thailand as a world-class tourist destination fed by intercontinental jet routes. In 1960, Thailand welcomed 100,000 international tourists to the kingdom, the first glimmer of what would become the kingdom's most important and lucrative industries.

Initially, Sarit tried to stay in the background and run the government through a surrogate prime minister. He held elections a few months after his coup and appointed the former ambassador to Washington, Pote Sarasin, as prime minister in September 1957. But Pote was little more than a place-holder. Three months later, in early 1958, Sarit put in his closest deputy, Thanom Kittikachorn. Shortly afterward, Sarit left Thailand for medical treatment for cirrhosis of the liver in the United States. When he returned eight months later, he almost immediately staged another coup. On October 28, 1958, Sarit overthrew the government he had set up and made himself prime minister. In this move, Sarit did away with all pretense of a representative government. He suspended the constitution and declared martial law. He opted to run the country through a so-called Revolutionary Council. As the name suggests, Sarit saw himself as a transformative figure who would rescue Thailand's unstable society by bringing it back to a state it had long abandoned. He used the Thai term *patiwat*, or revolution, to describe what he was doing. Sarit cited the threat of communism to Thailand's social, cultural, and political institutions as the reason for his self-coup. But Sarit's main goal was to undo the largely Western cultural and political norms that Phibun had promoted in the late 1930s and early 1940s. Sarit wanted to replace Phibun's civilization markers with Thai ones, even if he had to find them in an idealized version of the distant past.

Sarit was not interested in liberal democracy. The provisional charter he put forward in 1959 banned political parties and did away with an elected parliament. Having watched Phibun flail around as he tried to steer an often-unruly parliament, Sarit had decided that Thailand's governance required a ruler with more direct powers. Kingship of an ancient sort was his model. Sarit saw himself as belonging to traditional Thai leaders from the distant past who were believed to be charismatic and decisive, popular and authoritarian. The Thai-American political scientist and historian Thak Chaloemtiarana has written the most influential book on Sarit and his legacy, *Thailand: The Politics of Despotic Paternalism*. In Thak's analysis, Sarit models himself on the ruling style of King Ramkhamhaeng the Great from the thirteenth-century Sukhothai kingdom, a paternalistic style of warrior ruler called a *phokhun* in Thai. Others have suggested that Sarit was little more than a thug, a military strongman, who sought to legitimize his tyrannical rule by draping it in the romanticized historical trappings of a premodern system.

Perhaps because he did not study abroad or spend that much time living overseas, Sarit tended to blame foreign cultural and political implants for Thailand's problems. He stressed the idea of Thai-ness (*khwambenthai*) as a nearly sacred entity. He sought to convince the Thai people that the answers to their unstable government lay not in Washington or London but in Sukhothai and Si Satchanalai, in something like the Thais' collective unconscious, their barely remembered notions of formerly harmonious societies that were guided by uniquely Thai principles and traditions. He stressed the Thai people's pride in being neat in public and well-ordered in their social relationships. Sarit emphasized this penchant for neatness in both literal and figurative ways. He wanted to use development money to clean up and repair Thailand's streets and buildings. He banned human-powered pedicabs because they were old-fashioned. Having wrested control of the police from Phao's cronies, Sarit used the force to round up petty thieves and loiterers so that criminal types were less visible in public. He was ruthless in his treatment of arsonists by having them executed without the benefit of an investigation or trial. He had the police alter their approach to managing the sex industry so that prostitution was more discrete. He outlawed opium, which was legal in Thailand well into the 1950s, and made a great show for the press of shutting down opium dens and burning piles of opium pipes. Beyond the public's view, underground heroin exports to Asia and the West continued.

Sarit's efforts to make Thailand "clean" extended to the figurative. Many Thais consider orderliness (*khwam riaproi*) a quintessentially Thai value. Sarit stressed that self-conscious attention to neatness to denounce public protests and demonstrations as un-Thai and, of course, the work of foreign agents bent on imposing the un-Thai ideals of communism. Students and newspapers – the very same groups that had facilitated Sarit's rise – were pressed into conformity and support through violence, arrests, and the threat of further violence. Sarit's paternalism was such that all citizens had to be obedient and well turned out children who did their utmost to maintain peace and harmony within the national "family."

Enhancing the Role of the King

Sarit did not believe that Thai people could harbor love or loyalty for an abstract entity like a nation. Rather, in keeping with his development of the *phokhun* model of ancient kingship, he believed that Thai people could more easily feel love for a human embodiment of their country in the form of a sacred national father figure. For Sarit, this unifying person was the king. The government's function, in Sarit's view, was to carry out necessary tasks in service of that king. All the apparatuses of the state – the bureaucracy, the officials, the military – served the king, whose main function was to look after the well-being of his subjects. Sarit differed from Phibun in that he did not see himself as being in competition with King Bhumibol. In fact, Sarit's innovation was to stress his subordinate status to the king. He gave Bhumibol opportunities to emphasize his role as the father of the nation. He encouraged Bhumibol to revive many of the royal ceremonies dating from King Vajiravudh's nationalism-building period at the start of the century. Bhumibol now presided over the plowing ceremonies, where the king cast out various seeds in a specially prepared plot to the prayers of Brahmins. This ceremony was closely watched by Thailand's farmers who cherished the seeds touched by the king and quickly replanted them in the farms of Thailand's rural provinces. King Bhumibol also revived a more elaborate version of the royal *thod kathin* ceremony. Traditionally, Buddhist lay people performed this annual rite by offering new robes to Buddhist monks at the end of their rainy season confinement (*phansa*). In the royal elaboration of the rite, the king offers robes to monks mostly at royally sponsored temples. The palace marked the annual donation of new robes and other gifts to monks by treating the public to a grandiose ceremony in which a flotilla of ornate and colorful royal barges paraded up and down the Chao Phraya River while throngs gathered on both banks to catch a glimpse of the king.

Sarit increased the king's prestige by having the national day moved from June 24, the date commemorating the overthrow of the absolute monarchy and the start of the constitutional monarchy, to December 5, King Bhumibol's birthday. He also gave the king increased symbolic control of the armed forces by expanding the former oath of allegiance to the king to include a ceremony in which all soldiers now drank sacralized water in front of the king or, more commonly, a portrait of the king. Likewise, the king presented all university degrees to every college student upon graduation. Sarit increased the palace's budget and launched a major restoration of the king's palace.

Bhumibol embraced the opportunity presented to him by Sarit's coup. He used the restored power of the throne to pursue programs important to him. The king had long expressed an interest in the well-being of his subjects and had carried out development projects designed to improve their lives, but under Sarit these jaunts became bigger ordeals with farmers and laborers lining the roads to wave Thai and royal flags as they greeted their king. Fanfare aside, Bhumibol visited the rural areas to become more familiar with the problems facing his subjects. The camera and notebook Bhumibol carried on these tours became symbols of a new kind of Thai kingship. He was a monarch who sought to understand the challenges facing Thais everywhere so that he could do something to help them. Bhumibol also took more foreign trips. He and Sirikit visited Asian and Western countries in what was called royal diplomacy. Bhumibol met with foreign leaders to discuss the problems facing developing countries like his own and to affirm Thailand's anticommunist stance. In the United States, Bhumibol addressed Congress, received a ticker-tape parade in New York, and met with entertainment giants such as Elvis Presley, Walt Disney, Bob Hope, and Benny Goodman. His official visits to the world's great cities helped boost Thailand's image abroad. The young king and his striking wife became popular subjects for international newspapers and magazines. In the late 1950s and into the 1960s, Bhumibol became a compelling embodiment of Thailand in the Cold War period: youthful, talented, sophisticated, and elegant.

Despite his archaic model of leadership, Sarit was not a reactionary. He was committed to developing the country economically, educationally, and technologically. During the Sarit years, the word "development" (*patthana*) took on almost magical connotations. He formed a National Economic Development Board that oversaw a five-year plan to develop and improve Thailand's infrastructure. It focused on agricultural irrigation schemes for previously poor farmland, especially in the northeast, Sarit's ancestral home. Thailand improved electricity infrastructure. It added government schools to previously neglected areas, and built institutes of higher education in areas beyond Bangkok, such as colleges in Chiang Mai in the north and in Khon Kaen in the northeast.

Thailand prospered under Sarit's rule. His policies, combined with economic aid from the United States and other allied countries, helped Thailand's develop into a modern and economically vibrant nation. Beginning in 1960, Thailand's economy would grow by 7 percent annually for more than a decade. Its agricultural products and raw materials, mainly tin and rubber, found new markets abroad. Industrial production of items such as shoes, plastics, and electronics also grew exponentially. But in terms of civil liberties, Thailand seemed to be going in the opposite direction. Sarit fostered an oppressive and fearful environment for those who wrote about politics during this period. Military rule and the lack of a democratic constitution meant that only supporters of Sarit's regime could publish their books and newspapers and air their ideas in the realm of public discourse. No counternarrative was allowed. In trying to be "revolutionary" in his imposition of authoritarianism, Sarit set into motion a pro-democracy movement that would grow slowly in the 1960s, explode in the 1970s, and flourish as a social force in the 1990s and beyond.

A Leftist Hero

Chit Phumisak was among the most courageous political figures to emerge from the university political circles in the early 1950s. He was a scholar, poet, composer, and political activist. His influence on Thailand's political and intellectual history has been explored in groundbreaking articles by historian of Thai nationalism Craig J. Reynolds in his *Thai Radical Discourse: The Real Face of Thai Feudalism Today*. Reynolds' research has contributed strongly to the world's understanding of this enigmatic intellectual and his legacy, and is the source of some of the material here. As the son of a clerk in the Thai civil service, Chit grew up in the towns of Prachinburi and Samutprakan. But it was his father's posting to Battambang during World War II that affected his intellectual development most profoundly. Chit came of age there during Thailand's occupation of western Cambodia. As a teenager, he experienced Khmer resentment of Thai irredentism – he was even shot at on one occasion – and saw the early armed resistance to France's return. He returned to Thailand proper with Khmer language skills and a fascination with the region's premodern history. After studying at the government school at Bangkok's famed Wat Benchamabophit, Chit attended Chulalongkorn University, the more establishment of Bangkok's two elite universities, where he studied history and languages. He became obsessed with the purported origins of Thailand's nationalist history, studying the inscriptions and chronicles upon which it was based. Resented by some classmates for his iconoclastic views and suspected by others for harboring pro-communist sympathies, Chit became the target of right-wing hostility before earning his bachelor's degree. In 1953, he endured an ugly public assault in one infamous episode at the university. After rumors spread that Chit had designed an unflattering and satirical cover for the university yearbook, a space normally featuring a heroic representation of the school's namesake King Chulalongkorn, Chit was summoned to a student assembly to explain his actions. He used the opportunity to share his ideas with the entire university student body. As Chit eloquently defended his inclinations toward the historical avant-garde, a gang of enraged engineering majors rushed the stage and pushed him from the platform. Chit was knocked unconscious from the impact. His concussion was mild, but the episode laid bare the dangers that young non-conforming intellectuals like Chit faced when exploring alternative interpretations of Thailand's past.

During this period, the American linguist William Gedney hired Chit to help prepare the first Thai translation of *The Communist Manifesto*. The money for the project came from the United States Embassy. American officials in Bangkok wanted a Thai-language edition of this major political document because they thought it would help better expose the communists' goals for subverting Thailand's traditional social, political, and economic systems. Chit had already made a name for himself beyond his university circles by writing a Marxist critique of Buddhism in the early 1950s and was eager to contribute a Thai version of Marx that was not mediated by Chinese translations. Chit produced numerous essays, articles, and book and film reviews under his own name and various pseudonyms in the mid-1950s, especially after he was suspended for a year from Chulalongkorn University. His unusual take on Thai culture and arts generated admirers and detractors. But Chit's master work was a study called *Chom na sakdina thai*, which is usually translated as *The Face of Thai Feudalism*. It was published in 1957 during the brief period of democratic openness that Phibun declared before his regime was crushed by Sarit's coup. Chit took advantage of this fleeting openness to publish a Marxist critique of Thai history. In its structure, Chit's history of Thailand followed a conventional outline. He imitated the royalist historical framework that Chulalongkorn's half-brother Prince Damrong had first produced, a historical saga that traced Thailand's history from the Sukhothai period of the late thirteenth century and followed it through a line of kings spanning the four-century long Ayutthaya period all the way to the present Chakri dynasty. Chit's great feat was that rather than celebrating these many kings as the source of Thailand's strength and continuity, he argued that they had oppressed the Thai people throughout the centuries. Chit accused them of using aristocratic privilege to rob and abuse the Thai peasants. In picking up the Marxist historical framework, he argued that *sakdina*, the system by which human beings' status and rights were determined by this numerical expression of field power or how much land they could theoretically command, was as exploitative as European feudalism. Far from lionizing kings like Ramkhamhaeng or Borommakot, he suggested that these rulers were more like rapacious landlords than the "lords of life" that nationalist history books portrayed them as. The book caused a sensation that transcended even the somewhat constrained circles of politically minded academics. It outraged conservatives and royalists. The following year, Chit was arrested when Sarit came to power.

In 1958, Sarit's regime put Chit and many other dissident writers in jail. While in prison, Chit wrote and read prodigiously, and taught elementary school topics to both prison guards' children and fellow inmates. He was released in late 1964. Fearing for his life, he fled Bangkok and went underground. He joined the Communist Party of Thailand's insurgency operating in the northeast. A stubbornly original thinker, Chit was said to have clashed with other intellectuals and the seasoned cadre of the maquis. Although there is no definitive account of his death, the story goes that he was killed in Sakon Nakhon at the base of the Phu Pan mountains on May 5, 1966. The most reliable account says Chit was betrayed to village security forces after he asked an old woman for some rice. He was chased back into the mountains and gunned down. The spilling of blood in this woodland area, which included a reserve used for Buddhist meditation, caused consternation for the forest monks staying there. Later, the Thai communists played down Chit's ideological combativeness with its leadership and declared him a martyr to their cause.

The government kept Chit's killing a secret for many years. The ruling tyrants seemed to anticipate the fascination that would emerge around the brave young intellectual turned insurgent. Chit Phumisak became a hero to the more radically minded Thai students of the 1970s as they sought out progressive works in the twilight of Thanom and Praphas's authoritarian regime. Chit's ideas were intriguing because they presented an inverted view of the nationalist history that had been force-fed to these young people all of their lives. Although Chit's work has become a mainstay of leftist thinkers, most young Thais learn about Chit and his ideas from folk-rock songs written about him. One of his books, *Art for Life, Art for the People*, partly inspired the creation of a unique Thai music genre called "Songs for Life." The episodes of Chit's life have taken on a legendary quality, helped along by published recollections by friends and relatives of his principled work habits and prolific output. Chit himself made for a great visual icon as well. He did not have an unruly beard and radically chic beret like Che Guevara did in his famous portrait. He didn't have Mao's lunar gaze and bulwark collar in that famous image generated during the Cultural Revolution. Chit's iconic images are just as compelling, though. In one of the most famous images of Chit reproduced extensively since the early 1970s, he sports a full youthful head of hair and horn-rimmed glasses. His direct gaze into the camera lens projects intelligence and fearlessness – and hurt. In this school photo, he has the brooding charisma of a powerful but wounded spirit. His cool intellectual mien is a visual contrast, a reproach even, to the venality and menace evident on the faces of Sarit and the Thai strongmen who succeeded him.

Sarit's health had been bad throughout the period of his direct rule. His hard drinking and other dissolute habits had taken its toll on his health to the point that he had to be hospitalized repeatedly in 1963. There is a telling episode from that hospitalization period that reveals a lot about Sarit and his view of himself in transforming Thailand. When King Bhumibol came to visit him at his bedside as Sarit came closer to death, Sarit took the king's hand and pressed it to his forehead. This was an extraordinary thing to do because most Thais, even now, adhere to the old practice of avoiding physical contact with members of the royal family. But Sarit, who worked hard to elevate the status of the monarch, ignored protocol and risked insult to establish visible physical contact. He appears to have wanted to go to his death with the image of that increasingly powerful monarch transferring his karmic power, his *barami*, to him. The photograph of the king touching the ailing Sarit's forehead captured the relationship that Sarit had tried to foster between the monarch and the military strongman. The king blesses the general who worked hard to make such blessings meaningful to the point of sacredness. The photo was widely circulated in newspapers and memorial volumes.

In and out of hospital over the previous few years, Sarit succumbed to liver disease on December 8, 1963. He died a wealthy man; estimates put the total value at several hundreds of millions of dollars. In addition to cash, he had expansive land holdings, a brewery, and numerous homes and automobiles. After his death, scores of mistresses, his *mia noi*, came forward to claim a part of that fortune, with many being legally awarded a piece of his estate. The public was said to be shocked when tales of his vast fortune and many wives were revealed, but the surprise was more about the unexpectedly high figures rather than his pursuit of these prizes. Sarit had long styled himself as a figure known in Thai as a *nakleng*, a term that usually refers to a hard-living, hard-drinking man who thrives on risk and danger, an ultra-masculine swaggering hero who is above the law, fearless, and, ultimately good-hearted and just. Many in Thailand remember Sarit and his leadership fondly. The field marshal is a historical hero for many soldiers, especially those from the northeast. Sarit would have approved of the image he left behind in death.

CHAPTER 11

THAILAND IN THE VIETNAM WAR: ON THE FRONTLINES

Thailand was directly involved in the Vietnam War. It provided not only significant logistical support to the United States throughout the conflict but also committed its army, navy, and air force into direct combat in South Vietnam and Laos. Thailand was also the target of direct attacks, albeit uncommon, by Viet Cong commandos who crossed over from Laos to hit Thai military installations. Thailand's Police Aerial Reconnaissance Units had been fighting against communist forces, both Vietnamese and Laotian troops, inside Laos since the late 1950s. Thailand was thus a combatant in the Second Indochina War even before the United States committed troops. Thailand's air force had been using T-28 bombers inside Laos to hit positions several years before the United States officially started carrying out similar missions. Beyond its general wariness of the People's Republic of China and the Soviet Union, Thailand's leadership felt acutely threatened by the rise of the Pathet Lao, the communist Laotian units allied with the North Vietnamese, and eagerly entered the so-called secret war against them. Thai leaders focused on Laos because of its proximity and because of lingering notions of suzerainty over one of their historical "lost territories." Moreover, the specter of Isan separatism and pan-Lao nationalism sparked fear that these communist forces in Laos could inspire like-minded ethnic Lao in Thailand's northeast to launch a similar insurgency against Bangkok.

Thailand's Entry into the Vietnam War

Thailand's entry into the war was gradual but steady. Beginning in the early 1960s, the United States had pressed Thailand to play a direct role in the defense of the Republic of Vietnam (South Vietnam). First the Kennedy and then the Johnson administration put pressure on the United States' Free World Allies to contribute more to its effort to stabilize, defend, and develop the anticommunist nation. The United States asked its Asian allies to contribute human and material support to South Vietnam, especially military forces. The US foreign policy makers believed that these countries were the ones most directly threatened by what it saw as China's promotion of insurgency and revolution in South Vietnam. While the Domino Theory still held sway over the imaginations of anticommunists around the world, US leadership saw Thailand as the first domino to fall if Beijing's and Hanoi's allies in Laos, South Vietnam, and Cambodia succeeded in overthrowing the governments in their respective countries. Although many commentators poked holes in the Domino Theory almost as soon as it was articulated, the concept had a strong grip on Thailand's leaders, who embraced it as a legitimate model of what might occur if the communists succeeded.

A Domestic Communist Insurgency

Thailand's own communist movement was still miniscule.

The Communist Party of Thailand proper, a group specifically organized around issues concerning Thailand's internal affairs, had only been around since was formed at the start of World War II. This group did have a few more ethnic Thai members, especially from the northeast, but like the Chinese Communist Party of Thailand and Ho Chi Minh's groups, its membership was dominated by ethnic Chinese and Vietnamese. The prominence of outsiders in the CPT's leadership encouraged the enduring notion that communism was somehow un-Thai in its formulation. Many Thais said that communism's tenets made it incompatible with Thailand's most revered traditions, specifically Buddhism and the monarchy. This specious argument ignores the revolutionary nature of communism and the ability of its proponents to adapt communism to the local cultures in which they live and operate.

After World War II, and especially after the success of Mao Zedong's People's Liberation Army in 1949, the Communist Party of Thailand shifted its focus from urban-based activities to a broader program in the rural areas, especially in the northeast. The CPT was not specifically a guerrilla movement at this time. It did not immediately set out to try to overthrow the central government through a military insurgency. Instead, it concentrated on organizing and propagandizing in villages. It established cells in rural areas, and sent some of its recruits to the People's Republic of China and North Vietnam for education.

The military side of their struggle did not begin until the early 1960s. One of the events that triggered the switch involved a fascinating figure named Khrong Chandwong. He was a school teacher and headmaster from Sakon Nakhon Province in the northeast who had joined the Free Thai movement to oppose the Japanese during World War II. He got himself elected to the House of Representatives from his district in 1957, in what would be the last elections for more than a decade. In parliament, he supported measures to expand democracy at the village level and to lift the Anticommunist Act of 1952. Although he undoubtedly had leftist sympathies, he had never been a member of the CPT. Sarit arrested and jailed him shortly after taking control of Thailand in his coup. Eventually, he freed Khrong and allowed him to return to his home district in Sakon Nakhon, which is when and where his truly revolutionary activity began. Khrong started a movement he called Samakhi Tham (Solidarity of the Dharma) that promoted collective agriculture among the northeast's poor farmers. But more worryingly for Bangkok's leaders, he promoted a pan-Lao movement that might one day have Isan join Laos as a single country. The resulting nation would have been a kind of Laoland for the Lao set beside a Thailand of the Thais.

Sarit had Khrong arrested and killed. Predictably, this extrajudicial killing sparked more resistance to the central government. As in the case of Chit Phumisak, the CPT claimed Khrong as a martyr for their cause despite him never being a member of the party. Sympathetic northeasterners rallied to the CPT to avenge the slain schoolteacher. Among the most famous was Khrong's daughter Rasami, who became well-known for her underground activities after assuming a leadership role in the CPT. Thai newspapers in the 1960s often carried stories of her exploits in Sakon Nakhon, as well as efforts by the Border Police and Royal Army to capture her. The elusive guerrilla daughter fighting to avenge her father's killing cut a somewhat glamorous figure in the public imagination, but there were not many others like her until more than a decade later.

From Communist Movement to Armed Insurgency

The killing of Khrong in 1961, along with the escalation of the guerrilla warfare campaign in South Vietnam a year earlier, helped to transform Thailand's communist movement into an armed insurgency. Many rallied to the insurgents because of widespread corruption and abuse among local officials, the police, and the military. On August 8, 1965, a group of CPT guerrillas attacked security forces in Na Kae district in Nakhon Phanom in a brief engagement. The CPT counted the small-scale clash as the starting point in their military campaign against the central government. From the mid-1960s onward, they carried out attacks against police, army, and government targets throughout the northeast, but mostly in the areas around Nakhon Phanom, Sakon Nakhon, and Kalasin, which have always had a sizable Vietnamese minority. Early on there were about two hundred skirmishes between CPT guerrillas and government forces a year, but the scale of the fighting never matched the avalanche of anxious rhetoric pouring out of the military-dominated government of Thanom. The CPT worked to win recruits and support from the rural communities of the northeast. Beginning with a few hundred followers in the early 1960s, they claimed about four thousand by decade's end. Thanom's regime exaggerated the threat posed by the CPT when warning of the communist threat within Thailand's borders, but CPT influence and reach remained limited throughout the 1960s. The guerrillas generally benefitted from superior local knowledge and community support, and usually outmaneuvered the government's pursuing security forces. In one operation, the insurgents overran an RTA garrison in Chiang Rai and killed all its occupants. In another, they struck a US airbase at Udon Thani, damaging aircraft and inflicting casualties on its defenders. The relatively small number of clashes did increase over the years, though. By the early 1970s, the government was reporting more than six hundred engagements a year. The

CPT claimed a couple of thousand clashes occurred each year. Even if the larger number was true, the violence was tiny compared to that of South Vietnam, Laos, and Cambodia.

Thanom Kittikachorn Solidifies His Position

Thanom Kittikachorn used the growing national fears about communism to solidify his position as Sarit's successor and to hold off his two chief rivals, Praphas Charusathien and Krit Siwara. Thanom had followed a path similar to that which Sarit took to the top. A native of Tak, he grew up in the same remote western town that had fostered King Taksin's leadership skills nearly two hundred years earlier. He attended military academies for his secondary and postsecondary education, and went into the infantry after getting his commission. During World War II, he served in the Shan States, and after the war helped carry out the coup d'état of 1947. He rose through the ranks, often as Sarit's deputy, to become the 1st Infantry Division commander in 1950, the 1st Army commander in 1951, and a few years later, RTA commander in chief. With Sarit's ascension, he became defense minister, deputy prime minister, and while Sarit was abroad, prime minister. Field Marshal Thanom had little of the baroque thuggery of Sarit's persona. He maintained authoritarian control over Thailand's political scene without indulging in the public displays of dictatorial excess of the Sarit years. Thanom had a winning smile, good looks, and an affable manner. He used these assets, and his strong support of the army's leadership, to maintain his grip on the government. Thanom's biggest rivals, Praphas and Krit, shared the other major leadership posts between them. The two were ambitious, eagerly seeking opportunities that would carry them to the premiership. Praphas posed the biggest threat to Thanom. He was shrewd and cruel, with a well-deserved reputation for greed, while Krit remained more steadfast in his loyalty to Thanom. Thanom worked to maintain a distribution of power and spoils among the three of them and their respective factions. Just as Phibun, Phao, and Sarit maintained a triangular power balance, their successors found relative security in the same model. The huge influx of American aid increased the opportunities for enrichment, but it also generated friction and flare-ups among the competing power cliques.

American Assistance

American economic aid transformed Thailand dramatically during this period. From 1952 to 1972, the United States gave more than a billion dollars in military assistance, averaging about $52 million dollars a year. During the Vietnam War years, the United States provided more than half of Thailand's defense budget. The influx of American aid helped inflate the Thai military budget by a multiple of seventeen over this two-decade span. On top of this, the United States gave the Thai police $92 million. The United States Agency for International Development funneled in another $500 million in grants for development projects meant to improve the lives of rural people, with some of that money supporting semimilitary activities. In addition, US servicemen visiting Thailand from South Vietnam spent an estimated $110 million dollars in Bangkok, Pattaya, and other cities while on R&R.

Thailand was America's "aircraft carrier," to use one metaphor from the period, a stable launching pad for US operations, including aerial missions, in the region. Much of the Thailand-based aircraft bombed the Ho Chi Minh Trail, the logistical network of roads, bridges, and passes that stretched from North Vietnam to Laos and Cambodia and into South Vietnam. The United States also used Thailand as an R&R destination for its troops. While such an arrangement brought money to Thai businesses, the R&R industry debased the communities that hosted the bars, hotels, nightclubs and brothels catering to American GIs. Among the most visible legacies of this American presence were the many children fathered by US servicemen, what Thais called "red-headed children," who suffered poverty and neglect in the postwar years. The GIs' presence also boosted the commercial sex industry segment that catered to Western men. The many American-oriented go-go bars and other commercial sex outlets that sprang up during the 1960s and 1970s was the foundation for the sex tourism industry that arose in later decades.

As part of their partnership, the United States expected Thailand to play a leading role in opposing communism in mainland Southeast Asia. While the Thais were slow to contribute direct military assistance to South Vietnam, they acquiesced more quickly to US requests to host American military personnel and war planes on Thai territory. As early as 1960, the United States sent US Marines to Thailand's northeast to be ready for deployment if they were needed in the growing civil war in Laos. In 1961, the Americans put reconnaissance planes in Thailand. A year later, they stationed bomber units at newly constructed Royal Thai air bases in northern and northeastern Thailand. American personnel came with those aircraft in a gradual but steady increase in the American presence. By the end of 1964, the US had 200 aircraft with about 3,000 US personnel on hand. A year later, the total doubled to 400 planes with some 14,000 personnel. By the end of the 1960s, the US had more than 600 aircraft in Thailand and just over 45,000 military personnel and advisors stationed throughout seven air bases and one naval base, most of them specifically to support the mission of bombing communist forces and infrastructure in Laos and the two Vietnams. Other US personnel helped train the Thai troops in areas of counterinsurgency and counterguerrilla warfare. There were also many US citizens in Thailand who worked in a support capacity for the US military presence. They ran the Post Exchanges (PXs) or worked as skilled laborers on the massive construction projects that the US undertook to facilitate the aircraft and naval vessels. Adding to the ballooning American presence were the families of the American military personnel stationed in Thailand.

Before 1967, Thai leaders had tried to be discrete about the American troops stationed on its territory. While fully committed to Thailand's global partnership as a member of the Free World Forces, the Thais were also worried that if they were too overt in their support of the United States, they would invite direct attacks by Hanoi and China. This is a further example of what some have called "bamboo diplomacy." For a while, Thailand tried to maintain this delicate balancing act between supporting the American war effort and not antagonizing Beijing and Hanoi. Thailand was especially sensitive about the B-52 flights flying out of U-Tapao air base in eastern Thailand beginning in 1967. Because of the value of the aircraft created to counter a Soviet nuclear strike, Washington could not risk stationing them in South Vietnam or even in northeastern Thailand where their proximity to the border would make them vulnerable to communist commando squads. Likewise, the awesome destructive power of the B-52s and their association with nuclear counterstrike scenarios encouraged Thai officials to remain mum on the subject of their presence in Thailand. The Thais refused to confirm their presence even as the evidence of the loud and large planes taking off from U-Tapao could be seen and heard easily by anyone in the vicinity. They were a public secret. This obtuse denial of an evident fact irritated foreign correspondents in Thailand to cover the war whenever they asked about the flights.

Thailand was a willing if cautious participant in the war. While it did receive enormous amounts in assistance to join the United States in South Vietnam, it joined the effort out of self-interest. Bangkok adopted appropriately tough bargaining positions with Washington over the terms of its involvement, always seeking the best deal it could negotiate. But its leaders were not ambivalent about the geopolitical principles espoused by the Free World nations. By the mid-1960s, they felt increasingly threatened by what they saw as China's client state in Hanoi and, even more importantly, by communist gains in Laos. Beijing's support of revolutionary movements in the region, and the pledge of its foreign minister to make Thailand the next battlefield in the global wars of liberation, was truly alarming to the leaders of a country that had traditionally feared China, abhorred communism, and blamed ethnic Chinese for many of its economic and social ills.

Thailand's Troops in South Vietnam

Thailand was a frontline state in a regional war. Bangkok had been involved in Laos and Cambodia throughout the premodern era. It had also come into conflict with Vietnam in the early part of the modern era over control of Cambodia. Thai involvement in Laos in the early Cold War can be seen as an extension of earlier Thai notions of suzerainty and influence in the region. In the period of the Cold War, Thai leaders continued to see a noncommunist Laos as vital to their security. But Thai involvement in Laos remains a murky topic. Many archival documents on the topic in Thailand and in the United States remain off-limits to scholars. The Thais sent in irregular units funded by the CIA. They fought against the North Vietnamese and the Pathet Lao in the areas around the Ho Chi Minh Trail and other locations. They did not wear insignia to identify them as Thai. If they were killed in Laos, they did not have that place of death entered into their death certificates or into any army files. In fact, to this day, Thailand has not acknowledged sending any troops into Laos. The fighting was grim.

The Thai veterans I have spoken with described having to operate in Laos without external support. They recalled being frequently hungry, low on supplies, and often lost. When they did engage the enemy, the fighting was hellish.

In January 1967, about a year and half after the United States had started putting large combat units in South Vietnam, Bangkok agreed to send a token force to fight in South Vietnam. Initially, they offered a specially created unit of about 2,000 volunteers who would represent Thailand in South Vietnam alongside not only the United States but also South Korea, Australia, New Zealand, the Philippines, and a few other smaller contingents from Free World nations. The Thais agreed to send only a regiment-sized unit first. Thailand's military leadership feared that too large an expeditionary force, especially one that consisted of its most valuable and highly trained career army units, would leave the kingdom vulnerable to communist insurgents operating in the northeast. They also feared that sending big units would alarm Hanoi and Beijing. Thailand had not yet admitted publicly that it was hosting American B-52s, nor would it admit the degree to which it was involved militarily in the fighting against North Vietnamese troops and their Pathet Lao allies in Laos at the time. Discretion was Thailand's guiding principle.

Thailand's domestic political agenda was closely tied to its military involvement in the war. As the nation entered the war in 1967, it still had no democratic constitution or normally functioning political process. Nonetheless, Thanom tried to explain the dramatic shift in foreign policy to the Thai people in terms that would generate popular support, telling them that Thailand was sending troops to South Vietnam to protect its own security. He used simple words terms in an agricultural idiom to explain it. He posed rhetorical questions: if someone set your neighbor's crops on fire, should you wait around in your own farmhouse for the fire to spread to your land? Or would you help put out the fire and hunt down the arsonist before your fields were set ablaze? He argued that Hanoi was largely responsible for the communist-inspired insurgency in Thailand, and if it was allowed to succeed in crushing South Vietnam, then Thailand would be its next target.

Thais did not protest the kingdom's entry into the war. The absence of dissent, however, did not necessarily indicate support. Political protests were still rare in this period. But there was little evidence that the move was anything but popular in Thailand in 1967, especially in Bangkok. Newspapers and businesses greeted the news with enthusiasm. The Thai press, still not entirely free, was unstinting in its praise for development. Thailand's government and civic institutions seemed to like the move.

The special unit Thailand sent was called the Queen's Cobras. Its name was both an allusion to Thailand's earlier troop commitment to South Korea (the Little Tigers) and to Queen Sirikit, the honorary commander of the volunteers. The unit was not open to just anyone. The Royal Thai Army wanted soldiers with a particular set of qualities. The military launched a public campaign to encourage soldiers with a high school diploma and previous military training to volunteer. Radio and newspaper announcements spread the word. They stressed the voluntary aspect of participation, making it clear that the unit wanted civilians who were no longer active duty soldiers and had acquired specialized skills while in the army. They also drew volunteers from existing army units. The men who joined had to resign their spots in their regular forces before joining the volunteer detachment. On the first day of registration, some 10,000 men volunteered, more than five times the number needed. The papers carried photographs of snaking lines of young men waiting for their chance to apply. Some of the images showed Buddhist monks in robes queuing to volunteer to go and fight, strictly speaking something that is against Buddhist tenets. The presence of monks volunteering to fight perturbed leaders of Thailand's *sangha*, its Buddhist ecclesiastical hierarchy. They asked the volunteering monks to leave their temples and return to secular life before applying to fight. The press, however, loved the images of *bhikkhu* waiting in line to become soldiers. Newspapers used the image as their principal illustration for stories about the recruitment drive. The Thai leadership was likely heartened by the conflation of Buddhism with military service against communism.

Why did Thai men volunteer to fight in South Vietnam? One reason was money. The volunteers received bonuses nearly double the money paid to them by the Royal Thai Army. This focus on money spurred critics of the program to call these Thai soldiers "America's mercenaries." Certainly, some soldiers did volunteer to fight because they would benefit financially, but the first volunteers, more than sixty thousand qualified soldiers, did so without knowing how much compensation they would get. These men felt a complex sense of motivation, ambition, and obligation that captured their imaginations. Many expressed an apparently sincere desire, as Thanom had articulated, to protect Thailand from communism. Others said they wanted an adventure, as a place in the unit promised travel and other experiences that they would never otherwise get. Still others said they felt an almost mystical draw to serve on a battlefield. Some said they were desperate to carry and use the new M-16 Armalite rifle that the Americans had developed and about which they had heard so much. Many wanted to travel by aircraft for the first time, and they hoped that volunteering would give them that opportunity. Also, with news reports of the Vietnam War appearing in Thai papers daily, many wanted to participate in the big event of their day. Status was also important. The Royal Thai Army picked only the best to serve in this first volunteer unit, emphasizing education as much as military experience. None of them were draftees. All were highly motivated about fighting in South Vietnam.

The creation of the Queen's Cobra unit created enormous excitement in Thailand. The Thai press, and often the international press, carried stories about the extraordinary training that these soldiers went through to prepare. They trained at a special jungle warfare center that had been set up in Kanchanaburi, not far from the Death Railway bridge and cemetery. The United States sent some its best army instructors to train the Thais ahead of their deployment. These American trainers had already fought in South Vietnam, some for several tours, and gave the Thais the benefit of firsthand experience fighting the Viet Cong. Their send-off was equally grand. Huge crowds came to see them off. Field Marshal Thanom and the top military leadership addressed them at the departure ceremonies. And despite the Buddhist leaders' discomfort at seeing monks volunteering to fight, the Supreme Patriarch of Thailand's Buddhist clergy took part in the event by blessing all the soldiers as they marched past his spot on the grandstand. Airplanes swooped in from the sky to drop flowers and puffed rice on the soldiers as they paraded in front of cheering well-wishers. After the official ceremonies concluded, the volunteers all went over to Wat Phra Kaeo to pay their respects to the Phra Kaeo image, the so-called Emerald Buddha that Prince Chakri (Thong Duang) had captured from Vientiane.

When Thailand's troops arrived by ship at the port of Saigon, General William Westmoreland, commander of all allied forces in South Vietnam, greeted them personally. The American general shook hands with the Thai commanders and praised their troops. Vietnamese military bands played and Vietnamese actresses presented flowers. Although this official greeting was a scripted affair, there were signs that the Vietnamese people who turned out that day welcomed Thailand's participation in the war, perhaps because it suggested that the conflict could be ended more quickly with additional allied support. Vietnamese people waved and shouted greetings to the Thai troops as their convoys traveled from the port to their base camp. Their destination was the Bearcat Camp in Bien Hoa province, some forty kilometers from Saigon. It would be the center of Thai military operations during the four years they fought in South Vietnam. It sat beside National Highway No. 15 in a stretch that connected the huge American air base at Bien Hoa with the port of Vung Tau. Bearcat Camp had originally belonged to the US 9th Infantry Division, but they relinquished it to the Thai troops when the Americans moved on to other areas, specifically into the Mekong delta.

The Thai troops saw combat in South Vietnam, especially in the earlier deployments. They fought the Viet Cong in several battles that engaged the regiment-sized unit. In smaller actions, they appear to have been effective in disrupting the Viet Cong's logistical supply routes and underground sanctuaries in their area of operational responsibility. The Viet Cong tried to knock the Thais out early in their deployment. The guerrillas staged several large-scale attacks against the Thais field bases within a month or so of the Queen's Cobras' initial deployment. The idea was probably to try to land a psychological blow and a propaganda victory by overrunning a key Thai base. In December 1967, the Viet Cong tried it at Phuoc Tho village. They attacked the Thais' site at night with mortars and rockets, and then with waves of guerrilla commandos who attempted to pierce the Thai perimeter. The Thai troops fought well. With support from one American C-47 gunship providing firepower from above, the Thais held off the Viet Cong in a five-hour battle that lasted nearly until dawn. The latter stages involved close-quarter fighting after some Viet Cong commandos broke into the base.

There were other battles like this one in the years to come. A lot of the fiercest fighting took place around the airport at Binh Son. In all the clashes, the Thai troops appeared to have fought well. The Thai press carried accounts of these engagements with headlines that reflected the contemporary focus on body counts in numbers that always put the Thai troops overwhelming in the win column. The papers would be emblazoned with headlines touting the superior kill ratios that the Thais acquired in battles against the Viet Cong. The Thais often killed as many as ten times the number of soldiers lost from their own ranks. Most of the engagements were small. There were hundreds each year, but the rate of contact diminished as the years went by.

So, if the Thai troops fought well in South Vietnam, why did they get such a negative historical reputation? One reason has to do with the kinds of soldiers that were recruited for the later Thai deployments. Starting in August 1968, Thailand committed a larger unit to South Vietnam. For the next three years, they sent a full-sized combat division of about 11,000 men to replace the Queen's Cobra unit. The new unit was called the Black Panther division. Unlike the first group, the subsequent division included soldiers who were less professional in their conduct and outlook. Another change was motivation. Whereas the first wave of soldiers who volunteered did so without expectation of a monetary windfall, the latter stages came to expect a big payoff for their volunteer service.

American largesse was a significant factor in the Thai troop deployment. From 1968 onward, the United States covered the entire cost of putting the Thai troops in South Vietnam. They paid for all of the Thais' equipment, transportation, food, medical care, and salaries. The Royal Thai Army was allowed to keep the equipment they used in South Vietnam, as this had been one of the demands Bangkok made during their negotiations with Washington. All soldiers got combat pay on top of their regular salary. They also received a per diem while in Vietnam, and were given a mustering out bonus of about 8,000 baht when they left the special unit after a year. The extra income added more weight to the critics' contention that Thailand's troops were mercenaries.

One significant problem of the deployment was the Thai soldiers' preoccupation with the post exchanges, or PXs. These were shops selling imported goods that the United States set up for its troops and their allies. Many Thai soldiers had a fascination with the PX stores in Saigon and the one built specially for their use in Bearcat Camp while they were in South Vietnam. The PX shops had luxury goods and other consumer items that simply were not available to them in Thailand, including the latest big-ticket items, such as televisions, stereos, radios, refrigerators, and cameras being produced in the United States and Japan. They sold them at prices considerably lower than what was charged for the same imported luxury goods in Thailand, which imposed high import taxes and duties on these specialty items. Only wealthy Thais had the money for them. Thai soldiers in South Vietnam found that their combat pay and accumulated per diem money meant that they could easily buy one or more of these formerly prohibitive goods. They became protective of their items. A common story told over and over again about soldiers was that when under enemy mortar attack, some would put their flak jackets over their newly purchased stereos rather than risk having them destroyed. Foreign-made luxury items imparted status on the owners, a fact recognized acutely by those soldiers from impoverished families. The possessing and sharing of these items would elevate their social standing back home. But for foreign journalists observing the behavior of the Thai troops, the fixation on consumerism in the midst of a war was off-putting.

Another problem was what they did with that extra money they received while in South Vietnam. Some used it to set up black market schemes in which they would buy high-quality goods from the American-built PX stores to resell to Vietnamese middlemen who funneled them onto the black market. Some bought and sold beer, liquor, household items, and electronic goods to the black market. These Thai soldiers became enthusiastic black-market entrepreneurs when it became clear to them just how much money they could make from this practice. The foreign press noticed these schemes. *The New York Times* and other major American newspapers described Thai soldiers carrying stacks of toothpaste and soap from PX shops in Saigon to resell. These kinds of stories overshadowed the accounts of their combat, most of which appeared only in Thai papers. The result of this is a reluctance among American veterans to acknowledge that the Thai troops fought as bravely and as competently as did the soldiers from the United States, Australia, and, especially, South Korea, whose troops had a particular reputation for ferocity.

The Thai troops did not fight alongside the Americans. Although they had American liaison officers and translators attached to their units, they mostly fought independently of the Americans. When they did encounter each other, it was often in casual or non-military settings. Thai veterans said that the foreign soldiers with whom they had most contact were those who came around their camp looking to buy drugs and Thai whiskey. The American soldiers, according to many Thai veterans' recollections, wanted marijuana and harder drugs. They told the Thai soldiers that if they could smuggle these drugs back from Thailand after returning from R&R, they would pay them handsomely in items such as stereos and televisions. The other thing the Americans wanted from the Thai soldiers was Mekhong, the sugar-based spirit flavored with herbs and botanicals that is a staple of Thai drinking culture. Mekhong was generally not available in the American-managed PX shops, and those Americans who had developed a taste for it after visiting or serving in Thailand paid Thai soldiers a high mark-up for any bottles they could acquire.

The other item the American troops wanted most from the Thai soldiers were Buddhist amulets –small Buddhist statues encased in metal and plastic worn by most Thai men. It was common for Thai soldiers to carry dozens of amulets, with some around their necks and the rest hidden in their uniforms and packs. For Americans inclined to spiritual matters or superstition, the sight of the Buddhist amulets encouraged them to ask the Thai soldiers if they could buy them, thus promising another layer of protection from danger while in the warzone. Most of these Thai soldiers were amused that these soldiers from what they saw as Christian countries wanted to wear their Buddhist amulets. The Thai soldiers willingly gave away amulets to any American who seemed serious about acquiring one for protection. The Thais remember phrases from the Americans' Pidgin English that went something like, "Buddha Thai, No.1!" and "Buddha Thai! Very Good!"

Some Thais were ambivalent about bringing amulets with them, especially a lot of amulets, because they believed that they might make them look old-fashioned or, actually, un-modern. But the enthusiasm with which the Americans embraced these charms encouraged those doubters to see them as compatible with modern warfare. It also encouraged them to see the limitations of America's military sophistication. Many Thais concluded that in matters of spiritual protection, American soldiers, with their crosses and other Christian symbols, were vulnerable or even deficient.

Thailand kept that division in South Vietnam for three years. The final deployment rotated back home in 1972, less than a year before the United States took out the last of its combat troops. About 40,000 Thai troops from the army, navy, and air force served there. More than 500 died in combat. The Thai contribution probably did not change the course of the war significantly, but the Thai military's experience in South Vietnam, and in Laos, would have lingering effects on Thailand's politics and society for years to come.

CHAPTER 12

STUDENT DEMONSTRATIONS AND A RIGHT-WING BACKLASH

On October 13–14, 1973, the masses triumphed in the national political arena for the first time in Thailand's history by forcing a change in the government that many hailed as a "revolution." They stood up to an authoritarian and repressive regime and prevailed. In doing so, they demonstrated that there was popular support for the democratic ideals that have existed, at least in theory, within the various Thai constitutions that have come and gone since the overthrow of the absolute monarchy in 1932. They also showed that they were willing to risk personal danger to achieve democratic reforms, and many paid with their blood and their lives.

At the heart of this mass movement were the student organizations that had formed in the late 1960s during the period of the Vietnam War, a time that some academics call "the American era." These pro-democracy student groups marched, demonstrated, and died on the broad boulevards of Bangkok's Phra Nakhon and Dusit districts, home to many government offices and royal palaces. Their success would be a milestone in Thailand's political evolution. Although questions endure about the long-term success of the 1973 demonstrations, the immediate changes they brought about were almost unimaginable just a few years before. October 1973 was the starting point of one of Thailand's most turbulent periods. It was a time of great optimism for the pro-democracy forces. Their hopeful spirits would be tempered, however, three years later amidst horrific violence and repression. So controversial are the events of this period that Thai scholars are not yet free to publish research on the events in Thailand without fear of retribution by the ruling institutions. Foreign scholars have more latitude to publish on the bloodshed of 1973 and 1976, but they too face legal jeopardy in Thailand for writing about this period. In *Political Conflict in Thailand: Reform, Reaction, Revolution*, the political scientists David Morrell and Chai-anan Samudavanija produced among the earliest and most thorough analyses of the conflict between military autocrats and democracy advocates. Their landmark study is the source of some of the material in this chapter.

The political climate in the United States was an important factor in the development of this movement. As more American university students joined the growing antiwar movement in the United States in the late 1960s, descriptions of their dissent appeared in the pages of Thailand's newspapers. Another factor was the increasing numbers of Thai students who had traveled to the United States for undergraduate and graduate education. Many had spent years studying and living within American university environments in which campus demonstrations were regular occurrences. These Thai expatriates saw that American authorities largely tolerated open expressions of dissent on their campuses and streets. They also saw clearly the hypocrisy of their government's rhetoric about safeguarding Thailand's freedom from communism when that freedom seemed to omit basic civil liberties, such as the right to assembly, peaceful protest, and free speech. When they returned to Thailand, some of them tried to assert those theoretical rights only to suffer unpleasant consequences.

In this period, Thammasat University in Bangkok was the center of the student-led political movements. Pridi Banomyong had founded the university in 1934 as the College of Moral and Political Sciences. Thammasat had long attracted Thailand's more progressive students and faculty. In the late 1960s and early 1970s, it had spawned several student organizations, some of them leftist or Marxist in orientation, dedicated to expanding educational freedoms. Students had initially formed these groups to discuss political affairs in Thailand and, in imitation of student activist Chit Phumisak, to apply Marxist analyses to Thailand's history and its contemporary society. Other universities across Thailand, including the more conservative Chulalongkorn University, also saw the rise of student groups seeking expanded latitude in their curricula and campuses. These early participants were hardly firebrands. Many merely wanted the right to read, study, and discuss the political writings that the government had banned. The decade-long absence of a constitution that guaranteed basic civil rights had frustrated progressive students, but few had dared speak up against the government. In the 1950s and early 1960s, the rare student protest addressed immediate concerns, such as tuition costs, school regulations, or even cafeteria food. Some of these students expressed frustration at the absence of a constitution, but their concerns remained largely within the walls of the schools. The Thai government mostly ignored them.

According to official statements, the Thanom-Praphas regime had been working on a new constitution since Sarit had canceled the last one in 1958. In reality, the military clique preferred to maintain a constitutionless state under martial law. The leadership delayed completion of a new charter for years. Responding to pressure from the United States and King Bhumibol, the Thai government issued a new constitution on June 20, 1968. Its structure was similar to Thai constitutions issued by the military in the 1930s. While it included a bicameral legislature of both elected and appointed houses, its structure made it easy for the generals to control the body. With Thanom appointing all upper-house members (with the king's approval), he needed only a few dozen supporters in the lower house to dominate the parliament. Furthermore, the new charter maintained all measures issued under martial law, preserving the Anticommunist Act and other repressive decrees. Sweetening the deal for Thanom, the 1968 constitution gave the premier extralegal powers in times of national emergencies. There were some provisions for basic civil liberties, but their scope was modest. Compared to the constitution that Pridi drafted after World War II, and certainly compared to the constitutions of the Western democracies with which Thailand was allied, it was hardly a liberal document. The 1968 charter was more of a political fig leaf that Thanom donned to conceal his regime's tyrannical policies and to assuage foreign and domestic criticism. Rolled out to great fanfare, it failed, nonetheless, to conceal his contempt for democratic processes.

On June 21, a day after the new constitution was announced, a group of retired politicians and academics tested its provisions for freedom of assembly and freedom of speech. They gathered for an impromptu "Hyde Park Corner" at Sanam Luang, the expansive public lawn adjacent to Wat Phra Kaeo and the Grand Palace, and gave speeches that touched upon formerly taboo political topics. Almost as soon as the speakers started, police arrested and jailed them because they had assembled before the government had formally lifted martial law. Outraged, a couple of thousand demonstrators, including many Thammasat students, marched on Government House to demand the speakers' release. They also called for economic reforms to help Thailand's poor, and investigations into government corruption. Under pressure from the demonstrators, the government relented. It freed the jailed speakers and promised to make some policy changes that would help the poor. In this short exchange, the student demonstrators got their first taste of success as activists. Over the next few years, student leaders tested the boundaries of civil liberties contained in the new constitution with protests at the Ministry of Justice and other government offices.

Student Activists for Democracy
Although Thammasat University was the epicenter of student activism in Thailand at this time, progressive students at other schools played important roles in this historical drama. As Bangkok-based students formed political study societies at their schools, students across Thailand set up branches of similarly named groups. These groups explored new ideas and promoted change on their own campuses, and worked together when they identified areas of common concern. In late 1972, a Chulalongkorn engineering major organized a campaign to boycott Japanese goods sold in Thailand. As head of the National Student Center of Thailand (NSCT), Thirayuth Boonmee targeted the flood of inexpensive and often good quality Japanese products imported into Thailand over the previous decade as Japan's industrial output increased and its export markets in Southeast Asia flourished. The NSCT favored a kind of economic nationalism that would protect Thai industries from competition from Japan. Its members fanned out over Bangkok to distribute pamphlets and display

placards promoting the boycott. They hit the main shopping centers and busy traffic intersections of the principal commercial districts. Some of their concern for specifically Japanese products can be traced to World War II and the immediate postwar period of a generation ago. The students continued to associate Japan with the military men in power. Initially, the government was not concerned. Thanom's regime welcomed the students' apparent chauvinism as an endorsement of the government's policies. They saw their positions at the top as secure. Unlike foreign students in the United States or France, Thai students targeted foreign powers, not their own leaders. The boycott lasted ten days.

The government became concerned, however, when the students' ire extended beyond its original anti-Japan stance. One group at Chiang Mai University targeted the domination of the Thai government by active duty and retired army officers. They put out a publication called *Phai Khieu*, or "Green Menace," a twist on the idea of communism as the "Red Menace." It contained essays that decried the military's domination of politics. Another student group, the Marxist-influenced Sapha Na Dome at Thammasat, published *Phai Khao*, meaning "White Menace." This publication criticized the growing American influence on Thailand's government, economy, and culture. The "white" of the title referred to white people, the American *farang,* who they saw as the power behind Thailand's military government.

Feeling far more confident than even a year earlier, these formerly cautious and sometimes low-key student groups found they had a growing audience of similarly disaffected citizens who shared their disgust with the Thai leadership and their American allies. One factor that contributed to the growing sympathy for the students' causes concerned a shift in the power balance among the core of army officers running Thailand. By 1972, Colonel Narong Kittikachorn had replaced General Krit Siwara in the troika at the top. Narong was prime minister Thanom's son and, through his marriage to Supaporn Charusathien, deputy prime minister Praphas's son-in-law. Bound by blood, marriage, and mutual distrust, the three had acquired the derisive nickname "the Three Tyrants." Student demonstrators particularly disliked Narong. He was a career army officer, like his father, who had gravitated toward politics as an avenue to wealth and power.

Unlike his father, though, he came across as wild, coarse, and sinister. After serving as a Thai liaison to US forces in South Vietnam, Narong had returned to Thailand to continue the process by which Thanom and Praphas groomed him for future leadership of the country. Under parental supervision, he took charge of an antigraft agency called the Board of Inspection and Follow-up of Government Operations (BIFGO). The watchdog agency was empowered to root out corruption in the government, military, and private sector. The notoriously corrupt Narong used the BIFGO as a personal weapon to neutralize his military rivals, accusing them of corruption and abuse of power whether it was justified or not. Narong also took charge of the government's effort to suppress student demonstrators and others who challenged the government's policies and actions. In this capacity, he led the Committee to Suppress Elements Detrimental to Society. Dislike of Narong extended beyond the student activists. Unlike his elders, Narong had not built up a solid base of support in the Royal Thai Army. Many of his fellow soldiers despised him, especially his seniors, for his nepotistic rise and his reputation for cruelty and fecklessness. These career officers saw clearly how he had used the power of his parentally provided positions to crush anyone who might challenge him.

Under pressure from several sides, Thanom tried to regain the absolute control he had exercised before the 1968 constitution. On November 17, 1971, he staged a coup against his own government. He dissolved parliament, declared martial law, and moved to gain control of the hitherto independent judiciary. He created a National Executive Council from behind which he would run the country. The move outraged students, but their relatively staid demonstrations for a new constitution failed to rally the broad public support necessary to bring about a change.

October 1973

The story of the Three Tyrants' ultimate downfall began with a strange incident that literally fell from the sky. In April 1973, a military helicopter carrying army and police officers crashed into Thung Yai Naresuan Wildlife Sanctuary in Kanchanaburi Province killing six of the ten onboard. The dead officers were all associates of Narong Kittikachorn, who had come to Thung Yai to shoot exotic game from the air. The carcass of a gaur, a wild bison, lay near the crash site. News of the officials' illegal hunting trip outraged the public. The Thai government rushed to cover up the incident but only made matters worse. After a sham investigation of the crash, it announced that the group had been on a sensitive diplomatic mission along the Thai-Burmese border. The flouting of national laws to kill protected animals and the flimsy story fabricated to conceal it seemed to encapsulate the corruption, cruelty, and brazenness endemic in the Thanom-Praphas regime.

In the months that followed the crash and cover-up, young activists all over Thailand moved beyond their earlier circumspection to level criticism directly at the ruling military clique. The NSCT lambasted the regime in a publication about ecological conservation called "The Secret Account from Thung Yai." The document gained wide readership across Thailand, and the NSCT printed at least 100,000 copies to meet the demand. Students at Ramkhamhaeng University, Bangkok's open-enrollment university, produced their own "Secret Account" publication that lampooned Thanom and Narong. When school officials expelled the nine Ramkhamhaeng students responsible for the provocative publication, students from all across Bangkok protested on their campuses. The government shut down the universities in an effort to disburse the students. Instead of going home, the students took to the streets to join the demonstrations. Directed in part by the NSCT, students called for a constitution that would restore their right to assembly and expand basic civil rights for all Thai citizens.

The government now feared the student demonstrators as a real threat to their regime. To quell their growing national influence, the government went after student leaders. On October 6, 1973, police arrested twelve students near the Democracy Monument for handing out leaflets demanding a new constitution. Thai law limited gatherings for political purposes to no more than five people. One of the arrested, Thirayuth Boonmee, was the NSCT leader from Chulalongkorn University who had orchestrated the anti-Japanese products boycott. The government alleged that Thirayuth and his cohorts were part of a communist plot to overthrow the government. Their sudden disappearance in police custody led many to believe that the police had killed them, a fate that befell many suspected communists while under detention.

A portrait of King Chulalongkorn is displayed in Chiang Mai's train station. Chulalongkorn had his half-brother Prince Damrong dismantle the ruling houses of the northern kingdoms, including Chiang Mai, so he could put all of the independent kingdoms and principalities under Bangkok's direct rule.

In an age when naval fleets played an outsized role in determining a nation's status and power, King Vajiravudh invested heavily in building up the Royal Siamese Navy. After personally raising some of the funds to modernize the navy, he had Siam purchase a British destroyer that he renamed the *Phra Ruang*. The fleet he built was a significant improvement over the largely ceremonial coastal fleet of his father's reign, but it was no match for the French and British forces of the era.

Spendthrift, eccentric, and inspired, King Vajiravudh put state funds toward grand building projects and idiosyncratic programs. His excessive spending left Siam in precarious financial straits.

King Vajiravudh created the paramilitary organization the Wild Tiger Corps and its youth brigade, the Wild Tiger Cubs. Members of this royally directed organization gathered together for sporting competitions, military maneuvers, and cultural endeavors. The king designed their uniform, penned their oath, and directed nearly all of their activities. Members of the Royal Siamese Army resented the attention lavished on the unit.

To counteract Western ridicule of Thai femininity, King Vajiravudh encouraged Siamese women to grow out their close-cropped hair and to wear *phasin* tube skirts rather than *phanung* cloths around their waists

Siam's leaders tried to keep the kingdom neutral in the Great War. But following increased German U-boat attacks on civilian ships, King Vajiravudh allied his kingdom with the British and French in July 1917. Siam contributed an aerial detachment and logistical units to the warzone in Europe. Their participation was a source of great national pride for Siam. Still, some deployed soldiers, stung by French racist attitudes and unprepared for the cold temperatures, returned home embittered.

Until 1917, Siam's national flag had been a white elephant against a striking red background. The image presented Buddhist and royal symbols that were rich in meaning for the Thai people it represented.

(Photo: Kittipong Chararoj @ Shutterstock.com)

An unexpected monarch, King Prajadhipok had spent his adult life preparing for a career in the military before the early deaths of his brothers and half-brothers made him the seventh Chakri ruler. He inherited a kingdom in financial ruin caused by his brother's profligate spending. Modest and diligent, he stabilized Siam as it was beset by the consequences of domestic labor strife and a global economic depression.

After democratically-minded civil servants and military officers overthrew the absolute monarchy, King Prajadhipok chose exile with his wife, Queen Rambai Barni, and then abdication.

Pridi Banomyong left his mark on Thailand's history like few others. After masterminding the overthrow of the absolute monarchy and founding Thammasat University, he worked to reform Thailand's economic system for the benefit of farming folk and urban laborers. After being shunted aside by ambitious army officers, the brilliant lawyer and academic led the underground resistance against Japan's occupation of Thailand during World War II.

Pridi (pictured with his wife Poonsuk) helped Thailand avoid costly reparations demanded by Great Britain after World War II. But rightist forces led by a rapacious Royal Thai Army cabal forced Pridi to flee when they seized control in 1947. Pridi attempted a counter-coup in 1949 but failed to drive the generals from power.

Democracy Monument commemorates the change from absolute to constitutional monarchy in 1932. Resting atop a *phan* offering bowl is a representation of Thailand's first constitution; surrounding the center-piece are stylized wings representing Thailand's four military branches. *(Photo: Southtownboy Studio @ Shutterstock.com)*

David Lean's film *The Bridge on the River Kwai* has inspired many tourists to visit Kanchanaburi town. However, the railroad bridge there has little to do with events depicted in the film. *(Photo: Wuttichok Panichiwarapun @ Shutterstock.com)*

In 1935, the government elevated 9-year-old Prince Ananda Mahidol to the throne. The boy-king spent most of his reign abroad for schooling in Switzerland.

Phibun Songkhram helped overthrow the absolute monarchy in 1932 and put down a counter-rebellion. He took control of Siam in the late 1930s and changed its name to Thailand.

After avoiding persecution for his wartime activities, Phibun returned as Thailand's civilian prime minister in the 1950s. He sought to remake himself as a fierce anti-communist to win support from the United States.

After the tragic death of his brother, Prince Bhumibol Adulyadej was named king at age 19. Over the seven decades of his reign, he restored the power and status of the Thai monarchy in the constitutional era. Although he remained "above politics" officially, Bhumibol shaped historical events by interceding in times of national political crisis.

Sarit Thanarat (right), along with Phin Choonhavan (left) and other military strongmen, consolidated the Royal Thai Army's uncontested power in national affairs in the late 1950s.

Following Sarit's death in 1963, Field Marshal Thanom Kittikachorn, maintained the military's grip on Thailand's politics, extending martial law throughout the 1960s.

Thailand sent volunteer military units to South Vietnam during the Second Indochina War. Although the troops fought effectively against the communist guerrillas, their reputation was marred by the black-market exploits of some soldiers.

During the Cold War, Thailand was among the United States' closest allies. Thailand supported the American military in its efforts at preventing the spread of communism throughout the region. In 1969, Richard Nixon affirmed Thailand's importance by meeting with King Bhumibol during one of his first trips abroad as president.

Journalist, novelist, actor, and statesman, Kukrit Pramoj (pictured on a movie poster for *The Ugly American* with Marlon Brando) left his mark on numerous Thai institutions; however, his deft wit and closeness to the palace could not protect the multi-talented descendant of Rama II from a mob of right-wing vigilantes who attacked his beautiful Thai-style house in 1975.

Admiration for King Bhumibol grew steadily throughout his reign. Thai monarchists voluntarily displayed his image in their businesses and homes, while official policy dictated its presence in all government offices, schools, and facilities.

Armed *yaksha* (nature spirits) stand guard outside the temple. In the modern era, Thailand positioned itself as the world's principal defender of Buddhism, especially during the Cold War era. *(Photo: BerryJ @ Wikimedia Commons)*

Monks adorn a monumental Buddhist icon in the robes of a *bhikkhu*. The offering of new robes as part of the *thod kathin* ceremony endures as a solemn and cherished expression of support for Buddhist traditions and principles.

(Photo: Goldquest @ Shutterstock.com)

The Thai public did not believe the government's claims. Rather than hailing the police for their arrest of the activists, thousands of Bangkokians – laborers, merchants, professionals, and people from across all social strata – came out to join the student demonstrators in sympathy with their aims. They rallied throughout that week and by October 12 more than 400,000 demonstrators filled much of Ratcha-damnoen Boulevard in the areas around the Democracy Monument. The protest was peaceful and joyous (*sanuk*) as most participants marched, sang, displayed placards, and called out for democratic changes. They wanted the students released and a new constitution enacted. Many demonstrators put their hopes in King Bhumibol as democracy's savior. The monarch's speeches over recent years had condemned corruption and abuse while championing Buddhist prin-ciples as an antidote to the nation's ills, but there was little to suggest he favored greater democratic participation. Still, the students believed that the king's *barami*, and his institutional clout, made him the only person who could challenge the Three Tyrants' broad powers. They repeatedly turned toward his palace and sang the royal anthem while holding aloft images of the king.

Working from his palace, Bhumibol tried to defuse the crisis. He called in Thanom and Praphas to discuss the government's plan for meeting the demonstrators' demands. The two promised the king they would release the jailed students and prepare a new constitution for his approval within a year. Satisfied with their concession, Bhumi-bol met later that afternoon with NSCT representatives, reassuring the student leaders that democracy in some form would reemerge in Thailand within a year. The activists returned to the front lines and declared victory. Others were less easily placated. With the details of the future constitution still undetermined, some feared that Thanom and Praphas would engineer another charter that preserved their undemocratic powers. Others were convinced that the military men would renege on their promise as they had done throughout most of the 1960s. In the early hours of October 14, Bhumibol continued to meet with student leaders to urge an end to the protests. Some fifty thousand demonstrators opted to remain on the streets. Many camped overnight near Dusit Palace, with plans to reassemble at the royal residence in the morning.

On the morning of October 14, the remaining demonstrators got word from the palace that Bhumibol would not be coming out to address them. As the crowds tried to leave the area, police blocked exit points and manhandled some of the departing demonstrators. Police used tear gas on the students and the confrontations swiftly escalated into a melee. Then police and soldiers threw hand grenades and fired rifles into the crowds, killing dozens. As word of the police attack spread, thousands of Bangkokians rushed back onto the streets to renew their protest. Troops with automatic rifles, some atop armored personnel carriers and tanks, moved in to confront the demonstrators. From a helicopter hovering above, Narong orchestrated the army's actions. He ordered the troops to attack the demonstrators. The soldiers first launched tear gas into the crowds, and then fired volleys from their M-16 assault rifles. The armored vehicles advanced on demonstrators to drive them off Ratchadamnoen Boulevard. The attacks went on sporadically throughout the day, sending thousands of demonstrators fleeing in terror. Narong's personal contribution to the bloodbath was to shoot into the crowds from above.

Casualty figures from the October 14, 1973 violence remain disputed, but the consensus is that more than seventy demonstrators died and another eight hundred suffered injuries in the police and army assault. Many believe the death toll to be higher than the official count. Despite the threat of continued violence, many of the demonstrators continued to occupy Bangkok's administrative district. Some set government buildings on fire, including the BIFGO offices, and seized other buildings. They built barricades and cared for the wounded. Further military action became impossible, however, after General Krit intervened. As commander in chief of the armed forces, Krit refused to comply with another wave of assaults on the demonstrators. King Bhumibol was said to be horrified by the killing outside his palace, and let it be known that he opposed further bloodshed. He ordered Thanom, Praphas, and Narong to leave Thailand. Facing resistance from the army and the palace, the Three Tyrants resigned their leadership positions and fled the country.

The date October 14, 1973 would become a touchstone in Thailand's historical consciousness because of the killing of so many citizens by the forces entrusted to protect them. The photos of the demonstration, the nearly panoramic views of hundreds of thousands of people standing together in protest along Bangkok's grandest boulevard, are symbols of the frustrated desire for democracy in Thai political life both before and after this momentous event. While many people in Bangkok had never felt directly threatened by the communist bogeyman invoked almost daily for more than two decades, October 14 opened their eyes to the threat posed by the military regime. They now looked on in horror as their own government massacred young idealists who had only demanded that the government live up to the democratic rhetoric it espoused. This event, this day, was both a glorious moment and a frank view into the unpleasant realties that have remained a part of Thailand's authoritarian and frequently undemocratic system. It was a turning point in Thailand's political history.

A New Constitution

The period that followed was a heady time. Pro-democracy activists and other Thais who had craved greater political participation and civil rights believed they were looking at the start of a better age. Dozens of new political parties formed, and most candidates in the first election were political newcomers. It was also a time of relative intellectual freedom. The works of such formerly banned writers as Chit Phumisak and Kulap Saipradit were once again available in bookstores. Likewise, the works of Karl Marx, Vladimir Lenin, Mao Zedong, Che Guevara, and Ho Chi Minh were now accessible to Thais who wanted to study them. Political protests and demonstrations spread beyond the universities as many of the formerly oppressed found confidence to demand reforms in areas that affected them. Farmers, teachers, factory workers, and laborers all took to the public stage and demanded to be heard.

The prime minister overseeing the change was Sanya Thammasak. Sanya was a legal scholar and former rector of Thammasat University who had also served on the king's Privy Council. King Bhumibol had recommended him to lead the country in this transitional phase. Not since Pridi Banomyong had briefly held the premiership a quarter of a century earlier had someone so thoroughly civilian- and-legal minded enjoyed such powers. Bhumibol also oversaw the drafting of the committee that would create the new constitution. Sanya did not relish his entry into the political realm. He supervised tense and prolonged negotiations over the new charter. It was a time of open politics, when no single group had dominant control of the country. There were multiple interests and agendas competing to get their way. Despite the victory of the left-leaning demonstrators over the Three Tyrants, other military figures did not want to yield their dominant positions in politics. These military men were wealthy, plentiful, and entrenched. The police, too, remained unreformed and hostile to change.

The results of the first major election after the new constitution was uncertainty. None of the twenty-four victorious parties had a majority, and none looked strong enough to take the reins with any authority. Seni Pramoj's Democrats garnered the most seats, so the former ambassador and onetime prime minister cobbled together a center-left government from among the biggest vote-getters. His royal ancestry, familiarity with the United States, experience in officialdom, quick mind, and diplomatic demeanor should have been reassuring to most factions. But the aging Seni had a difficult time putting together a viable coalition. He faced challenges from the newly emboldened leftist parties that wanted, among other changes, to have Thailand distance itself from the United States. He also received criticism from rightist factions who opposed any rapprochement with communist regimes in Beijing and Hanoi. These groups wanted Washington to remove the tens of thousands of US military personnel stationed in Thailand. Although the US military had been pulling troops out of Thailand since the early 1970s, Thai military leaders did not want to see all of them go. The Thai armed forces had benefited greatly from American military aid in the Vietnam War years, and its leadership wanted the largesse that came with close military ties to continue. Furthermore, Thai military leaders feared possible clashes with North Vietnam and its patrons, notably the People's Republic of China, if the United States withdrew. Seni's coalition lasted just over a week before collapsing.

Kukrit's Political Balancing Act

With the failure of Seni's government, it fell to his younger brother Kukrit to form the next government. Kukrit Pramoj was a man of multifarious talents. Unlike Seni, who was a steadfast diplomat and lawyer, Kukrit seemed to do a lot, and do it all with flare. As a descendant of Rama II on his father's side and the Bunnag family on his mother's side, Kukrit made his lineage the cornerstone of his identity. Oxford-educated and cosmopolitan, he was a conservative who espoused monarchical sympathies in the quasi-mystical terms of the absolutist age. Kukrit worked in banking and commercial concerns, but was never far from the world of politics. His fame, however, came from his journalistic and literary pursuits. He founded the newspaper *Siam Rath* and used it as a vehicle for his ideas on culture, politics, and history. His editorials were as renowned as much for their acerbity as their erudition. He was a genuinely good novelist whose books earned praise from both Thai and foreign readers. His most famous work, *Si Phaendin* (*The Four Reigns* in its English translation), follows an aristocratic family like his own through the tumult of Siam's recent history. He was devoted to the Thai dramatic form *khon* in which costumed and masked dancers act out stories from the Indian epics. He was a stage actor as well and even turned up in a Hollywood movie. He played the prime minister of the fictional Southeast Asian kingdom of Sarkhan opposite Marlon Brando in the 1963 film version of *The Ugly American*. He was an advisor to King Bhumibol who knew firsthand how politics intersected with palace affairs. Many liked him for his sharp sense of humor, his distinctive looks, and his witty way with words. Thais recognized him for his cultural sophistication and commitment to traditional art forms.

In 1975, life imitated art when Kukrit assumed the premiership after his brother's second brief stint. Kukrit put together a shaky alliance from among three right-wing parties and his own Social Action Party. For more than a year, he used all of his talents and tricks to hold together a bumptious coalition. But despite his political savvy, intellectual prowess, personal charisma, and study of kingship, the job proved to be more difficult and dangerous than Kukrit could have ever imagined.

Kukrit made a good attempt to address many of the most contentious problems facing Thai society. Thailand's population had grown rapidly since the end of World War II, and the growth put pressure on available lands for farming. Many rural laborers left the countryside to seek work in the factories, construction projects, and service jobs of urban zones. Many languished in poverty as the economic growth failed to keep pace with the rise in the non-agricultural labor pool. The newly formed Farmers Federation of Thailand worked to protect the rights of the poor in matters of rent control, access to government-protected lands, and protection from graft demanded by local officials. They pressured the government for change. Kukrit believed that improved economic and social circumstances would end Thailand's rural insurgency by taking away the root cause of the Marxist-inspired guerrilla forces. He carried out land reform measures and other programs designed to aid the rural poor, including free health care. Kukrit instituted a national minimum wage and had rice donated to the urban poor. He also sought to decriminalize Marxism by abolishing the Anticommunist Act of 1952 that the police and army units had used to persecute many in these rural areas.

Kukrit's most controversial initiative concerned the United States and its military presence in Thailand. Over the course of the Vietnam War, more and more Thais had come to resent the tens of thousands of Americans stationed in Thailand and those visiting for R&R. Some Thais benefitted greatly from the American presence. Savvy entrepreneurs and business people, as well as military and government officials, found ways of reaping high profits from all of the American money spent in Thailand. Most Thais, however, did not see any benefits. Instead, they experienced, or read about, examples of social disruption and debasement caused by an increase in prostitution, drug sales, and other crimes. Many resented the irresponsible behavior of American servicemen who fathered children with Thai women, only to abandon them without support. Some Thais saw the foreign soldiers' presence as an affront to Thai sovereignty. Student groups organized increasingly large anti-American rallies during this period. They blamed the US military for enabling the corrupt military government of the Thanom-Praphas era and decried American influence on Thai social and cultural norms. Kukrit set about negotiating the removal of the 25,000 American military personnel and their 350 aircraft that remained in the first part of 1975. He gave the United States a one-year deadline to get all of them out. The Thai public largely supported the move.

Despite the popularity of his policies among the Thai public, Kukrit accomplished little. The same right-wing political parties with whom Kukrit had formed an alliance to build his government opposed him at almost every turn. Their resistance to his minimum law made it largely unenforceable. The government agencies and landowners he needed to donate land for his land-distribution scheme gave little or nothing. Many powerful people who had benefitted from the American alliance tried to derail the negotiations with US officials over removing the American troops. The pending loss of US dollars so angered the Thai military that the threat of a coup d'état constantly hung over Kukrit's head. His anticorruption committee floundered after his top choices to run it refused to take on the herculean task. Even King Bhumibol, who had appeared to favor many of the changes pushed by Kukrit, backed away from him. The conservatives may have had their grip on power loosened by the events of October 1973, but they were not going to let go of it.

Vigilante Terror

Right-wing social groups came forward to oppose Kukrit. The most famous of these was the Village Scouts (Luk Sua Chao Ban). Established by the Border Patrol Police (BPP) in 1971, the Village Scouts were a jingoistic organization dedicated to fighting communism in rural areas by promoting "Thai cultural values." The Village Scouts underwent semireligious initiation ceremonies in which they pledged themselves to defending the monarchy, Buddhism, and the nation against the Communist Party of Thailand and other leftists. The anthropologist Katherine Bowie has produced the most comprehensive study of these movements. Her *Rituals of National Loyalty: An Anthropology of the State and the Village Scout Movement in Thailand* was born out of her time studying rural political organizations in the mid-1970s. The study shows how the Village Scouts and other groups exploited the Thai public's anxieties in the aftermath of the fall of Saigon and Phnom Penh to the communists in April 1975. One of their main messages was that Thailand was in imminent danger of being overrun by local communists working for Hanoi and Beijing. Initially, the BPP had encouraged the Village Scouts to act as a counterinsurgency unit by collecting information on their neighbors about potential communist activities. As the movement grew, the Village Scouts engaged in more overtly political activities beyond rural villages and small towns. They trained together at retreats that combined courses in camping skills with intense nationalistic indoctrination rituals. They were highly moralistic. Members were supposed to abstain from alcohol, keep fit, eschew individualism, and live simply. They marched through towns and villages denouncing leftists and celebrating symbols of Thai-ness in their narrowly conservative conception of the term. They promoted a chauvinistic view of Thai identity that rendered ethnic minorities, especially Thai-Vietnamese, as suspect citizens. Both King Bhumibol and Queen Sirikit became their official patrons. The royal couple presided over many of the Village Scouts' initiation ceremonies and rallies. The knotted bandanas they wore around their necks were said to have been blessed by the king before being distributed to new members. The king's endorsement encouraged the urban and the middle class to support them with donations. Eventually, the government gave them financial support as a kind of official national institution. Membership grew swiftly. At one point, nearly 10 percent of the adult population belonged to the Village Scouts.

Other right-wing groups with even more sinister motivations emerged during this period to block Kukrit's policies and undo the October 1973 "revolution." The most notorious of the vigilante organizations was a group called the Krating Daeng, or "Red Gaurs" in English. A gaur is a large and notoriously ill-tempered forest bovine. A command of the Royal Thai Army had set up the Krating Daeng group to terrorize student demonstrators and hunt down suspected communists. Krating Daeng members hurled bombs into protests to kill and maim participants. They were also the likely culprits responsible for killing the head of the short-lived Socialist Party of Thailand (STP). The Krating Daeng's core were former soldiers who feared the military losing its power and prestige. Many had fought in South Vietnam or Laos and brought combat experience to the group. They openly carried assault rifles, grenades, and other war weapons. Unlike the ostensibly abstemious Village Scouts, the Krating Daeng made heavy liquor consumption an important part of their public appearances. The group's reputation for brutality and drunkenness attracted other sociopaths, including ex-convicts and vocational school hooligans, who expanded its membership and amplified its destructive pursuits. Group members reveled in violence, savagely beating students and attacking striking laborers.

If the translated name "Red Gaur" seems familiar, it is because the famed energy drink Red Bull, a beverage now consumed in almost every country around the world, had its start in Thailand during this period. In the mid-1960s, a Sino-Thai pharmacist named Chaleo Yoovidhya created the tonic as a sweeter imitation of imported Japanese pick-me-ups. He masterfully marketed his concoction to laborers in provincial towns and cities by stressing the restorative properties of its chemical additives. The vigilante group appropriated the name and iconography of its packaging. In the early 1980s, a visiting Austrian businessman discovered the drink while vacationing in Thailand. He bought the rights to sell a slightly altered version of the beverage around the world. Most non-Thai fans of the energy drink are unaware of the connection between the beverage and the brutal organization, but it easy to imagine that former students targeted by the Krating Daeng might feel uneasy by the current ubiquity of the name and logo.

Another rightist group, Nawaphon, was the creation of military intelligence specialists from the Internal Security Operation Command (ISOC). Nawaphon means "the Power of Nine," an allusion to King Bhumibol's reign title as Rama IX. Nawaphon organizers asserted that Hanoi and Beijing had instigated the protests of October 1973, and that the student movement was a communist program designed to overthrow the monarchy and destroy Buddhism in Thailand. Nawaphon recruited provincial bureaucrats, civil servants, and business people to attack leftists and demonstrators in the provincial cities and towns. They targeted leaders of the rural-rights group Farmers Federation, many of whom were later assassinated by unidentified gunmen. By mid-1975, all of these right-wing vigilante groups found that they could act with impunity. They attacked college students, set off bombs and threw grenades into demonstrations, assaulted union leaders, and assassinated farmers' rights activists throughout the country. Thai-Vietnamese suffered from organized attacks in areas of Isan where ethnic Vietnamese had lived for generations.

The most audacious attack by these right-wing vigilante groups was against Prime Minister Kukrit himself. In August 1975, Kukrit criticized the police for its complicity in the extrajudicial violence. In response, a mob of angry policemen and right-wing thugs, many of them intoxicated, stormed the prime minister's residence and ransacked it. They smashed many of his beloved antiques and prized art objects. Kukrit was powerless to stop them. Afterward, the three groups – Village Scouts, Krating Daeng, and Nawapon – joined forces to protest Kukrit wherever he went. It was clear that these right-wing groups could unleash mayhem wherever they wanted and no one was going to stop them.

Surprisingly for many inside and outside Thailand, some Buddhist monks incited violence during the right-wing backlash phase. The most notorious was Kittivudho Bhikku, a charismatic monk who had been preaching an anticommunist alarmist message since the 1960s. He had established his own college in Chonburi and had acquired many influential supporters, including King Bhumibol, along the way. Kittivudho infamously stated that killing communists was not a sin in Buddhism. He likened communists to rabid dogs that threaten the well-being of a village. He preached that it was a Buddhist's duty to kill those communists. Kittivudho became a kind of holy figurehead for the right-wing groups, and Nawaphon adopted him as their spiritual guide. The monk led increasingly large demonstrations of Nawaphon members and their supporters to demand that Kukrit resign and turn over his government to the military so that they could protect Thailand from what he said was an imminent Vietnamese invasion.

Kukrit's end came about when the chief of the army, Krit Siwara, abandoned him. General Krit refused to support the one-year deadline that Kukrit had issued to the United States for the removal of its military forces. Thai and US military intelligence reports warned of Hanoi's alleged plan to invade Thailand and conquer all of mainland Southeast Asia after the Americans left. Kukrit's turning out the Americans, they argued, would facilitate the loss of Thailand to the Communist bloc, the destruction of the monarchy, and the eradication of Buddhism. Kukrit was portrayed by his enemies as a dupe or, worse, a communist agent. The Thai military pressed Kukrit to resign so that they could save the nation. Kukrit was unbowed by the threats made against him and his government. He worked to maintain a close relationship with Washington even while he oversaw the removal of US troops. He continued his diplomatic outreach policies toward Thailand's communist regional neighbors, visiting Beijing to meet China's communist leadership and then hosting Cambodia's Khmer Rouge foreign minister in Bangkok. Kukrit's courage and talents were not enough, however, to hold together his government while under pressure from the army leadership. In January 1976, several rightest parties fled the coalition and Kukrit dissolved his government.

The scale of the right-wing mayhem and the impunity with which the vigilantes acted might give the impression that these were somehow popular movements. This is wrong. In the first elections after Kukrit's premiership, his brother Seni Pramoj's Democrat Party received the most votes and Kukrit's Social Action Party got the second most. The unrelenting fearmongering had not dissuaded the Thai population in its preference for a civilian-led democracy. The election results of 1976 suggested that Thai voters did not welcome a return of the tyrannical army generals to the premiership. They also indicate little public support for the violence unleashed by corrupt police officers and right-wing hooligans. These groups, however, had exercised power for so long that they had the durable institutional and infrastructural advantages to maintain their extraconstitutional privileges. And they would soon use them to wreak terrible revenge on the students who they blamed for their diminished reputation.

CHAPTER 13

MILITARY RULE AND THE GROWTH OF A RURAL INSURGENCY

By August 1976, key members of the deposed military ruling circle seemed to believe that they were strong enough to restore the pre-1973 regime. The first step was to bring back Thanom Kittikachorn and Praphas Charusathien, the disgraced field marshals who, along with their mentor Sarit Thanarat, had run Thailand for almost two decades. Praphas returned first, ostensibly for medical treatment. Some 20,000 students rallied at Thammasat University to protest his homecoming. Krating Daeng thugs threw homemade bombs into the crowds and killed four protestors. Thanom returned shortly after. The exiled field marshal came off the plane dressed in the orange robes of a Buddhist monk and went straight to a Bangkok temple. Thanom declared that he was returning home to live as a *bhikkhu*. Almost immediately, King Bhumibol visited him at the temple, signaling the palace's approval for the return of the tyrants. Thanom's choice of the temple itself was, in fact, royally significant and conveyed a powerful message to the Thai public. Wat Bowonniwet Vihara was the same temple complex at which King Mongkut had served as abbot in the late 1830s. Since then it had become the *wat* most associated with the Chakri kings. King Bhumibol himself spent most of his brief time as a monk at that temple. Thanom underwent ordination there in a private ceremony in the evening. Traditionally, monks conduct ordinations as public events so that community members can have the opportunity to object if they know the novitiate to be unqualified, criminal, or a danger to the temple.

Shortly after Thanom's and Praphas's return, a horrific act of violence occurred in Nakhon Pathom, a province just outside Bangkok and among the capital's residential suburbs. Two students who were hanging up posters protesting the tyrants' reappearance were beaten to death there. Their mangled bodies were hung from a wall as a gruesome warning to other students inclined to protest a return to the status quo. The initial outrage at the killings turned to anger when it was discovered that it was the police who had lynched the students. Students and labor activists organized protests in late September and early October at Sanam Luang. They also marched on Wat Bowonniwet. At Thammasat University, they staged a reenactment of the police lynching of the two students in Nakhon Pathom. The student portraying one of the victims bore a slight resemblance to Crown Prince Maha Vajiralongkorn, the king's only son, who was twenty-four at the time and not surprisingly resembled many Thai college students of the era. One right-wing newspaper, *Dao Sayam* (Siamese Star), published a photograph of the mock hanging and asserted that the students had deliberately selected a young man who looked like the prince. The paper argued that the students had meant to transmit a threat to the palace by suggesting they could kill the crown prince. Other papers and radio stations took the bait and made their own increasingly wild announcements about the students' alleged plans to storm the palace and kill the royal family. The right-wing media organs, many of them the mouthpieces of one or more of the vigilante gangs, called on their followers to go to Thammasat University and stop the students before they could hatch their regicidal plot.

The result was a massacre of almost unimaginable horror. More than four thousand men, among them representatives from the Village Scouts, Krating Daeng, Nawaphon, the army, and the police, descended on Thammasat University on the evening of October 5, 1976 as the students were preparing to leave the campus. To call the group that surrounded the school a mob is to ignore how well-organized and coordinated their violence was. Many had come by helicopter and deployed to set positions. These rightist forces bottled up the terrified Thammasat students in their school for the night. At dawn on October

6, the massed gunmen opened fire on the exhausted students with an array of war weapons. They shot the students with assault rifles, pistols, and even 105mm recoilless rifles. They dropped grenades on them from M-79 grenade launchers. The students who came out to surrender were shot with their arms raised in the air. The students who leapt into the Chao Phraya River from Thammasat's western wall were gunned down by the boats. Gangs of these right-wing groups, police, and military men then rushed onto the campus to assault the students with clubs and iron bars. Students who lay down on the ground to signal their surrender were stomped to death. Others were hanged from trees. Some were set on fire and burned alive. Female students were raped on the lawns. The massacre went on for hours. In the early afternoon, thousands of Village Scout reinforcements arrived on site and resumed the bloodbath. Other hooligans gathered just down the road from the royal palace chanting "kill the communists" and awaiting orders. But before they could move out of the Thammasat University area to attack another location, radio reports brought news that army officers calling themselves the National Administrative Reform Council (NARC) had overthrown Seni Pramoj's government in a coup. Thanin Kraiwichien, a civilian lawyer with connections to the palace, was made prime minister. Like the political slogan of the previous year, the right had literally killed the left.

The phrase "October 6" has entered the Thai collective historical vocabulary as shorthand for the horrific slaughter of the students that day. It also alludes to the terrible lengths that rightist forces are willing to go to halt the democratic gains promoted by these student activists and supported by the people. The phrase also must stand for a broader narrative that cannot be published or stated publicly in Thailand as there is no authoritative or official account about what happened that day. The survivors have a difficult time writing about it because even now they fear for their lives, worried that they will be assassinated by surviving members of the organizations who carried out the attacks. One of the best contemporary accounts of that period is "History Must Be Retold" by Atsiri Thammachot. In it, the writer describes the events as witnessed by the journalists who covered the massacre and the carnage. It ends with the line, "In this 'short story,' I did not add or even make up one single line." The writer has to present a piece of "fiction" about a massacre that happened on October 6, 1976, but says, "This work of fiction was all true." The lingering fear remains so strong that few Thai academics have written about it with any depth or specificity. Many are afraid that if they implicate any of Thailand's ruling institutions in the violence they will be accused of lèse-majesté and jailed for harming the reputation of the monarchy. Various governments have come and gone during the subsequent decades in Thailand, but none has been eager to get a full accounting of what happened. A painful silence remains around the events of October 6. It haunts the generation that endured its horrors. It will probably remain that way for the foreseeable future.

Student Activists as Insurgents

The students reacted to the violent crackdown in 1976 by running away. Many literally fled for their lives. But where could they go? In a country that was increasingly under the influence of several nationwide rightist organizations, it was difficult for them to go anywhere and be safe. Fearing for their lives and disgusted by the depravity of their right-wing persecutors, many students joined the Communist Party of Thailand and fled into the jungle.

To combat the communist activity, Thanom had created the Communist Suppression Operations Command (CSOC) in 1965 and put Praphas in charge of it. The CSOC was supposed to teach the security forces sophisticated methods of counterinsurgency, such as communications and psychological operations, to undermine the appeal of the guerrillas. Under Praphas's leadership, the CSOC eschewed political messaging and developmental models of counterinsurgency for brutal violence, including summary executions, against suspected communists and their sympathizers. Among its excesses were a spate of extrajudicial killings carried out in the early 1970s in the south. After arresting suspects, security forces interrogated them while beating and torturing them, often to the point of unconsciousness. When the interrogators had finished, they dumped the captives into empty 200-liter gasoline barrels, colored red in the day, to be doused with fuel and set alight. Thai soldiers who had fought in Vietnam had seen American soldiers use this method to eliminate excrement from base latrines. These veterans knew the method to be a fast and effective way to destroy matter, and the fuel fumes covered the smell of burning flesh. Those suspected communists who had died during interrogation were said to be the more fortunate ones. Their end was more merciful than those who awoke inside the barrels as their bodies burned. The security forces ran loud diesel-engine trucks to drown out the cries of the burning victims. When the barrel fire had consumed all of the body within it, the security forces dumped the ashes into nearby rivers. The anticommunist squads ended these "red barrel killings" only when the government changed in 1973. In 1974, after Thanom and Praphas had fled, the CSOC changed its name to the Internal Security Operations Command (ISOC). At that point, they switched to other methods of killing, such as shooting suspects or tossing them from helicopters. Despite the changing methods, the term "red barrel incident" gained currency as shorthand for all kinds of state-sponsored violence during this period, including torture, mutilation, assassination, and forced disappearances.

When the students first protested Thanom and Praphas in 1973, they did so without any meaningful contact with the Communist Party of Thailand. Even though the government labeled them dupes of various domestic and foreign communist organizations, the student leaders, even the leftist ones, were largely independent of CPT influence. The political scientists David Morrell and Chai-anan Samudavanija point out that the CPT was surprised at the students' success in bringing down the military-run government. What the CPT had fought so hard to do – they had suffered 1,400 casualties in eight years of fighting up to that point – the students were able to do overnight. Interestingly, the government's persistence in labeling the students communists turned out to be even more mistaken than most of its often hysterical and paranoid labeling of anything oppositional as communist. The students of 1973 had little idea about Marxism or communism, in part because of the government's suppression of its study. Certainly, some had come into contact with Marxist literature while studying overseas, and some did bring these works back with them, but this would have been a small minority of the students in the movement. Most would not have read these works because few Thais possessed works by Marx, Lenin, or Mao. The students themselves may not have been drawn to them either. Many associated communism with the bloodshed and chaos of South Vietnam and of the scary social experiment of China's Cultural Revolution, the details of which were coming increasingly to light in Thailand during this period. Many were just not interested in communism before 1973. They were more interested in reforming the oligarchic authoritarianism of the present Thai leadership into democracy. Most wanted Thailand to have elected representatives under a constitutional monarchy. They were certainly not the brainwashed communist fifth column that the military-led government had conjured in its propaganda.

After 1973, more and more student activists became familiar, if not enamored, with Marxist ideology and its egalitarian promises. When the rightist repression exploded in horrible violence in October 1976, many students fled to the CPT. To the students, the antigovernment insurgency with its proclaimed commitment to opposing the extralegal tyranny of the military-dominated government, represented their best hope. It not only promised a place of refuge for those being hunted by rightist gangs, it was also a cause that held out the promise of regaining the democratic momentum they, and the rest of the country, enjoyed after October 1973. As many as 3,000 students fled the universities and went into the jungle. The CPT's ranks swelled to its biggest size ever, with approximately 10,000 members.

Families were ripped apart by these divisions. Predictably, the tears were along generational lines. When I first lived in Thailand I knew a young woman, the older sister of a friend, who had gone to school to become a nurse. Disgusted at what she had seen of the military-dominated government and the horrible brutality of the right-wing gangs, she fled her native Ayutthaya and joined the communists in the jungle, not immediately after 1976, but a few years later. Her father had been a government official, and his beloved daughter's decision to join the communists made him extremely distraught and damaged his health. In fact, it may have killed him. He had a stroke shortly after she sneaked off to join the insurgents. His stroke was debilitating, and as he drew closer to death, his children sent word to the missing daughter about what had happened to their father. After a few weeks, the daughter returned from the underground and slipped back into Ayutthaya in the middle of the night. She was pale and thin, and shivering violently from the malaria she had contracted in the jungle. "She looked like a ghost that had appeared in the night," her younger sister recalled. The revolutionary daughter stayed a few hours overnight with her ailing father. She tried to explain her decision to join the guerrillas, and then said goodbye to him, before vanishing ahead of the coming dawn. Her father, still broken-hearted, died a few weeks later.

The students who fled into the jungle after 1976 were not great guerrilla fighters. Although they were ardent and determined, these middle- and upper-class students lacked the life experiences necessary to prepare for the grueling work of guerrilla warfare. Most were put to work creating propaganda material that would appeal to urban-based, educated people like themselves. The mixing of these groups – hardened CPT guerrillas and university students – was not a harmonious process. The two groups carried with them many of the social divisions and class differences that are deeply rooted in Thailand's social hierarchies. They came from two different worlds and they found it hard to get along. The old CPT members had been fighting for nearly two decades. With their roots in the Chinese communist organization inspired by Mao, they had merely copied Mao's critique of Chinese peasant society as "semifeudal and semicolonial" society and applied it to Thailand with little adjustment. This rather unsophisticated approach bothered the new student arrivals. They saw it as inappropriate to the historical and social circumstances of Thailand. They pointed out that Thailand of the late 1970s was not China of the 1930s. Thailand was far more developed economically and technologically than was China when Mao formulated his ideas. The students were intellectuals, they were thinkers, who chafed at being told to adhere to party discipline without question. These young idealists felt like they had fled one authoritarian environment for another. Seksan Prasertkun, a student leader, said of his time with the CPT that he had to fight for democracy there just as he had fought for it in Bangkok.

The students' enrollment in the CPT breathed life into the moribund insurgency. The movement also gained sympathy from the many Thais disgusted by their government's violent reprisals and by the encouragement and protection it gave to the right-wing vigilante mobs. But the CPT insurgency sputtered along with only limited success in the late 1970s. The source of the CPT's problems came from both within Thailand and without. The external problems were related to dramatic changes in the global alliances that occurred after the Vietnam War. When the students first joined the CPT, the organization received support from both the People's Republic of China and from the newly unified and communist Socialist Republic of Vietnam. But the already uneasy relationship between Beijing and Hanoi deteriorated shortly after the end of the Second Indochina War, particularly over China's support of Pol Pot and his Khmer Rouge regime in Cambodia. Vietnam and China eventually went to war with each other after Vietnam invaded Cambodia at the end of 1978 to overthrow Pol Pot. China responded a few months later with its own month-long invasion of Vietnam. The CPT found itself between warring patrons. It had to choose between one or the other of the quarreling communist countries. China was stronger in its support for the CPT, and it had a longer and deeper relationship with the Thai communists than did Vietnam. The CPT chose the PRC. Hanoi responded by cutting all support to the CPT and by pressuring Laos, over which Vietnam had considerable influence, to stop giving sanctuary to the CPT's insurgents. Cut off from their safe havens in Laos, the CPT guerrillas found themselves increasingly vulnerable to Thai military and police attacks.

Abandoning the CPT

There were other problems related to the broader global strategic relationships that were evolving at this time. President Richard Nixon's efforts to reach out to China had eventually brought a rapprochement between the United States and the People's Republic. By 1978, China and the United States had established diplomatic relations. Bangkok, like Washington, normalized relations with the communist giant around the same time. One of the conditions of that normalization was that Bangkok had asked Beijing to end its financial and ideological support of the CPT. It also wanted Beijing to shut down the Voice of the People of Thailand, a radio station located in Yunnan Province that broadcast programming attacking the Bangkok regime in Thai. In return, Thailand agreed to give assistance to Beijing as it struggled to prop up the dispersed Khmer Rouge armies that had fled into Cambodia's western jungles following Hanoi's invasion. Thailand's proximity to the contested battlefields of Cambodia made it an ideal staging ground to get arms to the Khmer Rouge and other anti-Vietnamese groups. As part of their new partnership, the United States joined China in helping get aid to the coalition of Cambodian guerrilla groups fighting the Vietnamese invaders. Within a year or so, the CPT found itself almost completely abandoned. The students who had joined the guerrillas likewise found the harsh world they had joined had become almost intolerable.

Back in Bangkok, changing dynamics within the government and the military affected the fate of student insurgents. A group of young army officers from Class Seven of the Chulachomklao Military Academy had formed a kind of secret society in the mid-1970s called the Khana Thahan Num, or "Young Officers Group." In English, they came to be known as the Thai Young Turks. Their core group included 6–8 young officers depending on the period, but dozens more joined them over the years. They were motivated to start the group by the widespread loathing that many Thai citizens felt for the Royal Thai Army during the end of the Thanom-Praphas period. The Thai Young Turks despised Narong Kittikachorn for his corrupt schemes and boorish behavior, and cheered his forced exile. But they also worried about the public relief that greeted the downfall of the military-dominated government in 1973. These young officers wanted to halt the army's continued diminishment in Thai public opinion and bring about a return of military leadership to the government. The Khana Thahan Num had all fought in South Vietnam or Laos, and had all received military training in the United States. They opposed Kukrit Pramoj's efforts to push out the Americans. They were all high achievers, smart and capable, and generally sterling in their conduct. By the late 1970s, all had ended up with good positions within the Royal Thai Army. They used these billets to guide events within the army that had spillover effects in the political arena. They wanted Thai military leaders who matched their collective self-image. To bring this about, they began to organize in secret.

In October 1977, the Khana Thahan Num convinced General Kriangsak Chomanan to stage a coup. Kriangsak was deputy director of the NARC cabal that have overthrown the government a year earlier. He and other prominent military leaders resented Prime Minister Thanin Kraiwichien for failing to give the army a bigger role in the government despite their part in overthrowing Seni's government.

They recognized that Thanin's rigid anticommunist rhetoric – he labeled all demonstrators "communist terrorists" – was damaging the military's efforts at neutralizing support for the CPT. Furthermore, the NARC leadership and the Young Turks had grown impatient with the Tanin government's half-hearted initiatives in addressing rural poverty. They saw firsthand that the government's anticommunist strategy was ineffective and even counterproductive.

By the late 1970s, the Thai military had come to acknowledge the shortcomings of American counterinsurgency doctrine after years of following it in rural Thailand. They had also seen the limitations of American methods while fighting in South Vietnam. Under Kriangsak's new government, two generals, Prem Tinsulanonda and Chavalit Yongchaiyudh, who had served in South Vietnam, had begun exploring various new strategies for ending the insurgency in Thailand. They concluded that the Royal Thai Army would never eradicate completely the guerrilla movement by military means only. Prem and Chavalit knew that in trying to kill the insurgents, the Thai security forces' heavy-handed tactics generated sympathy for the rebels among Thai villagers. Napalm strikes and bombing raids on villages aroused hatred for the government and the military while feeding support to the insurgents. Their ill-disciplined troops who raped and robbed confirmed the CPT's propaganda. Villagers came to fear the arrival of Bangkok's forces more than they did the CPT. Thus, when China and Vietnam abandoned the CPT, Prem and Chavalit took advantage of the insurgents' dwindling resources and collapsing morale to convince the new recruits to abandon the cause.

Thai Young Turks

The new anticommunist methods would focus less on direct military confrontation and more on strategic opposition. The security forces knew from interviewing defectors that many of the new recruits wanted to leave the insurgency. One new tactic was to deny the insurgents their hiding places. The government constructed roads leading into the densest jungle strongholds used by the guerrillas. The roads allowed logging firms to get their crews, equipment, and trucks into formerly inaccessible areas so they could cut down the forest. The loss of forest cover denied the CPT guerrillas their protected sanctuaries, leaving them exposed and vulnerable. Military figures associated with the logging operation also benefitted financially from the arrangement as the felled hardwood trees hit world markets hungry for Thai timber. The logging kickbacks and other military-run schemes rankled the idealistic Khana Thahan Num. They viewed Thailand's poor farming folk through a sympathetic lens and believed that the military's role should be to protect and aid the farmers in whatever ways it could. They saw that the villagers aided the communist guerrillas in rural areas because the army, and the army-dominated government, had been so grossly corrupt and abusive. The Royal Thai Army's involvement in shady business deals like the logging kickbacks tarnished its image and fed the insurgency. The Khana Thahan Num pledged to eschew these sweetheart business deals that so many of their senior officers had used to enrich themselves.

The Khana Thahan Num admired General Prem for his apparent incorruptibility and his effectiveness in mitigating the CPT's power without resorting to more killing and destruction. They threw their support behind him and helped him become the RTA commander in chief. He, in turn, helped them get into ever more important spots within the higher ranks of the army. Meanwhile, Kriangsak worked to calm the simmering national conflicts. He lifted marshal law and won amnesty for the eighteen student protest leaders jailed since the October 1976 massacre. He reined in the rightest vigilante groups by cutting their ties to state entities and sending some of them out of Bangkok. He made diplomatic overtures to Thailand's former foes in Vietnam, Laos, and the PRC. Despite these positive steps, he remained on shaky ground. Kriangsak could not manage restive and competitive military factions vying for government positions, nor could he do much to improve the Thai economy hurt by a global downturn. In early 1980, he stepped aside to allow General Prem Tinsulanonda, a favorite of the palace, to take over as premier.

Prem continued the process of national reconciliation started under Kriangsak. He expanded the areas of his counterinsurgency program to include more of the northeast. He added new elements to his strategy for undermining the CPT. Most effective of these new elements was his offer of amnesty to the students. He had noticed that many of them were defecting from the CPT because of arguments over ideology and strategy, and because they were bored, sick, and disillusioned with life on the run. Prem offered the students a blanket amnesty if they would come out of the jungle and surrender their weapons. He told them they would be able to rejoin society without facing legal repercussions for joining the communists or for any guerrilla activities. The new approach was almost immediately effective. The government played up these defections in grand ceremonies in which groups of bedraggled students assembled before military officers who welcomed them back into the national family. The ceremonies projected the paternalistic nationalist propaganda favored by the military-dominated government. And while the army's orchestrated fanfare may have been insulting to the young idealists, the amnesty prevented further deaths among guerrillas, and the soldiers who hunted them, in what had clearly become a losing cause for the communists. Prem's plan worked well. By the end of the 1980s, the communist insurgency was a hollow shell of its former self with only a smattering of holdouts remaining under arms. The returned students went back to school to resume their formal education. Later, many of them became academics, social activists, writers, poets, artists, and even politicians. The largely peaceful neutralization of the insurgency made Prem's star rise ever higher on the nation's political horizon. But he had his detractors.

Throughout the 1980s, Prem's leadership was challenged repeatedly by coup attempts. Notable were efforts led by the Khana Thahan Num, the same young officers who helped put him into power. On April 1, 1981, the Thai Young Turks tried to overthrow Prem's government. The "April Fool's Day Coup" fell apart when the palace intervened to support Prem. The entire royal family flew with the prime minister to a military base in Korat as the coup was unfolding. With the king squarely behind Prem, the coup had little chance of attracting support from other military units. A few years later, the young officers tried again. This time, they made their move while Prem was abroad. The coup attempt of September 9, 1985 failed largely because General Chavalit Yongchaiyudh, one of Prem's closest allies, rallied enough troops to neutralize the Young Turks' forces. The following year, Prem helped Chavalit become commander in chief of the Royal Thai Army.

A Global Tourist Destination

The Thai economy struggled in the late 1970s as the rising cost of oil and the surging US dollar and other strong currencies took their toll on Thai exports. The Thai government responded, in part, by promoting tourism. During the Vietnam War, Thailand had welcomed around 300,000 foreign tourists a year. In the 1970s, that number grew to 1 million tourists a year. In the early 1980s, the kingdom attracted 2.5 million a year. By the end of the decade, that number had doubled to 5 million. In the first decade of the twenty-first century, the number was 14 million tourists a year. How did that come about? Throughout the 1980s, the government promoted tourism vigorously through the Tourism Authority of Thailand (TAT) and gave generous incentives to those businesses that opened new hotels and started enterprises related to accommodating and entertaining foreign visitors. The amount of money generated by tourism grew sixfold in that period. Around the same time, tourism overtook rice exports to become Thailand's biggest foreign exchange earner. Thailand came to be seen as a tourism haven because it did tourism well. Foreign visitors embraced Thailand as a safe and stable country to visit. It had warm weather, scenic beaches, cultural sites, good cuisine, lively nightlife, and, not least, a population that was generally friendly, tolerant, and patient. Some of this collective impression was illusory, especially the stability part, but the industry's phenomenal growth remains a testament to the government's expert promotion campaigns and Thai entrepreneurs' genius for catering to foreign tourists' myriad desires.

Prem stepped down as premier in 1988. In the press and in political circles, there was a lot of excitement about the relatively smooth transition of governments at that time. Although Prem had been an authoritarian prime minister who came to power undemocratically, his willingness to allow lower house elections and the transition of power to an elected representative seemed to augur well for a possible resumption of democracy. Many in the Thai press announced that the days of military coups were finally behind Thailand. There was a general feeling that the main sources of instability that had generated the military coups in the second half of the twentieth century were gone for good. Political structures looked stable, even durable. The prime minister who replaced Prem, Chatichai Choonhavan, was associated with the oft-stated intention to turn the former battlefields of Indochina into a marketplace for all of Southeast Asia, with Thailand playing a dominant role. Chatichai was the only son of Field Marshal Phin Choonhavan, one of the big four in the Coup Group of the late 1940s. Chatichai himself had fought in Burma and China during the war, and, following a stint as a military attaché in Washington, DC, served with Thai forces in the Korean War. After leaving the military, he joined the diplomatic corps, partly because his father's faction had been banished by Sarit. He was ambassador to Switzerland, an important posting owing to Thailand's strong historical ties to the alpine country, and several other countries in Europe and South America. Back in Thailand, he was elected to parliament and to several important positions in various administrations. He had a well-deserved reputation as a cosmopolitan bon vivant and playboy who enjoyed expensive cigars, fine wines, and Harley Davidson motorcycles. His background in the military, foreign service, business, and even luxurious living made him seem like an appropriate leader for a globalizing Thailand in the 1980s.

Thailand's economy and stock market boomed. Everyone at the top, in politics, business, the military, and the bureaucracy, seemed to be profiting from the good times. In May 1988, Thailand's entrant in the Miss Universe contest took the crown. Twenty-year-old Porntip Nakhirunkanok was only the second Thai winner of the worldwide pageant. Beauty contests are enormously important in Thailand, and the global victory seemed like further evidence that things were going Thailand's way.

Long before mass tourism came to Thailand in the 1980s, Thailand had been a site of inspiration for numerous writers, musicians, and artists who traveled the world. Bangkok, in particular, has fed the imaginations of countless creative visitors, many of whom knew little about the kingdom before their arrival. They used the stimuli of Thailand's intricate cultural tapestry to feed their imaginations and restart their creative engines. For many years, the epicenter was The Oriental Hotel, a Western-style grand hotel on Charoen Krung Road overlooking the Chao Phraya River. Although the exact date of establishment has been lost to history, the storied inn was probably opened sometime in the early 1860s by a British merchant. In its earliest days, it was the temporary home for sailors willing to splurge on a bed and meals ashore while in port for a few days. During this phase, Joseph Conrad took meals and drinks at The Oriental. Conrad visited in February 1888, when the vessel he commanded, the three-masted iron barque *Otago*, stopped in Bangkok for supplies and repairs on its voyage from southern China to Singapore. The Polish Ukraine-born Conrad, who would later come to the world's attention with his English-language masterpieces *Heart of Darkness* and *Lord Jim*, had not yet started his writing career when he stopped in Siam. But his time in Bangkok coincided with the pinnacle of his seagoing career, a time when he was considering leaving life on the seas to try his hand at fiction. Conrad's short stay in Siam, and especially the stories he collected over drinks at The Oriental, provided source material central to his novels *The Secret Sharer* and *The Shadow Line*, as well as elements found in *Lord Jim, Typhoon, Victory*, and *Falk*. As steam-powered ocean-going vessels made travel to Asia a comfortable experience for well-to-do Westerners, The Oriental went upscale. It grew from a boarding house for scrappy merchants and seafarers to a proper luxury hotel. For many a weary Western traveler, rejuvenation was found inside the hotel's breezy suites and private verandas with views of the river. Others got it from the hotel's teakwood bar and plush chairs of the drawing-room.

Like Conrad, the British writer W. Somerset Maugham got a lot from The Oriental Hotel during his stays there. Throughout his career, Maugham had regularly traveled to Asia to gather material for his short stories, novels, and plays. A shy interlocutor, Maugham took advantage of the garrulousness of travelers in hotel bars, where alcohol and loneliness encouraged fresh acquaintances to unload their tales and spill their secrets. During Maugham's first visit to the hotel in 1923, The Oriental gave the best-selling writer of the era more than story ideas: it gave him a new lease on life. Traveling down from Chiang Mai by rail, Maugham had contracted malaria during one of his stopovers. He was checking into The Oriental when the first symptoms of the ailment hit him. Despite generous doses of quinine and cool baths, Maugham remained under the grip of the often-deadly disease. He suffered days of delirium and agony. When it appeared that Maugham would likely succumb to malaria, The Oriental's manager came forward with an idea. She suggested to the attending physician that the famous writer be moved to a nearby hospital lest his impending death hurt the establishment's reputation for hospitality. The doctor inveighed upon her to let Maugham stay while he clung to life. Maugham, who overheard the conversation about his precarious state, recovered soon after. As Maugham regained his strength, he sat on the veranda outside his room to bask in the sunlight and take in the sights along the busy river. The tales he set down in his convalescence, including his "Siamese Fairy Tale," became the heart of his omnibus travelogue, *The Gentleman in the Parlour*.

For several decades after World War II, the German avant-garde photographer and memoirist Germaine Krull ran the hotel. During that spell, other greats from the world of popular Western literature, including Noel Coward, James A. Michener, John le Carré, and Paul Theroux, stayed and wrote at The Oriental. Graham Greene stayed there several times in the early 1950s as he was putting together what would become his Cassandran novel of US intervention in Vietnam, *The Quiet American*. Three decades later, when The Oriental named a suite after the author in one of its newly constructed wings, Greene sent a note of appreciation, adding his recollections of the older building: dousing himself with buckets of water for "baths" and dodging swarms of ravenous mosquitos that appeared on the veranda at nightfall. Greene remarked appreciatively on the interesting fellow guests from those days, which included, in his recollection, authors and crooks. Over the last few decades, The Oriental has acquired several new buildings, a couple of swimming pools, and all the modern amenities found in every high-end hotel the world over. The grand old building that charmed Conrad, Maugham, Greene, and others is still there under the many layers of renovation, and a keen eye and a patient soul can just about separate the architectural treasure from the luxurious sprawl that surrounds it.

Around the same time the world was discovering Thailand as a tourist destination, Thais were changing the world's culinary tastes. In North America, Europe, Australia, and New Zealand, Thai immigrants who opened restaurants made Thai cuisine the most recognizable and admired element of Thai culture. As the Thai-American cultural studies scholar Mark Padoongpatt points out in his study *Flavors of Empire: Food and the Making of Thai America*, the Cold War was responsible for transferring a uniquely Thai configuration of flavors to the tongues of Western nationals. In the United States, an updated immigration act in 1965 overturned the Asian Exclusionary Act that had long limited the number of Asian immigrants coming to America. Within a few years of ending the racially discriminatory policy, Los Angeles became the center of a culturally vibrant and influential Thai-American community. By the early 1970s, many of the Thais who had come to the United States on student visas were settling throughout southern California and other areas of the West Coast. One survey from the decade showed that three-quarters of all Thais who came to the United States on an education visa ultimately decided to stay. The students cooked for themselves and their friends initially. Ingredients needed for curries, stir-fry dishes, and the chilis found in so many Thai favorites did not exist in North America. Thais found substitutes in Chinese and Mexican ingredients, but these alternatives produced rough approximations at best. Through ingenuity, networking, and sometimes even smuggling, they helped each other locate the precious components that would allow them to eat Thai food on the other side of the world.

Lacking work visas or permission to stay after earning their degrees, these Thai expatriates had difficulty finding jobs in their fields of expertise. To make ends meet, many turned to business opportunities that they could run on their own. These educated Thai immigrants established restaurants, food markets, food-production enterprises, and import–export concerns catering to other Thais and to the growing population of Southeast Asian immigrants who came to North America during the Vietnam War and its aftermath. In the mid-1970s, perhaps one-third of all Thai businesses in southern California were Thai restaurants. The *nakrian nok* entrepreneurs were joined in this period by more Thai immigrants who came to the States lacking English-language proficiency, advanced degrees, and professional specialization. Some of these later arrivals had married Americans and settled in the United States with their spouses. Many found it difficult to find work in all but the most menial jobs. But these newcomers did have the highly technical knowhow and experience needed to make authentic Thai food. They went to work in the newly opened Thai restaurants. With the help of investment capital from more established Thai-Americans, these various groups of Thai immigrants joined together to feed a growing appetite for Thai food on the West Coast. Beyond the need for employment, these Thai restaurant workers brought more than their labor to their jobs; many had something akin to missionary zeal in their efforts at introducing Thai food to the people of their adopted country. As in California in the 1970s and 1980s, a similar pattern of Thai food introduction occurred in the college towns and bigger cities of the United States. With obvious Thai-locating words such as "Bangkok" and "Thai" in their names, the earliest restaurants combined simple sit-down elegance with modest prices in a formula that was often a guaranteed success. American eaters, while ostensibly embracing the piquant challenge that some spicy Thai dishes posed, learned to order milder versions of chili-rich Thai dishes. Over time, Thai restaurants and Thai food expanded outward from these introduction areas into all parts of the nation. Americans ate better for it.

More so than *muay thai* or even Thai Buddhism, food has been Thailand's most affecting cultural export. The delicate blending of sweet, sour, salty, and spicy that is the cornerstone of Thai cookery has expanded the food vocabulary of the *farang* nations more so than any other cuisine in the latter half of the twentieth century. This intriguing amalgamation of tastes, which Thais call *yam* ("mixture") or, as it is often appropriately spelled, *yum*, found its way onto the palates and cravings of the Western eaters through Thai restaurants. Western diners found the unique flavors – many of which owe their origins to specifically Southeast Asian ingredients and preparation methods – offered a sharp contrast to more familiar Chinese, Japanese, and Indian foods. Mainstays such as *pad thai, kaeng khieu wan*, and *kaeng massaman*, helped win over even spice-phobic and picky eaters to Thai food. In recent times, the arguably more challenging Thai-Lao fare, such as *som tham* and *larb*, is routinely eaten around the world. Beyond the Thai-operated restaurants, mainstream supermarkets of the West have also embraced Thai cuisine of a sort. In any aisle of any grocery, a shopper is bound to find a few products marketed as "Thai-flavored," "Thai-spiced," or with the name "Bangkok" on the label. Soups, spiced cashews, frozen foods, premade curries, simmer sauces, tea blends, spicy potato chips, and many other packaged comestibles carry the Thai-taste endorsement. Furthermore, the produce needed for such Thai staples – unripe papaya, Thai eggplants, and "mouse shit" chilis, to name a few – can now be found in "ethnic" or "international" groceries of the West without much difficulty. In fact, in a matter of a decade or so at the turn of the new millennium, Thai food enthusiasts went from making do with whatever *nam pla* (fish sauce) they could find to having their choice of all of the major brands found in Bangkok's supermarkets. Recently, American meal-prep companies have added even Thai regional fare, such as northern Thailand's *khao soi*, to their rotation of home-delivered meal kits. The process of Thai food transfer described here has unfolded similarly in Europe, Australia, and New Zealand, with minor differences in the overall immigration story. Despite these variances, it is probably accurate to say that Thai food has won over much of the world in the last couple of decades.

Suchinda's Power Grab

The atmosphere of political stability celebrated when Prem Tinsulanonda stepped down as prime minister in 1988 and Chatichai Choonhavan took over did not last. Chatichai's business-friendly government faced repeated accusations of corruption, but the booming economy and surging stock market suggested that few would contemplate any rash action that might derail the good times. But when the Persian Gulf War of 1991 caused a dip in the global economy, Thailand, and its prime minister, suddenly looked vulnerable. In February 1991, the Royal Thai Army's chief-of-staff Suchinda Kraprayoon led a group of generals to overthrow Chatichai's government. They arrested the prime minister as he was boarding an airplane bound for the north, the purpose of the trip being to present the king with a plan for reshuffling the military leadership. The generals jailed Chatichai briefly before allowing him to leave Thailand for exile in London.

General Suchinda promised an end to corruption and new elections within a year. But when Suchinda tried to have himself appointed prime minister a year later, Bangkokians came out into the streets to protest the power grab. At the height of the protests on May 17–18, 1992 some 200,000 Thais gathered in the historic district around Sanam Luang to voice their opposition. Led by former Bangkok governor (and Khana Thahan Num member) Chamlong Srimuang, the protestors marched toward Government House. A cordon of soldiers and police blocked their procession along Ratchadamnoen Avenue with a barricade of razor wire. In the clashes that unfolded, the security forces blasted water cannons into the crowd and used batons to beat those who tried to get past the barricade. Some protestors responded by throwing rocks and even Molotov cocktails at the police lines. The troops opened fire on the demonstrators. Officially, fifty-two people died in the clashes and many thousands were injured. Unofficially, stories about scores of victims vanishing in the aftermath of the violence circulated for years. A persistent rumor was that the Thai military had flown the bodies of the massacred demonstrators to the jungle borderlands adjoining Burma and dumped them there. King Bhumibol was instrumental in ending the crisis. After several days of escalating violence, the king called the leaders of each faction to his palace. As Suchinda and Chamlong knelt before him, Bhumbiol told the two to cease their confrontation for the good of the kingdom. Television cameras recorded the extraordinary encounter, and the royal scolding was broadcast to the nation later that evening. The conflict ended almost immediately after the royal intervention.

For a brief period following the violence of 1992, Thailand appeared to be on the way to building a sound democratic political system. In this atmosphere of rising expectations, Thailand created a new constitution. A body known as the Constitutional Drafting Committee (CDA) generated one of the most extraordinary political documents in Thailand's often frustrating and heartbreaking history of democratic government. The CDA consisted of one elected representative from each of Thailand's 76 provinces, as well as an additional 23 constitutional experts selected by parliament. The constitution it drafted gave Thai voters the ability to vote for a single candidate running in their now smaller constituencies rather than voting for a two- or three-block list of candidates running in formerly larger constituencies. Thai voters could directly select the 400 seats of the House of Representatives from the single-seat constituencies via the plurality rule and another 100 seats elected from a nationwide constituency via proportional representation. More remarkable was the election of Thailand's 200 senators. No longer were senators appointed. Instead, they were elected by a single nontransferable vote electoral system like that used in Japan, South Korea, and Taiwan. Each voter cast one vote for a senatorial candidate running in their province. Such provisions would make vote buying more difficult. Another provision designed to develop stronger, more enduring political parties was the new requirement that MPs relinquish their seats in parliament if they joined the cabinet. Similarly, new restrictions on party switching were put in place. The document added unprecedented protections for human rights. It also created government agencies such as the Constitutional Court, the Anti-Corruption Commission, and other bodies meant to check the abuses of power committed so frequently by Thai leaders in the past. The size and representation of the drafting committee, the numerous public hearings that preceded its adoption, and the unprecedented power it entrusted to individual voters, helped give the 1997 charter its "People's Constitution" nickname. It was evidence that the Thai people wanted to participate in a political system that was clean, responsive, and truly democratic. However, the new constitution did not survive even a decade.

CHAPTER 14

POPULISTS AND ROYALISTS IN CONFLICT

By the end of the twentieth century, it might have been tempting to imagine that Thailand was more resilient politically, economically, and socially than all its neighbors in Southeast Asia. It had endured the most tumultuous periods of the century without the catastrophic consequences suffered by the countries around it. The kingdom had escaped the worst of Western imperialism, a global economic depression, World War II, postcolonial wars of liberation, and most Cold War strife with far less upheaval that that found in nearly every other country in the region. While not isolated from these disruptive events, Thailand seemed to pass through one perilous period after another with relative national calm and continuity. This extraordinary good fortune might tempt a student of history to judge Thailand as exceptional. Was it the wisdom and courage of its kings and prime ministers? Did figures such as Mongkut, Chulalongkorn, Vajiravudh, Phibun, Pridi, Sarit, Prem, and Bhumibol have superior leadership qualities? Did they have unusual wisdom that helped them maintain Thailand's independence, peace, and stability? Was their history of relying on "bamboo diplomacy" and appropriated civilization markers the key to protecting the people and the land? Was it the cultural and social qualities derived from a specifically Thai-inflected Theravada Buddhism that inculcated the population with an uncommon equanimity and resilience in the face of major challenges? What were the secrets to this unique sociocultural confidence that extended from the leadership all the way down to the humblest subject? Such questions could be asked without embarrassment in the final days of the twentieth century. But they would soon seem naïve. In the first decades of the twenty-first century, Thailand endured continuous cycles of political unrest. Rather than sidestepping the external and internal challenges bedeviling other Southeast Asian states in this era, Thailand seemed to suffer more profoundly than almost all of its neighbors. Rather than be unified in the face of foreign-born threats, Thai society seemed to turn against itself with a ferocity perhaps never seen before in the modern era. Amidst seemingly endless periods of political demonstrations and street violence, Thailand would find itself on the brink of civil war. The turmoil of this age, the great conflicts in the realm of politics, economics, social strata, and culture, has largely buried any lingering notions of Thai exceptionalism.

Political Turmoil Continues

At the center of this dispiriting age was Thaksin Shinawatra, an extraordinary figure who seemed to possess the intelligence, courage, and charisma to unite all social classes in a new democratic age. Instead, he became the focal point of a national struggle between rival social classes that tore the kingdom apart. Following General Suchinda Kraprayoon's power grab of 1991 and the massacre of demonstrators the following year, the Thai electorate appeared interested in rescuing its democracy from the strongmen and fat cats who threatened it. In 1992, Thais elected members of parliament from a broad array of parties representing numerous social, economic, and regional constituencies. Chuan Leekpai and his Democrat Party were the biggest winners. Chuan built a coalition government with members of some of the other parties, namely New Aspiration and Phalang Tham ("Power of the Dharma"). Chuan was not a forceful leader, but he seemed to be what Thais wanted at the time. He was a low-key brainy lawyer who had been involved in the Democrat Party for most of his adult life. Never a grandstander, the Sino-Thai southerner had a reputation for being sincere and hardworking, if not a little boring. In the postabsolutist age, most Thai leaders had been forceful men with larger-than-life public personas. Chuan seemed drab but honest, a reassuring combination for many fed up with years of corruption and violence. Just as importantly, Chuan and the Democrats had the support of the palace. Chuan's enthusiasm for King Bhumibol's development projects put the new government behind several high-profile royal development schemes under way in the countryside.

Despite its promising beginning, Chuan's administration was quickly beset by problems. Accusations of corruption leveled against those around him undermined his authority. His government fell in 1994. In quick succession, Thailand saw the election of two more governments, those of Banharn Silpa-archa in 1995 and Chavalit Yongchaiyudh in 1996. Both were as weak and wobbly as Chuan's. And like Chuan, both Banharn and Chavalit were seasoned and skillful politicians who were nonetheless incapable of presiding over administrations that met the people's new expectations for clean and responsive government. They were also incapable of dealing with crises when they occurred.

The Asian Financial Crisis

Thailand was a principal flashpoint of the Asian Financial Crisis of 1997, and its effects were felt most acutely there. The financial press labeled the catastrophic economic downturn that devastated economies throughout Asia as the "Tom Yam Kung Crisis" after the Thai spicy shrimp-based soup of that name. The crisis was a terrible setback for a region that had become synonymous with remarkable growth. Throughout the 1980s and '90s, economies in East and Southeast Asia had boomed. Institutional investors from around the world poured funds into the "Four Asian Tigers" of Hong Kong, South Korea, Taiwan, and Singapore, fueling their economic growth. Economic planners in the newly industrialized countries of Southeast Asia, especially Thailand, Malaysia, and Indonesia, tried to imitate the models offered by the Four Tigers. By 1997, foreign investors had inundated Thailand with "hot money," investment provided in an atmosphere of unrealistic optimism with an expectation of a fast return. In this money-rich atmosphere, Thailand's financial institutions loaned money more freely, even recklessly, than at any point in the past. Many of the loans went to prominent figures in business, politics, and the military. This "crony capitalism" made it possible for influential people to borrow huge sums easily and on generous terms. Many lacked sufficient collateral for these hefty loans.

The financial crisis damaged not only Thailand's economy but also its global reputation as a stable and profitable place to do business. Thailand's economy had boomed since the Vietnam War. With American economic aid and advice from the World Bank, the Thai economy grew between 4 and 7 percent in the 1960s and 1970s. It bounded upward by double digits for much of the 1980s. In the early 1990s, Thailand's economy continued to grow by almost 9 percent. Inflation was low. Thailand moved away from its exclusive reliance on agricultural exports to include manufacturing and other industries. The per capita income of Thailand in 1965 was US$138; by 1996, it was $3100. Thailand's economy had been so good for so long that its economic planners seemed unprepared for change. Growing trade competition from China, a stronger US dollar, a contracting real estate market, and a fall in demand for semiconductors at a time when they were one of Thailand's principal exports all played a role in weakening the economy.

In late 1996, Thailand's stock market and real estate prices declined rapidly. The heavy losses drove currency speculators to put pressure on the Thai baht which, at the time, was pegged to the US dollar and other stable currencies. The Thai government stepped in to prop up faltering Thai finance companies whose holdings in bad real estate properties threatened to bankrupt them. The move added further pressure to an already stressed baht. When Thailand's finance minister sought to alleviate the pressure, he discovered that most of the kingdom's $30 billion in foreign reserves had been paid out to future contracts, while another $8 billion had been put toward saving faltering finance companies. With so little money at his disposal, he was unable to commit funds to propping up the other endangered finance companies, and had to let them fail. The result meant that foreign investors, who had been reassured by Thai leaders that the nation would protect their investments, lost a sizable chunk of their investments. The dramatic collapse of these giant financial institutions scared away foreign investors. To relieve pressure on the baht, Thailand unlinked the baht from the dollar on July 2, 1997 and let its value fall. The currency fell from about 25 baht to one US dollar to almost 49 during 1997. Desperate for help, Thailand called in the International Monetary Fund (IMF) to rescue its economy.

Thais suffered. Businesses that had appeared robust went bankrupt overnight. Personal fortunes, both real and on paper, evaporated. The upper echelon and those who worked for their companies got hurt. Newspapers ran stories of former bosses who were now doing such unskilled labor as selling sandwiches on the streets to get by. Many construction projects ground to a halt. A symbol of Thailand's abrupt downturn were the skeletons of unfinished skyscrapers dotting the Bangkok skyline. For Bangkokians, these ghost buildings, with their exposed beams rusting in the onslaught of several seasons of monsoon rain, were stark visual reminders of the swift turn of fate that had befallen their red-hot economy. Thailand looked sick and vulnerable.

A Populist Tycoon

Thaksin Shinawatra emerged as a national figure in this period of crisis. He was a new kind of leader that had strong appeal to many Thais who had come to expect more opportunities for political participation from regular citizens. He had no royal ancestry, he did not descend from a line of bureaucratic officials, nor did he come from the upper ranks of the Royal Thai Army. He was a business tycoon who successfully presented himself as a populist. Businessmen had long been involved in Thai politics. But tycoon figures like Thaksin had usually remained in the National Assembly, leaving the top leadership slots to their military partners. Thaksin was a new political-business figure who sought the same control over the nation that he had wielded over his businesses.

Like many tycoons, Thaksin portrayed his rise to power as a rags-to-riches success story. In speeches, interviews, and memoirs he described a childhood of difficulty and want. His alleged origins were distortions of a more complicated family story. He did this to emphasize a populist persona that was capable of understanding the plight of the rural poor. Thaksin's autobiography highlighted his education in a rural temple school, a circumstance often associated with extreme poverty or even orphanhood. As historians Pasuk Phongpaichit and Chris Baker show in their study *Thakisn*, the truth is that Thaksin came from one of the most prominent Sino-Thai business families in Chiang Mai Province. His grandfather had laid the foundation for the family's fortune by building a silk company in the early decades of the twentieth century. In the following two generations, the extended Shinawatra family built up other businesses across the northern Lan Na region and beyond. Some of his relatives from his grandfather's generation had become leading figures in the Royal Thai Army before moving into national politics. Thaksin himself opted to go into the police. He studied at the police academy where he developed personal connections that would aid his rise in business and politics. Like the *nakrian nok* of old, Thaksin went abroad for graduate school. He earned two advanced degrees in the United States, including a Ph.D. in criminal justice at Sam Houston State University in Texas. The time abroad opened his eyes to coming trends brought about by globalization.

Thaksin built his own fortune in telecommunications. Although not exactly rags-to-riches, Thaksin's rise to super wealth and national leadership was marked by cycles of opportunities, failures, and persistence. His biggest success came from the launch of telecommunications satellites. Competing in the often-ruthless contest for government concessions made Thaksin adept at politics. He fostered relationships with ministers and other high-ranking members of the government. He also recognized the advantages of being an insider in a system where reciprocity and cronyism lay at the heart of many successful bids. In November 1994, Thaksin joined the government as a cabinet appointee from the Phalang Tham Party. At the time, Chamlong Srimuang, the Bangkok governor who had led the protests against General Suchinda Kraprayoon in May 1992, dominated the party's affairs. Chamlong was famous for his abstemious habits and frugality for which he had become somewhat of a folk hero to Thais who had grown sick of venal politicians. Thais saw his Buddhist-guided example as a potential antidote to the scourge of money politics. But Phalang Tham was not strictly an ascetic's party. Its "temple wing," led by Chamlong, was offset somewhat by some ambitious businessmen who, like Thaksin, hoped the party's share of cabinet posts and other leadership positions would benefit their businesses. Phalang Tham's rivals objected to Thaksin holding a cabinet position while profiting from companies that were essentially state concessions. The conflict drove Phalang Tham from the coalition government. But Thaksin's loss of prominence was only temporary. When Chamlong resigned the party leadership shortly after withdrawing from the coalition, the reins of Phalang Tham fell to Thaksin. The hubbub over Thaksin's concessions seemed to help him. The press reports describing him as a communications tycoon made him a familiar and admired public figure. When he ran for parliament in July 1995, he easily won a seat representing central Bangkok. The former construction magnate Banharn Silpa-archa, as leader of the Thai Nation Party, made Thaksin deputy prime minister in his coalition government. Thaksin remained as deputy prime minister when former RTA commander in chief Chavalit Yongchaiyudh of the New Aspiration Party became prime minister in late 1996. But, just as before, Thaksin found his efforts to use his political power to further his business interests were thwarted by political rivals.

Thaksin was stymied by men who were a lot like him. The unstable coalition governments of competing businessmen-politicians produced too much rivalry, jealousy, and scrutiny for him to gain the insider advantages he sought. If anything, the high profile he had attained inspired imitators to set up their own telecommunications businesses to compete against him. It took the economic crisis of 1997 to give him the advantages he needed to vanquish his rivals.

While the crisis devastated Thai businesses in nearly every sector, Thaksin's companies suffered far less than most. His rivals suggested that he had used his insider's knowledge as deputy prime minister to put his companies on a better financial footing ahead of Thailand letting the baht float. Thaksin's ventures had more cash, better-established projects, and stronger stock shares than any of his rival companies had. While others saw their fortunes ruined, Thaksin saw his position in all markets strengthen. Within a few years, he would be counted as among the world's richest people.

Thaksin's growing prominence as a "money politician" ultimately destroyed the party that took him in. Thai voters drawn to Phalang Tham's Buddhist-inspired ideology withdrew their support when Thaksin supplanted Chamlong as the face of the party. With Phalang Tham in disarray, Thaksin resigned. He used his time out of politics to plan his comeback. He later claimed to have traveled the country talking to people – laborers, academics, and journalists – about the challenges they faced in a rapidly changing Thailand. He finished his nationwide listening tours convinced that globalization, environmentalism, digital technology, and information revolutions made the old Thai political paradigm obsolete.

Thaksin's idea was to reframe Thai political systems along lines of the business world. He presented Thailand itself as the company whose fortunes were hurt in regional and global competition by internal strife. Rather than have Thai politician-businessmen compete ardently against each other, they would now seek a means of cooperation that would allow Thailand to compete against its rivals in Singapore, Hong Kong, Taiwan, the Philippines, and beyond. In July 1998, he launched his own political party. He called it Thai Rak Thai (TRT), meaning "Thais Who Love Thais." Thaksin built the party membership with friends and associates, mainly from the business world. He also brought in associates from the police, the military, and his former political party. Surprisingly, he invited a few former pro-democracy activists from the 1973–76 period, some of whom had spent time with the antigovernment rebels in the jungles before amnesty. With some of their youthful idealism still intact in middle age, these former activists saw in Thaksin a chance to transform the Thai government's power from serving mainly the elite to serving a broader spectrum of social classes.

Thaksin gained political stature by presenting himself and his party as defenders of Thai businesses, both big and small, against a rapacious external threat. He declared himself an opponent of the International Monetary Fund (IMF) and the Democrat-brokered plan to rescue the Thai economy. The Democrat-led government of Thailand had brought in the IMF to rescue the devastated economy and to prevent it from further hurting the economies of the region and the world. The IMF provided the loans necessary to stabilize the economy. With the necessary cash came advice about how Thailand should restructure its economy to prevent further devastation. The IMF blamed Thailand's financial crisis on what it identified as Asian modes of business. It saw crony capitalism as the source of the excessive and reckless lending that brought down the economy. It also faulted Thailand and Thai companies for poor investing strategies and bad planning. IMF strategists pressed Thailand to lift the restrictions on foreign ownership of businesses. In this state of financial crisis, foreign buyers would be able to buy the imperiled businesses at rock-bottom prices. Some

Thai business leaders, politicians, and journalists sought to fuel public indignation toward the IMF advisors by describing the rescue plan in xenophobic tones. Thaksin invoked the historical specter of Western imperialism and its odious extraterritoriality provisions to argue that foreigners once again threatened Thai sovereignty through the IMF's bailout plan. Thaksin tapped this anti-Western message by presenting his fledgling party as a movement of Thais who defended Thais from foreigners. Later, when Thailand repaid the last of its IMF loans in July 2003, two years ahead of schedule, Thaksin declared an "independence day" for Thais.

Authoritarianism and Extrajudicial Killings

While major political parties had focused almost exclusively on urban voters, Thaksin took his message to rural people. His party's platform in the lead-up to the 2001 elections featured debt forgiveness for farmers, expanded educational opportunities for the poor, an anticorruption drive, and broad economic policies that appealed to the growing nationalistic mood. Two planks stood out especially for rural people. One was a war on drugs, the second a health care system. In the 1980s and 1990s, methamphetamine use had become a scourge throughout Thailand. While touching all social classes and regions, it had a particularly devastating effect on the working poor. Truck and bus drivers, cabbies, farm workers, manual laborers, and even students relied on the drug to work long hours on little rest. The pills meant that they could work superhuman shifts to get ahead. The drug also became a party drug for young people of all backgrounds. In some cases, the consequences of drug use were severe. Rural communities saw increased crime, horrific accidents and injuries, and drug-related deaths. Newspapers carried sensational stories of drug users who committed atrocious crimes, gory suicides, and other desperate acts while on the drugs or in withdrawal. Thaksin's promise to fight drugs resonated strongly with those who wanted the government to do more to combat meth production, distribution, and use. He also promised a health care scheme that would allow the poor access to basic medical care for only 30 baht (about US$1 at the time) a visit. Thai Rak Thai broadened its appeal by supporting candidates in local elections throughout the country. Ultimately, it registered some eleven million Thais to its organization.

Thaksin's strategies paid off. In the 2001 election, Thai Rak Thai candidates took 248 of the 500 seats. They did particularly well in the north, Thaksin's home region, but also in central and eastern Thailand. And because success breeds success (and because politics attracts opportunists), Thaksin attracted politicians from rival parties to bolster his strong victory. He also drew upon his family's extensive network of contacts in the army, police, national bureaucracy, and business world when appointing officials to key government posts.

As planned, Thaksin asked Thais to see the nation as analogous to one of his companies. He and his advisors promoted the idea of the country as a company in which he was the chief executive officer (CEO). As "CEO prime minister," he saw his primary role as formulating policies and directing branches that would rejuvenate the economy. He gave some "CEO governors" special training in management principles and practices so that they would administer their provinces like moneymaking businesses. Their mission was to funnel capital and resources to key sectors of the national economy. In addition to boosting national enterprises and strengthening the banks, Thaksin directed resources toward programs designed to help the poor. He sought to help them gain access to capital and opportunities hitherto unavailable to them. He created schemes to give villagers funds that they could devote to developing small-scale enterprises or improvements in local infrastructure. He pushed the "One Tambon, One Product" (OTOP) program that encouraged each subdistrict (*tambon*) to develop, promote, and market a distinctive product or craft. He financed a moratorium on farm debts. The government facilitated the sale and distribution of affordable computers to rural schools. Many of the programs seemed designed to make Thai voters see themselves as potential entrepreneurs, and potential success stories, like the romanticized version of Thaksin's life story.

True to his word, Thaksin launched a war on drugs. But in zealously prosecuting the antidrug campaign, Thaksin's administration pursued methods that appeared to cross the line from tough tactics into extrajudicial killings. Thaksin declared openly his support for killing drug dealers. Under the direction of the minister of the interior, Wan Muhamad Noor Matha, district chiefs drew up lists of known and suspected drug dealers. In short order, many on the lists were killed. In most cases, they had been executed by unidentified assailants who shot them with handguns while riding pillion on motorbikes. The government blamed drug dealers for the spate of killings, asserting that the criminals were silencing associates and underlings who might identify them to the police. Others were not so sure. Newspapers noted the execution methods bore the hallmarks of professional gunmen used by authorities in the past to carry out assassinations. In the first three months of the campaign, some 2,800 were killed. In heart-wrenching testimonials to the news media, families of some of the victims asserted that their executed loved ones were not drug dealers or had ever used drugs. Subsequent investigations by human rights organizations revealed that half of the victims had no connection to the drug trade.

Thaksin clashed with domestic institutions as well. His rhetoric during his early political career labeled politicians as corrupt and unsophisticated. He also derided most politicians as ignorant of the forces transforming Southeast Asia – globalism and technology – and thus incapable of leading the nation. Once in power, he criticized the institutions set up to remedy the problems he decried while running for office. He complained about the Election Commission, the National Counter Corruption Commission, and the Constitutional Court, three institutions empowered to check the abuses of Thai political leaders. Despite his assault on democratic watchdogs, Thaksin remained popular with the Thai people.

Thaksin's expressed concern for the common people, however, did not extend to broadening participatory democracy. Once in power, he used his position to attack many of the institutions that had protected the poor and disenfranchised. His strategy was to neutralize those entities that challenged his increasingly autocratic methods so that he would have a freer hand to act as he chose. He attacked the news media, especially the foreign press, for writing critically about him and his programs. He lashed out at Thai journalists, labeling anyone who questioned his actions as ignorant or unpatriotic. He derided nongovernmental organizations (NGOs) as little more than gangs of rabble-rousers and anarchists whose stated concern for the environment, the poor, and the voiceless concealed seditious purposes. He ridiculed and threatened public intellectuals and other prominent figures who spoke critically about his policies. Thaksin's intimidation tactics largely silenced his detractors. But he remained hugely popular with the rural voters and urban poor who had brought him to power.

By 2004, many Thais had come to see Thaksin as a miracle worker. He convinced many that he had remedies for all of Thailand's problems. Handsome and decisive, he appeared on television and the press to offer his ideas for fixing Thailand's economy, political process, cultural mores, and diplomatic relations. For many Thais, things seemed to get better under his leadership. The national economy had regained much of its precrisis vigor, growing by more than 6 percent in 2004. The Stock Exchange of Thailand rebounded strongly. Poor people liked his 30-baht health care scheme, village loan program, and other initiatives aimed at rural people. Many of his supporters felt proud of Thaksin's personal success. His businesses flourished in step with his soaring political fortunes, with some reports estimating that he was worth at least $5 billion. Thaksin used his popularity to broaden his political base. He neutralized most of his former opponents by getting them to join his movement. The Thai Rak Thai Party had drawn in so many former rivals that only the Democrats remained as credible challengers to single-party rule.

In the 2005 election, Thaksin's Thai Rak Thai Party scored a landslide victory with a stunning 377 of 500 seats. He had the strongest parliamentary majority of any Thai leader in history. For many who had lived through periods of semidemocratic and democratic governments marked by weak political parties and wobbly coalition governments, Thaksin's forceful victory seemed to promise stability and unity. For some, though, the one-party domination by a populist leader with enduring business interests throughout the country and the region, Thaksin appeared to be a more powerful version of the absolute monarchs and military tyrants who had stifled political participation in the previous half century. His wealth, party apparatus, and business networks made him look as rich and as powerful as a king. That perception of apotheosis may have been ultimately fatal to Thaksin's time on top.

Challenging the Palace

The beginning of the end for Thaksin occurred on December 4, 2003, King Bhumbol's birthday, in a very public setting. In the middle of the king's televised speech, Bhumibol singled out Thaksin by name when declaring that no one was above criticism. In the same address, the king expressed concern over the violence in Thaksin's antidrug campaign. With the nation looking on, Thaksin grinned uncomfortably throughout the royal dressing down. Many observers concluded that Bhumibol disliked the brash populist.

Thaksin was reportedly furious about the incident as he had tried to ingratiate himself with the palace. He promoted economic and social programs that seemed to match Bhumibol's interests in self-sufficiency and moral rectitude. He also tried to buy influence with the palace through financial assistance, especially after the economic crash in 1997. But it was his purchase of a stake in iTV, which at the time was Thailand's only independent television station, that alarmed the people around the king. By acquiring the kingdom's sole independent broadcaster, Thaksin gained a powerful and uncritical outlet for his views. Even better, he stopped any potential critics from using the station to challenge him. With all the other stations already under his sway as government-controlled broadcasters, Thaksin now had something like a monopoly on television programming in the kingdom.

Reportedly, the former generals, princes, and statesmen who comprised Bhumibol's Privy Council also did not approve of Thaksin's apparent efforts at supplanting the king as the symbolic father of the nation. Thaksin fed this impression by presiding over religious ceremonies at Wat Phra Kaeo, the Temple of the Emerald Buddha, in a manner similar to that of the king. His powerful detractors saw in Thaksin's efforts to rearrange the kingdom's leadership, including his appointment of top military leaders, as an effort to shift real and symbolic power away from the palace, as Phibun Songkhram had tried a half-century earlier. They also feared the power structures built around Bhumibol since the early 1960s would be destroyed.

Further complicating matters, Thaksin had angered senior military commanders with his selections of candidates for promotions and top military positions. They saw in his choices a disregard for seniority and achievement while promoting those connected to him by family ties and political connections. Through his heavy-handed management of military promotions, Thaksin had earned the enmity of the commander of the army, General Anupong Paochinda. Anupong had formerly been commander of the Queen's Guard, an elite infantry regiment that has historically been close to the throne. The unit's members maintained close connections with Privy Council chair and former prime minister Prem Tinsulanonda, and shared his antipathy for Thaksin. For all of his political acumen and business savvy, Thaksin had failed to master critical elements of Thailand's tutelary democracy. As political scientist Paul Chambers has outlined in his scholarship, non-elected elites from three important intuitions exerted powerful influence over Thailand elected representatives in this age: the king, members of the king's Privy Council, and military leaders (mostly the army). Although Thaksin was a popular elected representative of the people, he had overestimated his ability to cajole and control the people who exercise unofficial power over the nation's affairs.

Thaksin also attracted criticism for his handling of the reenergized Muslim-led separatist movement in the south. He had dismantled the military's joint-services command responsible for neutralizing the insurgents. He turned over security duties to the police. Almost immediately, the relative calm of the south exploded. On January 4, 2004, a group of militants overran a military weapons depot at Narathiwat and got away with 400 rifles and ammunition. The stolen arms fed an escalation in violence across the four most southern provinces. Rebels hit police stations, government offices, schools, and even temples. Gruesome attacks on monks and novices, including beheadings carried out by machete-wielding assailants on motorcycles, shocked the kingdom. The situation deteriorated further in 2004, with two notorious incidents emblematic of Thaksin's mishandling of the southern insurgency. On April 28, a band of Islamic insurgents that had earlier attacked a police station at Pattani took refuge inside the town's Krue Se mosque. Pledging themselves to martyrdom, the group refused to surrender or release the hostages they held. In the ensuing battle between separatists and security forces, some 108 people were killed. The fighting destroyed the historic mosque. Later that year, in October, security forces attacked a group of peaceful protestors at the town of Tak Bai in Narathiwat. Government forces killed seven people in their initial operation, and then caused the death of another 74 while transporting them in overcrowded trucks to a detention center. Most of the dead suffocated under the weight of their fellow detainees stacked on top of them. These and other incidents throughout the year convinced many that Thaksin's policies were exacerbating tensions in the south. His most important critics were in the palace. The king and queen gave advice for defusing the situation, while some of their most trusted advisors rebuked Thaksin for his apparent bungling of the sensitive situation.

The taint of corruption clung to Thaksin's administration. Just as Thaksin had made his first real money through winning government concessions, his family and associates seemed to benefit greatly from the government's policies and initiatives. His critics decried numerous examples in which someone associated with the extended Shinawatra family had seemingly profited by his or her proximity to the prime minister. The construction of Bangkok's new airport was a focal point for many of the corruption accusations. The sprawling Suvarnabhumi International Airport appeared to be a fruitful opportunity for many TRT-connected figures to enrich themselves further on graft. The most damaging of these were stories about the outrageously high bribes demanded by Thaksin's own children for airport-related concessions. Stung by continued accusations that he was using his office to enrich his family's business ventures, Thaksin sold the family's Shin Corp to Singapore's Temasek Holdings in early 2006. This should have helped him move past the growing chorus of criticism over how he used the prime minister's position to grow his business, but instead the exact opposite occurred. With a price of $1.8 billion, the sale of Shin Corp was the largest private business deal in Thailand's history. Thaksin had arranged the sale through a tax haven he had set up in the Virgin Islands. Other opaque maneuvers helped him maximize the profit from the sale. His children, the listed owners of the company, avoided paying any capital gains taxes on the huge profits they reaped in the deal.

Thaksin's critics pounced on the apparent tax avoidance as evidence of his malfeasance and corruption. They organized anti-Thaksin demonstrations that drew surprisingly large crowds in Bangkok. Two former Thaksin allies, media tycoon Sondhi Limthongkul and Phalang Tham chief Chamlong Srimuang, led the protests. They called their movement the People's Alliance for Democracy (PAD). They drew support from Democrats, southerners, and other Thaksin opponents. Their stated goal was to oppose corruption, defend democracy, and protect the monarchy. In marching against Thaksin, they exploited the rumored antipathy between Bhumibol and Thaksin by dressing in yellow, the color of the monarchy. Their adoption of the royal color gave PAD demonstrators their nickname, "the Yellow Shirts." Their slogans included such phrases as "Fight to Protect the King" and "Love the Father." While the palace did not initially give overt signs of approval for the PAD demonstrations, its silence on the yellow-garbed protestors' actions led many to believe that the king and his senior supporters welcomed the campaign.

Under intense pressure over the tax issue and growing demonstrations, Thaksin called for a snap election. His chief rivals in the Democrat Party knew they would lose badly to Thai Rak Thai. To avoid another crushing defeat, the Democrats sought to spark a constitutional crisis by refusing to post candidates in the contest. In the election of April 2006, Thai Rak Thai once again cruised to an easy victory. TRT candidates captured 53 percent of the votes cast, but a sizable number of abstained votes and invalid ballots threw the outcome into question. Thailand's government remained in limbo as various factions argued about the legitimacy of the contest. Bowing to pressure from palace insiders, Thaksin initially announced he would not become prime minister in the next government. Soon after, though, Thaksin backtracked and tried to reclaim the premiership. Because Bhumibol had played a decisive role in settling similar political crises in 1973 and 1992, many Thais anticipated his intervention. When Bhumibol did weigh in publicly on the developing constitutional crisis, he suggested in a speech that the Constitutional Court should settle the matter. A month later, the court declared the election invalid. Thaksin announced that he would stay on as a caretaker prime minister until the next election later in the year. He never got that far.

CHAPTER 15

RED SHIRTS AND YELLOW SHIRTS: DEFINING THAI-NESS?

Generals linked to Privy Council Chairman Prem Tinsulanonda carried out the coup d'état of September 19, 2006 that toppled Thaksin. General Sonthi Boonyaratklin, commander in chief of the Royal Thai Army, led the group. These generals had opposed Thaksin's choices for the military's top leadership positions. They objected to Thaksin favoring military men connected to him by marriage or politics over more senior and accomplished career soldiers. Thaksin's efforts were ultimately unsuccessful, but his heavy-handed interference in military affairs pushed the active-duty generals into action. They joined with prominent retired generals and statesmen surrounding King Bhubmibol to topple Thaksin. The military cabal also opposed Thaksin for bungling the antiinsurgency efforts in the deep south. While rumors of an anti-Thaksin coup had long circulated among the Thai population, the compromised election in April and growing antigovernment demonstrations gave the move an air of inevitability. The generals struck while Thaksin was abroad to speak at the United Nations in New York City.

In their address to the nation, the coup leaders said they acted because Thaksin was corrupt and because he was dividing the people. Their announcement alluded to the tax-avoidance issue and recent demonstrations. In overthrowing a democratically elected prime minister, they acted in statement and deed on behalf of the king. The generals called themselves the Council for Democratic Reform (CDR). They promised a new constitution and elections at some point in the future. In the meantime, they targeted Thaksin and his supporters, first by banning them from politics. They passed decrees disbanding Thai Rak Thai. They unleashed the military's Internal Security Operations Command (ISOC), the army's political and intelligence units that had once hunted suspected communists in the 1970s and 1980s to track down and intimidate Thaksin supporters. Later, they passed a Computer Crimes Act and a Broadcasting Act that gave the government new powers over political expression.

Red Shirts Take to the Streets

The coup-makers proved inept at administering Thailand. Operating under the new title of Council of National Security (CNS), they appointed retired army general Surayud Chulanont as the interim prime minister. Surayud had been commander in chief of the RTA in the early 2000s, and after retirement he joined the Privy Council. Surayud, Sonthi, and their allies defended the assault on democracy with accusations of Thaksin's malfeasance and disloyalty. Their argument did not convince the many Thai voters who had welcomed the democratic reforms of the 1990s that had helped bring Thaksin to power. Even many who disliked Thaksin for his autocratic tendencies and apparent corruption felt Thailand had lost the ground it had gained as a democratic society when the military reasserted itself into national leadership through a coup. Following the brief interlude of coup-inspired public frivolity described in this book's opening chapter, the electorate expressed their disapproval of the army's meddling. Tired of coups d'état and the elusive promise of participatory democracy, many Thais took to the streets to protest the persecution of Thaksin and his supporters. Borrowing a page from the PAD's Yellow Shirts, they adopted their own sartorial political signature by dressing mainly in red. Some said the choice of color alluded to Thailand's tri-color flag on which red symbolized the people. Red was also a good contrast to yellow. Over time, the red of the Red Shirts became identified with Thaksin more narrowly and pro-democracy support more broadly. Thaksin's allies called their red shirt grouping the United Front for Democracy Against Dictatorship (UDD).

The Red Shirts were the working poor and the newly middle classed, segments of the population that had benefitted from Thailand's economic growth in the last quarter century but continued to suffer from problems such as debt, lack of educational opportunities, and poor health care access. Their core elements were farmers, merchants, service workers, and salespeople. Many came from rural families who, in a generation or two, had seen their quality of life rise from destitution to something like the lower middle class. They had acquired access to education, material goods, capital, and mobility. Formerly remote from Bangkok, they had been largely ignored by governing institutions and political parties. With their entry into the lower tiers of the middle class, they now wanted economic security and a social safety net like those enjoyed by Bangkok's middle and upper classes. Since the 1960s, many of these upwardly mobile workers had split their time between the provinces and the capital. For part of the year, they worked on their families' farms, especially during the planting and harvesting periods, and during other parts of the year they came to Bangkok to work as taxi drivers, laborers, house cleaners, prostitutes, service workers, and factory employees. As more farms mechanized, these migrant workers stayed on in Bangkok and in provincial capitals to do other work. They melded with existing urban communities to create a working class that was more increasingly aware of national affairs and the world beyond Thailand. With their rising incomes and new perspectives, they also wanted to play a greater part in the political processes that the upper middle class and the elite had long dominated.

Thaksin and Thai Rak Thai had strong appeal for the working poor. Thaksin offered national policies that seemed designed with them in mind. The 30-baht medical visit, OTOP initiative, village loan scheme, and debt-repayment program addressed their concerns for continued improvements in their quality of life. While having less formal education than their Yellow Shirt counterparts, they had acquired more schooling and vocational training than the previous generations of rural folk. In Thaksin they saw someone like themselves – an outsider who came into money and power through hard work and risk-taking. His ascendency seemed analogous to their own upward mobility. Best of all, he spoke to them directly as potential entrepreneurs and stakeholders in the nation. When Thaksin was removed, they saw it as an attack on their burgeoning civil rights and economic elevation. The Red Shirt movement spurred a political awakening that had been growing gradually over the previous three decades. Inspired by the example of the Assembly of the Poor's rallies in Bangkok in the 1990s and 2000s, these pro-Thaksin demonstrators had summoned newfound courage to speak up for their own interests. They were willing to break social taboos by openly challenging representatives of the government and, by extension, the monarchy and its military backers. The Red Shirts saw themselves as citizens with rights, not merely as *phrai*, a feudal-era word denoting lower-class commoners. They wanted the Thai upper classes to stop taking their labor for granted. They wanted to speak directly to the political leadership about their desires and hopes. They wanted a say in national affairs, especially in terms of economic policy. They also resented the characterization hurled at them by some Yellow Shirt opponents that portrayed them as ignorant "buffalo" who were easily manipulated, or bribed, into mass political action by Thaksin and his surrogates. They wanted the Thai state to treat them with dignity.

The Yellow Shirts represented the established order. They were primarily the middle and upper classes of Bangkok and its environs. They came from the ranks of the professionals, the civil service, state enterprises, and medium- and large-scale businesses. They had long worked for and benefitted from the dominant political and economic systems of Thailand. They had easier access to capital, higher education, and foreign travel than did their Red Shirt counterparts. As the quality of life in Thailand improved, the upper middle class increasingly identified with the elite. They resented the suggestion from Red Shirt organizers that their higher status or comparative security meant that they had unduly prospered or had few worries. Many had suffered in the economic crisis of 1997. They feared that the fiery rhetoric of the Red Shirt demonstrations would bring about more economic crises. Initially, the Yellow Shirts did not target democracy per se. But their strong opposition to Thaksin made them fear for the tyrannical behavior of an elected figure like him. The leadership called their movement the People's Alliance for Democracy (PAD), although their principles were certainly less democratic than the movement they opposed. When their campaign to disabuse Thaksin's supporters of their veneration for the tycoon proved to be difficult, the PAD leadership began to question openly whether the democracy of one vote for one person was suitable for Thailand.

Many in the PAD looked askance at the provincial rural poor and lower middle class that made up Thaksin's base. Having heard for years about vote buying in the provinces, they believed that Thaksin's TRT could easily buy the votes of the rural poor for small sums or unrealistic promises. They resented Thaksin for his rhetoric that seemed to pit rural against urban, working class against upper class, and new money against old. They saw their own hard work and reliability as important drivers for Thailand's strong economy over the last half century. They valued their cosmopolitan outlook and advanced skills as vital for making Thailand a regional and global economic power. The ranks of the Yellow Shirts did not benefit to the same degree as the Red Shirts from Thaksin's policies.

The Yellow Shirts objected especially to Thaksin's seeming disregard for King Bhumibol. They rallied around the monarchy as a stabilizing force in society. Although the foreign press often labeled them "monarchists," it is more accurate to say they were "Bhumibol-ists." PAD supporters saw in Bhumibol a moral leadership, wisdom, and a paternal care for the kingdom's subjects that unified the nation. As stories about Bhumibol's declining health appeared in the press, they feared for his death. Like the old guard in the Privy Council, many among the Yellow Shirts wanted the monarchy to endure as a check on Thaksin or other authoritarian leaders like him. They viewed such leaders as a threat to their continued prosperity, social dominance, and even their understanding of "Thai-ness." They were also concerned that the enormous wealth of the palace would be diverted away from Bhumibol's idealistic projects, initiatives, and favored programs and redirected to the businesses of Thaksin and his cronies. Such a radical shift, they reasoned, would undermine their economic well-being and social status. These sentiments evolved over time into what PAD leader Sondhi Limthongku began to call "new politics," a restriction on directly elected representatives and a move away from the one person/one vote standard Thais had come to appreciate. It also welcomed intervention by the military, which would be placed under control of the king in times of political crisis. The "new politics" were actually more like the limited democracy of old.

More Protests and Another Coup

The PAD staged bigger and more frequent anti-Thaksin protests throughout the first half of 2006.

While the September 2006 coup d'état occurred without violence, the conflict it caused generated bloodshed that was genuine, shocking, and persistent. On New Year's Eve 2006, several bombs detonated in two waves around Bangkok. The first three bombs exploded early in the evening at a shopping mall, supermarket, and bus stop at the Victory Monument. A second wave hit a flyover and a popular seafood restaurant in the Central World shopping area. The blasts killed three and injured dozens, including foreign tourists. Bombs like these had become an almost daily occurrence in the southern provinces following the revival of a Muslim insurgency there, but Bangkok had largely been spared this kind of terrorism. The interim government blamed Thaksin and his supporters for the attacks. Despite an intense investigation, no person or group was ever positively linked to the bombs, and no one claimed responsibility. The ruling junta tried to cope with the growing violence both in Bangkok and nationally through the Internal Security Act (ISA) in 2007. The act revived the military's role in maintaining internal security. The ISA's purpose was to quell violence in the south and other parts of the country, but also to suppress antigovernment protestors in Bangkok.

In the months following Thaksin's removal, the coup leaders scrambled to prevent his return. In May 2007, they dissolved Thai Rak Thai and banned more than a hundred of its leading members, including Thaksin, from politics for five years. They applied new laws retroactively to find Thaksin and his associates guilty for actions related to the election of April 2006. The CNS froze Thaksin's assets valued at $2.3 billion. After acting under an interim constitution that concentrated power in the CNS, they rushed through a new constitution that stripped away many of the democratic elements that made the previous one so popular. The new charter cut the number of directly elected senators, limited the prime minister to two terms, prevented parliament members from easily switching parties, and contained other provisions designed to prevent Thaksin's return to power. It also strengthened the judiciary as a check on the power of the political parties. In promoting the draft ahead of a referendum, the government linked resistance to the document with opposition to the king. Slogans such as "Love the king ... vote for the draft charter" accompanied its roll-out. The Thai public approved the new constitution in a national referendum, but it was not popular as its passage owed more to a collective desire to end political strife than any popular support for increased authoritarianism.

Thaksin loyalists fought back by appropriating an existing political party, the People's Power Party (PPP), as a replacement for Thai Rak Thai. They set up offices in the old Thai Rak Thai headquarters, and to ensure their purpose was crystal clear, they created a new party logo that closely resembled the distinctive TRT symbol. Thaksin himself, banned from participating in the election, orchestrated the PPP's campaign from exile in Hong Kong. The PPP tapped Samak Sundaravej to be their standard-bearer in place of Thaksin. He was an unlikely champion for democracy. A staunchly right-wing lifetime politician who had held leadership positions in various governments in the 1970s and 1980s, he also had close ties to the palace and the military. He had played a role in inciting the violence of October 1976 by using a radio program to goad vigilante groups into attacking student demonstrators. A few years later, he formed his own far-right party. His other dubious credentials included strong support for the military's massacre of demonstrators in 1992.

In the lead up to the December 2007 election, the CNS pushed hard to discourage voters from supporting the PPP. It used its influence over the military and the national bureaucracy to undermine the appeal of Thaksin's proxy party. But despite the CNS's best efforts to thwart a Thaksin comeback, and despite Samak's largely undemocratic resume, the People's Power Party came out on top with more than 36 percent of the constituency polls and 233 of 480 seats in parliament. PPP won the northeast and the north handily, and made the strongest showing in the central region. The Democrat Party, favored by the establishment, fared better than it had in any election since the rise of Thaksin a decade earlier. It won the south and Bangkok, but also did well in the central region. The Democrats' improved fortunes were a pale victory, though, for the establishment. The 2007 election results showed that Thaksin, while considerably weaker than in his heyday only two years earlier, still had a strong appeal to Thai voters.

Thaksin Returns from Exile

Samak's administration rushed to undo the CNS's anti-Thaksin campaign. It formed a government with all the other parties except the Democrats, and set about trying to help Thaksin return from exile. Samak restored Thaksin's passport. He ordered personnel changes at the various government entities examining the Shinawatra family businesses for corruption and other crimes, purportedly to derail their investigations of Thaksin. By February 2008, Thaksin and his wife Pojaman Shinawatra felt secure enough to return to Thailand. Although Thaksin claimed to be out of politics, he did not act as such. After pressing his head to the ground at the airport for the benefit of reporters and supporters who had gathered for his return, he embarked on a tour of 99 Buddhist temples in the north and northeast. The trips, while ostensibly religious, included official greetings from leading politicians in his former electoral strongholds. Thaksin's efforts appeared aimed at rebuilding the coalition that brought Thai Rak Thai to its unparalleled political domination. Further worrying his opponents was a rumor that Thaksin planned to return not as prime minister but as the president of a newly republican Thailand. Such a scenario suggested the eradication of the monarchy. Thailand's Assets Examination Committee (AEC) investigated the Shinawatras for violations of the National Counter Corruption Act. The Criminal Court took on the tax evasion charges while the Supreme Court considered abuse of power.

Alarmed by Thaksin's return and Samak's victory in the elections, the anti-Thaksin PAD ramped up its activities. Sondhi Limthongku's Yellow Shirts held academic conferences and rallies throughout the city. Although such moves did not enjoy widespread support among Bangkok's politically weary denizens, PAD leaders pushed for more and increasingly heated confrontations with the government. In May 2008, some ten thousand Yellow Shirts had set off from the Democracy Monument to march on Government House, the complex housing the offices of the prime minister and the cabinet. Police stopped the marchers at the Makkhawan Bridge. Unable to advance, they set up a camp that became the focus of noisy antigovernment protests for several months. The camp also became a gathering place for well-to-do women, who arrived daily in luxury cars accompanied by their servants. They were sincere in their devotion to the PAD cause, but they also embraced the rallies as a newly fashionable activity, like a street fair or neighborhood picnic. Vendors sold food, pro-monarchy merchandise, and music CDs of royalist songs. Speakers stirred up the crowds with warnings about the danger that Thaksin posed for the establishment, especially the monarchy. A symbol of these often loud and spirited events was a noisemaker shaped like two plastic hands that made a clattering racket when shaken back and forth. Later, the Red Shirts produced their response to the yellow hand-clapper in the form of a red foot-shaped noisemaker. In Thailand, the foot is the lowest part of the body, both physically and spiritually. In polite company, one must never point a foot or bare a sole at another person. To do so intentionally is a deep insult, akin to the Western taunt of raising a middle finger. The irritating rattle of the plastic noisemakers became the sound of dissent for both sides.

In July 2008, the Criminal Court found Thaksin's wife Pojaman guilty of tax evasion on profits of 546 million baht earned from stock sales. The court issued a three-year sentence but allowed her to remain free while appealing the verdict. The Supreme Court considered whether Thaksin's premiership had aided Pojaman in her 2003 purchase of Bangkok business real estate at what appeared to be a fraction of its market value. In Beijing for the Olympics that summer, Thaksin and Pojaman chose exile in London rather than return to Bangkok to face the court's verdict. In October 2008, the Supreme Court found Thaksin guilty of abuse of power and sentenced him in absentia to two years in jail.

A Fight for Ruins

During this period of domestic turmoil, the Samak government stumbled into a conflict with Cambodia over the Angkor-era ruins that Thailand calls Phra Wihan. Although the origins of the conflict dates to events from the colonial age and the Cold War, the dispute escalated largely because of the PAD's antigovernment rhetoric. In 2007, Cambodia proposed listing the contested ruins, which it calls Preah Vihear, as a UNESCO World Heritage site. Noppadon Pattama, Samak's foreign minister (and Thaksin's lawyer), agreed that Thailand would co-sign the application in a joint communique to the

UN agency. The move inflamed Thai chauvinist sentiments that have their roots in a dispute dating from the early 1960s. The remains of the twelfth-century temple sit astride the Thai-Cambodian border on the edge of the Dangrek mountains above a steep and breathtakingly beautiful watershed. But because the temple complex is located on a cliff's edge above Cambodia's plains, visitors must pass through Thailand to gain access to it. French colonial administration surveyors had drawn the border to put Phra Wihan in Cambodian territory. In signing treaties that fixed the border in 1907, Siam's leaders failed to notice that the borderlines deviated slightly to give France the scenic temple. They did not understand the implications until several decades later when they conducted their own surveys.

Thailand regained the territory when it annexed sections of Cambodia during World War II. After the war, the international community forced Thailand to return Phra Wihan when it gave up its territorial claims on Cambodia. In pressing its claim on the site after the war, Thailand invoked the history of its "lost territories" to French colonialists. Thailand and Cambodia negotiated their competing claims to the site in 1957–58. When negotiations ended in a deadlock, Prince Norodom Sihanouk, Cambodia's leader, sought to present Cambodia to the world's press as a victim of Bangkok's regional imperialist claims. While this campaign won some sympathy for Cambodia, especially with Communist bloc states and nonaligned nations, it did not deliver Phra Wihan to Phnom Penh. Sihanouk took his case to the United Nation's International Court of Justice (ICJ) at the Hague. In 1960–61, the ICJ heard claims from both countries' representatives. In June 1962, the court delivered its decision with a nine to three vote in Cambodia's favor. An ICJ judge cited several previous Franco-Thai negotiations, in 1937 and 1946, during which Thailand could have disputed the border but had failed to do so. The ICJ ordered Thailand to withdraw its troops from the site, and delivered full sovereignty to Cambodia. The court's decision stunned the Thai public. They felt betrayed by Cambodia, a country they had come to view as Thailand's weaker sibling. Under pressure from an angry Thai populace, Thai leaders vowed that they would one day get Phra Wihan back.

The opportunity came in the aftermath of the Indochina Wars. Heavy fighting in Cambodia and along the border had made any visit to Phra Wihan/Preah Vihear almost impossible for Thais between 1973 and 1991. Following the peace agreement between Cambodia's warring factions in the early 1990s, tourists eager to see this formerly closed-off site began visiting it again. Foreign tourists entering from Thailand had to present their passports to Cambodian officials at the northern entrance of Phra Wihan/Preah Vihear to pass into what was technically Cambodian territory. Both countries collected visitors' fees, and the arrangement worked well for more than a decade. But when Noppadon agreed on behalf of Thailand to support Cambodia's World Heritage initiative, the PAD pounced on the agreement as evidence that Thaksin had sold out Thailand's territorial claims for his own gain. Thaksin had business interests in Cambodia, including a stake in a casino. To the PAD, the acquiescence to Cambodia's plans looked like Thaksin's proxies were using their positions to further his business interests abroad. The political spat would fester in the coming months before erupting in fighting between Thai and Cambodian troops near the site in 2008. Both countries put troops into the disputed area while political activists in Phnom Penh and Bangkok whipped up jingoistic ire among their respective citizens. From 2008 to 2011, Thai and Cambodian armies clashed at the border, firing assault rifles, M-79 grenades, and mortar rounds at each other. At different points in the dispute, both sides accused the other's troops of invading their territory. The ongoing fighting added international tension to the domestic political conflict between the Red Shirts and Yellow Shirts, with both sides accusing the other of selling out the nation to Cambodia.

Protest Camps

Throughout the country, the PAD Yellow Shirts clashed with groups of UDD Red Shirts. At first, the conflicts involved shouting and the occasional fight. When the PAD staged rallies in the northeast, in the heart of Thaksin's electoral base, the violence escalated. At rallies in Udon Thani and Sisaket, factions from both sides went at each other with sticks, causing a few dozen injuries on each side. In August, the level of violence escalated following the PAD seizure of Government House. In the rallies surrounding this operation, the well-heeled ladies in yellow were joined by gangs of armed young men who served as guards. These ad hoc security teams wielded arsenals of Molotov cocktails, air rifles, slingshots, swords, homemade bombs, and every kind of truncheon, stick, or bludgeon. The Thai police disarmed some of the guards, but the Thai government did not move to evict the protestors or dismantle the protests. Even when the demonstrators violated injunctions and broke other laws, the authorities did little to counter their provocations. By the end of August, PAD groups had occupied provincial airports and train stations. Government leaders under Samak appeared unable to order the military to strike against a movement pledged to defend the king. But their patience and their cautiousness were running thin in places high and low.

Indirectly, the palace tried to signal its disapproval of the escalating violence of the PAD rallies. Princess Maha Chakri Sirindhorn, the closest of the royal children to King Bhumibol, suggested in a televised interview that the PAD leaders were acting on behalf of their own interests and not those of the monarchy. Others close to the king sent messages to PAD leaders encouraging them to end the confrontations. Much of Bangkok, including many who had supported the PAD's original aims, had grown frustrated by the disruptions and delays caused by the occupation of Government House, airports, train and bus terminals, and rally sites around the city. They were also increasingly alarmed by the apocalyptic tone emerging from the PAD's rhetoric. The PAD leadership seemed to ignore the entreaties of the palace and the frustration of the people. Rather than back down, Sondhi raised the pitch of the antigovernment message.

In June, Samak's government survived a censure motion of no confidence brought by the opposition Democrat Party. But his People's Power Party was barely holding itself together. Amidst the pressure brought on by the PAD protests and opposition motions, it suffered from high-level defections and the loss of other party leaders to political bans brought by the Supreme Court for such violations as concealing assets and vote buying. A couple of months later, Samak himself was ousted as prime minister for a more unusual violation. In September 2008, the Constitutional Court found Samak had violated conflict of interest laws by continuing to appear on televised cooking shows while he was prime minister. (It is unconstitutional for the prime minister to receive a salary for other work while in office.) Beset by growing challenges from within his own party and suffering from liver cancer, Samak did not fight to regain the spot.

The PPP replaced Samak with Somchai Wongsawat, a retired senior civil servant and former judge who was Thaksin's brother-in-law. In late September, the National Assembly elected him prime minister, beating out his closest Democrat challenger. Somchai struggled to lead the country. PAD activists sought to stop his cabinet from convening, a constitutional requirement for all new governments, by blockading the parliament. The police ordered them to dismantle the armed camp, but to no avail. Finally, police fired explosive tear gas canisters directly into the crowds and broke into the PAD encampment. Yellow Shirt guards responded by hurling homemade bombs, powerful firecrackers, and other explosive devices at police. A chaotic battle ensued with both sides attacking the other. Many suffered serious injuries, including the loss of limbs. The Yellow Shirts drove cars and trucks into police lines. A few blocks away from the main conflict, a PAD leader was killed when his Jeep exploded, probably from accidently detonating explosives he was transporting. But the casualty that drew the most attention was the death of a 28-year-old woman. The college-educated middle-class Yellow Shirt died from catastrophic internal injuries caused by a bomb blast. Public outrage over her death drove many to condemn the police for using force indiscriminately and excessively.

With the deaths and street violence, many Thais expected the king to intervene to stop the confrontations. They expected a declaration like the one he had made in 1973 and 1992 to pressure both sides into backing down. Many hoped he would make some grand gesture before the kingdom that would ease tensions between the color-shirted factions. King Bhumibol made no public statement, but Queen Sirikit came forward and inserted herself directly into the PAD's campaign. Sirikit helped cover the cost of hospital care for the PAD wounded. She attended the dead young woman's funeral, and even praised her for seeking to protect the monarchy.

After delivering a policy address at the Parliament in October, Prime Minister Somchai was forced to flee when PAD demonstrators besieged the building in an attempt to take the assembled lawmakers hostage. With the power cut and the exits blocked, Somchai escaped by climbing over a fence behind the building. Unable to enter the prime minister's office during the siege, he tried to continue working from offices at Don Mueang Airport. But PAD demonstrators pursued him relentlessly, hounding his public appearances. When Somchai tried to visit a telecommunications office, Yellow Shirts pelted him with shoes and water bottles as he left the building. Finally, Somchai withdrew to the north to work out of Chiang Mai. In the midst of the crisis of 2008, the National Counter-Corruption Committee found him guilty of dereliction of duty from his days working for the Department of Justice eight years earlier.

In November 2008, PAD leader Sondhi Limthongkul pushed his followers into a "final battle" against the PPP-led government. His strategy was to escalate the mayhem and violence to the point that the military would intervene and overthrow the government in a coup. Gangs of PAD provocateurs armed with clubs, slingshots, and even firearms pursued ministers and surrounded government offices throughout the city. In some cases, violence erupted between the armed PAD gangs and government supporters. As if in response to the escalation in tactics, anti-PAD forces struck back at the Yellow Shirt sites. In two separate nighttime incidents, unidentified assailants threw grenades into the PAD's armed camp inside Government House, injuring several. Other attacks against PAD sites caused injuries and deaths. Army officers sympathetic to the PAD began to give the movement's armed guards training in military tactics.

Things came to a head in late November. On November 24, the day Prime Minister Somchai was due to return to Thailand from an overseas trip, a group of PAD activists occupied Suvarnabhumi International Airport. With photos of King Bhumibol and national flags held aloft, they pushed through security cordons and poured into the airport. Wielding iron bars, bats, and golf clubs, mobs of Yellow Shirts stormed the complex. During their week-long occupation, they vandalized rooms, seized ammunition and weapons, stole valuables from shops and offices, destroyed monuments, and even set up bomb-making works. Thousands of foreign tourists found themselves stranded when it became clear that the PAD had shut down the airport. Airport authorities tried to shift flights to the domestic airport, Don Mueang, but PAD activists rushed there and occupied it as well. Their occupation disrupted international passenger and cargo flights, stranding some 350,000 foreign travelers. At risk also were ninety international aircraft grounded on the tarmac. Foreign embassies pressed the government to lift the siege. Thai authorities evacuated some of the stranded passengers from the military's U-Tapao air base outside the capital, but most remained trapped in Thailand while the siege continued. Demonstrators attacked police checkpoints and clashed with security forces throughout the occupation. PAD leader Sondhi threatened to "shoot back" if the police fired upon the attacking Yellow Shirts. The police did little in response to continued provocations. They were concerned with potential injuries to the occupiers if they struck back. They also feared possible retribution from those high-ranking officials who sympathized with the pro-monarchy mob. When a bomb explosion at the airport injured fifty Yellow Shirt occupiers, four of them seriously, the PAD's other leader, the political ascetic Chamlong Srimuang, called on the police to provide protection. Throughout the siege, rumors circulated that a coup led by the military was imminent. But army intervention never materialized. Instead, a combination of court decisions and pressure from the palace and business leaders helped end the siege and halt the escalating violence.

Tarnishing a Global Image

Over the past thirty years or so, in a period coinciding with Thailand's rise as a global tourist destination, Thai leaders have been especially concerned with the kingdom's image abroad. The assault on the international airport dealt a blow to Thailand's reputation as an ideal destination for international tourists. Foreign news coverage of the airport seizure showed frightened and angry tourists fretting for their safety as they searched for ways to get home. Background features on the related political violence painted a picture of a fractured and violent society that undermined the Tourism Authority of Thailand's carefully orchestrated advertising campaigns showing a stable, safe, and welcoming society. With foreign tourism as a cornerstone of the economy, these stories threatened to cause severe harm to the kingdom. Thailand had long held a near monopoly on foreign tourism to mainland Southeast Asia, but by the early 1990s the kingdom had to compete increasingly with its neighbors. With the peace treaty between its warring factions in 1991 and elections in 1994, Cambodia welcomed tourists who had long wanted to see the ruins of the mighty Angkor-era empire. Vietnam, too, saw a spike in tourist arrivals after the United States and other countries lifted their trade embargo and normalized relations in the mid-1990s. Laos had also emerged as a favorite destination for those foreign tourists who had found Thailand's tourist sites to be overly commercialized, inauthentic, or crowded. Apart from tourism, the disruptions also threatened to scare off foreign investors, especially important as Thailand's economy was still rebounding after the financial crisis of 1997. Disruptions in cargo flights hurt importers, manufactures, and other businesses that relied on the airport for timely arrivals. Ultimately, the occupation would cost Thailand an estimated 290 billion baht or 3 percent of its GDP.

Leaders of the business community and the military pressed the two sides to end the conflict. Together they offered a deal to the battling factions in which the PAD would end their occupations and the government would resign. Both sides rejected the proposal. In the end, though, it was the judiciary that brought about an end to the crisis of 2008. On December 2, 2008, the Constitutional Court dissolved the PPP. It based its decision on the July 2008 conviction of PPP deputy chairman Yongyuth Tiyapairat for vote buying. The court also banned Somchai and other party leaders from politics for five years. Chavarat Charnvirakul stepped in as acting prime minister. After a tumultuous few months at the top, Somchai seemed to welcome his exit from politics. His departure and the dissolution of the government allowed Sondhi and the Yellow Shirts to proclaim victory. After some hesitation, they ended their siege of the airports and government buildings.

Thaksin's allies tried to reconstitute their ruling coalition by creating a new party, the Phuea Thai ("For Thais") Party. Despite having Thaksin behind it, the new party lacked the organization and funding to make it a credible opposition to the Democrats. With so many of the People's Power Party's MPs having defected to other parties or been banned from holding office, Thaksin's successor party was a shell of what Thai Rak Thai had been. The rival Democrat Party was able to lure away enough of the minor parties that had formerly supported the PPP to claim a majority. On December 15, the Parliament elected

Democrat leader Abhisit Vejjajiva prime minister, the fourth in a year.

Abhisit was the quintessential establishment political figure. He came from a prominent Sino-Thai family who had received their family name, meaning "medical profession," from King Vajiravudh himself. His great-grandfather and father had held important positions in the Ministry of Public Health at different points in the twentieth century. Abhisit was born in Britain and was educated at Eton College and Oxford University. He relocated to Thailand in his twenties to take up politics. In 1992, he was elected to parliament at age twenty-seven. Within a few years, he had become a rising star in the Democrat Party, and in 2005 became its leader.

Once installed as prime minister by military and judicial intervention, Abhisit appeared reluctant to return the country to democracy. Despite decrying the street violence and army intervention, Abhisit chose to put off national elections for more than two and a half years. His cabinet was also checkered and suspect. Some were familiar names who were better known for their survival instincts than their integrity. Others were new and inexperienced. The cabinet included a Yellow Shirt leader, a beer heiress with royal blood, an Oxford classmate, a massage parlor tycoon, and a couple of wives of disgraced politicians who came aboard as proxies for their banned husbands. He granted cabinet seats to the military-connected Bhumjai Thai ("Thai Pride") Party. The Democrat-Bhumjai Thai cabinet increased military spending and gave top military positions to officers close to General Anupong Paochinda. Abhisit came across as honest but unimaginative. He lacked charisma and the common touch. In public appearances, he was stiff and scripted. His efforts to generate public support for the government's position mostly failed.

In the meantime, Thaksin worked to destabilize Abhisit's government by inciting his Red Shirt followers into demonstrations. Taking a page from the PAD violence of the previous year, the United Front for Democracy Against Dictatorship's Red Shirts staged disruptive demonstrations throughout Bangkok and other Thai cities. From his exile, now in Dubai, Thaksin addressed Red Shirt rallies via a video-link carried on giant screens. He boldly denounced key figures in the king's Privy Council, the military, and the courts for their role in removing him from power and allegedly trying to assassinate him.

Invoking the history of antigovernment demonstrations from 1973 and 1992, he called on his followers to rescue Thailand's democracy from the institutions – the military, the palace, and the bureaucratic elite – that have thwarted it. Heartened by his words, the antigovernment demonstrations grew. Many who had voted for Thai Rak Thai candidates hoped their street protests would facilitate Thaksin's return to Thailand. They took to the streets in noisy demonstrations to protest Abhisit's administration and to demand elections. Their rallies gained momentum during the first part of the year, with participation growing from about 20,000 to 100,000. In one protest, they rallied at the prime minister's office to demand he resign. In another, they converged on the home of Prem Tinsulanonda to accuse him of orchestrating the coup that removed Thaksin from power.

During the second week of April, the Red Shirts staged their most ambitious protest activities. The timing for their street actions was significant. Traditionally, Thailand has marked the start of the new year with its Songkran Festival on April 13. Most people celebrate for several days before and after the date. During this period, nearly all the work of the nation comes to a halt. Businesses close, factories shut down, and offices are abandoned to allow people time to relax and reflect. Many migrant laborers travel from the cities back to their family homes in the countryside. The religiously minded seek an auspicious start to the year through good work and devotions. They make merit (*tham bun*) at *wat* by donating money, offering food and supplies to monks, doing needed repairs, and washing the sacred icons there. In modern times, young people pursue fun in the streets with water. Coming at the hottest time of the year, when the rains of the monsoon are still a month or so away, the youngsters douse each other with water hurled from every possible conveyance. From midday into the wee hours, they use cups, buckets, barrels, high-velocity squirt guns (sometimes loaded with chili-spiked water), and hoses to splash friends and strangers alike. Usually, the water assaulters finish off their soaking victims by rubbing talcum powder into their faces. Increasingly, revelers have upped the mayhem by hurling firecrackers and other pyrotechnics. It is a wild, fun, and sometimes frenzied celebration that is, for the most part, a socially healthy pressure release in a still highly hierarchical society. Unfortunately, some revelers become excessively intoxicated, and every year sees injuries, accidents, fights, and sexual assaults.

In the days before Songkran 2009, Thaksin's supporters launched their most ambitious demonstrations against Abhisit's government. The holiday season and extra trains and buses operating for Songkran made it easier for people to move. On April 8, tens of thousands of Red Shirts rallied in central Bangkok. Bolstered by thousands from the north and northeast, they demonstrated outside Government House and, once again, Prem's house. Taxi drivers parked their cabs on the vital road arteries around the Victory Monument to bring the city's traffic to a halt. Bangkok's already terrible traffic remained gridlocked for more than a day. Thaksin's supporters coordinated similar rallies in cities and towns throughout the country. On April 10, Red Shirts descended on the beach resort town of Pattaya, a couple of hours' drive from the capital. Abhisit was there to host a summit of the Association of Southeast Asian Nations (ASEAN). In an atmosphere of rising tension, Thaksin exhorted his supporters to "swarm the summit venue." On April 11, thousands of Red Shirt demonstrators smashed through the glass doors of the Royal Cliff Beach Hotel, where nine of Asia's leaders and their delegations were staying and occupied the building. Waving Thai flags, overturning tables, and blowing horns, the pro-Thaksin crowd moved through the building chanting "Abhisit get out!" Outside the hotel, pro-government groups wielding clubs, bricks, and slingshots fought with Red Shirts. Someone threw smoke bombs into the battle lines.

In the midst of the chaos, helicopters airlifted the visiting leaders, including those from China, Japan, and South Korea, from the hotel's roof. Abhisit's administration was deeply humiliated by the attack, and was forced to cancel the summit. A principal focus of the summit was a discussion of strategies for protecting the region's fragile economic recovery. Thailand, which neighboring countries blamed for the economic meltdown in 1997, was now accused of harming the recovery effort because it was incapable of providing adequate security to the assembled leaders. Back in Bangkok, Abhisit himself barely escaped falling into the hands of a mob. Demonstrators attacked his motorcade as it left the Ministry of the Interior. The crowd smashed up his car before his driver was finally able to ferry him to safety. In personal and political terms, Abhisit came across as weak and bumbling.

On April 13, Songkran, the government struck back. It deployed thousands of soldiers in full combat gear to the capital to break up the protesters. The troops marched through the areas occupied by the Red Shirts, launching teargas canisters and firing rifles at the demonstrators. Later, the army would claim that they fired blanks at the crowds and live fire only in the air, but scores died from gunshot wounds that day. The Red Shirts responded with Molotov cocktails, burning tires, slingshots, and even bombs fashioned from propane gas canisters. They sent commandeered city buses into the advancing army lines. After a day of street fighting and explosions, the Red Shirt defenses crumbled. Most protesters slipped away to avoid the army's advance. Those who chose to remain at Government House surrendered the following day after the army had surrounded their positions. The government shut down the Red Shirts' radio and Internet broadcasts, then rounded up the UDD leaders and charged them with rebellion. In doing so, they set the stage for the Battle of Bangkok.

CHAPTER 16

A STRUGGLE FOR THAILAND'S POLITICAL FUTURE

In 2010, political violence in Thailand hit its nadir in the modern era. It began with Abhisit Vejjajiv ordering tighter security on Red Shirt activities in the lead-up to a Supreme Court decision on $2.3 billion in frozen Shinawatra assets that the government had seized in 2006, which Thaksin sought to regain. Even before Thaksin called for new protests, his followers had gathered throughout the city, including at the Supreme Court, to demand he be allowed to return. Thaksin called for calm ahead of the decision, still hoping for a favorable resolution, but tensions ran high. The judges were reported to have worn bulletproof vests when entering the courthouse. On February 25, 2010, the court found Thaksin and his wife guilty of concealing assets and abusing power. The ruling allowed for the seizure of $1.4 billion of the frozen assets while returning about $900 million to Thaksin. Angered by this loss and by his inability to return to Thailand, Thaksin called for more protests in March 2010. Like the year before, his appeal for political action drew tens of thousands of supporters to Bangkok. On March 14, they set up a camp at the Phan Fa Lilat Bridge before extending their sites into the government district around Government House. Acting on Thaksin's behalf, Red Shirt leaders demanded that Abhisit dissolve parliament immediately and call early elections ahead of a vote scheduled for late 2011. Thaksin's supporters saw Abhisit as an illegitimate prime minister who had come to power through the extralegal influence of the military and the palace on the courts, a view not exclusively theirs. Many Thai voters who cherished democracy, even those who abhorred Thaksin for his plutocratic tendencies, resented the intrusion of the military and the palace into political affairs. After two weeks of noisy protests, including one in which some Red Shirts threw their blood at Government House, Abhisit and the UDD leaders met to negotiate. Television stations broadcast the meetings live to the nation. Abhisit offered elections in late 2010, a year early, but demanded an immediate end to protests. Thaksin instructed the Red Shirt negotiators to reject the offer and the talks stalled. Both sides remained steadfast in their original demands.

In the days that followed, the protestors occupied Ratchaprasong Intersection, right at the heart of twenty-first century Bangkok. The site includes some of the most popular high-end shopping centers and tourist hotels, but also the Erawan Shrine, Wat Pathum Wanaram, Princess Sirindhorn's royal residence, and several important police buildings, including the Royal Thai Police Headquarters. With the seizure of the shopping districts, the protest sites grew substantially, and the Red Shirt camps claimed more of Bangkok's center. Over time, the Ratchaprasong encampment grew to include Lumpini Park and parts of the financial district. The more militant Red Shirts constructed defensive perimeters around the camps using giant tires, boards, debris, and sharpened bamboo poles pointing outward. These fearsome-looking ramparts were four meters high in some parts.

Inside the camps, the Red Shirts built a city within a city. They set up tents, food stalls, shops, and sleeping quarters. Supporters listened to pro-democracy speeches and musical performances. They sang Red Shirt anthems and made pro-democracy placards. Speakers denounced Abhisit's government and called for Thaksin's return. Many of Thaksin's followers had come from the northeast. The food they ate and the music they danced to originated in the ethnic Lao areas of the Isan region. Their political slogans were earthy, even coarse, compared to those that the city protestors had used in 1973 and 1992. The ethnomusicologist Benjamin Tausig's study *Bangkok is Ringing: Sound, Protest, and Restraint* explored how these rural people used the sounds of their folk songs and improvised speeches within the skyscraper valleys of Bangkok's urban environment to convey their opinions and hopes to the capital, the government, and the nation as a whole. Many of Bangkok's urbanites looked down on these rural people as hayseeds who were incapable of understanding complex political affairs. Some resented the occupation for disrupting their daily routines. The Red Shirts had set up roadblocks at key intersections around the camps, further slowing Bangkok's already sluggish traffic flow. Locals tried to disband the protestors. One Saturday in the middle of the occupation, thousands of Bangkok residents gathered in Lumpini Park with signs that expressed their anger at the disruptions. Others found the vehemence of Red Shirts' convictions to be unsettling. Formerly, educated city-dwellers had taken the lead in bringing about political change through mass protest. These urbanites could not yet accept their rural compatriots as equal partners in the political arena. It was common for many residents to dismiss the protestors as "poor and stupid."

As temperatures rose in April, Bangkok's hottest month, both sides grew more provocative. On April 8, some 5,000 Red Shirt protestors stormed the Parliament building, just after the cabinet had voted to extend the Internal Security Act that guided official responses to the protests. Besieged by the occupiers, the cabinet ministers escaped out the back of the building, climbing over a rear wall and hopping aboard a waiting Blackhawk helicopter that spirited them away. After the incident, Abhisit declared a state of emergency, a move that outlawed any gathering of more than five people. The government added more security forces to encircle the roughly 100,000 demonstrators near Government House. The Red Shirt leadership believed that they could win public support and sink Abhisit's government if the army were to attack the demonstrators. History guided their conclusions. They saw the army's bloody crackdown on unarmed demonstrators in 1973 and 1992 as potential models for their success in 2010. They believed that the public would rally to their side if the army shed blood. As Abhisit added more troops, the Red Shirt leaders' rhetoric grew more defiant. Red Shirt leader Jatuporn Prompan openly challenged the soldiers, demanding that they either attack or disperse.

On April 10, the army attempted to dislodge the protestors from their camps, attacking the demonstrators initially with batons, rubber bullets, teargas, and water cannons. The protestors fought back with clubs, iron bars, and slingshots. The army brought in helicopters to drop teargas into the camps. As the fighting intensified, black-shirted militants among the protestors threw petrol bombs and fired guns at the military lines. Gangs of youths, mostly boys and young men, joined them. The urban battles raged into the evening with both sides accumulating casualties. As night fell, Red Shirt militants ambushed an army unit on Dinso Road south of the Democracy Monument. They struck with grenades, killing an army general and wounding his deputy. Rattled by the attack, troops fired wildly into the crowds surrounding them. They killed twenty civilians in their reprisal, including a Japanese journalist.

The armed resistance among the protestors routed the attacking army units, but many demonstrators fled the camps during the clashes. In the following days, the Red Shirts abandoned their redoubt near the government offices on Ratchadamnoen Avenue and consolidated their positions in the Ratchaprasong shopping district. Pools of blood, bullet casings, and burning debris littered the site of the now-abandoned camp. The news media transmitted images of the violent clashes to the world via television and the Internet. The bloodshed stunned the world, especially those who had come to know Thailand only as a vacation spot. Thailand's reputation as the land of *mai pen rai* ("never mind") was another casualty of the April fighting. Many holidaymakers, medical tourists, and business delegates postponed or canceled their trips to the kingdom. A month into the demonstrations, the government set up blockades on the main routes from the northeast into Bangkok. To counter such moves, antigovernment activists sought to block soldiers boarding trains at upcountry rail stations to prevent them from deploying to Bangkok.

A militant faction among the Red Shirts set about reinforcing the defenses around the camp located at the southern section of Lumpini Park opposite Silom Road. The area is among the most popular with foreign tourists because of the many bars, restaurants, and shops found along Silom and its side streets. The camp became the nucleus for the more provocative Red Shirts who favored violent confrontation over peaceful protest. These rogue militants had earlier attacked a Yellow Shirt office with gunfire and grenades, wounding a police officer. The militants became known as "Black Shirts" or "Men in Black" for the black military tunics, long-sleeved shirts, and bush hats that many of them wore. They brandished pistols, military assault rifles, and grenade launchers to provoke the army and police by firing upon their ranks from within a human screen of unarmed demonstrators. At night, some would slip out of the camp to strike at the security forces in surprise attacks. In response to the attacks, the army brought in even more troops to its massive security perimeter. The military also put snipers in the buildings and pedestrian walkways overlooking the camp. When fired upon from the camp, the troops shot back. A no-go zone of a few hundred yards separated the two groups. As the occupation wore on, casualties mounted. Nearly all of the dead were civilian protestors.

The conflict between the Red Shirts and Yellow Shirts had parallels in Thailand's security forces. In the simplest terms, the police stood with Thaksin while the army supported the royalists. The divide reflected Thaksin's origins in the police, while the army's stance mirrored the dominance of retired army generals on the king's Privy Council. When security forces clashed with protestors, army units led the forays while the police units reportedly slipped away in the confusion. There were exceptions on both sides of the army-police divide. In the army, some enlisted soldiers and junior officers, especially those from low-income families, admired Thaksin for his stated devotion to the poor. Some police, especially those who were ardent royalists, favored the Yellow Shirts against Thaksin. But, institutionally, the two groups remained loyal to their respective factions. One of these exceptions played a prominent role in the violent clashes of 2010.

During the crackdown of April 10, assailants killed one high-ranking army officer and injured another in Bangkok in a street attack. The victims had links to General Anupong and the army faction that dominated the king's Privy Council. The attack appeared to be the work of pro-Thaksin troops known as "watermelons" because they were said to be green on the outside and red on the inside. Many believed that these troops served a charismatic renegade army officer who led the Red Shirts militant faction.

Maj. Gen. Khattiya Sawatdiphon was the rare Royal Thai Army officer who openly supported Thaksin. Khattiya was a career soldier who had started as a Thahan Phran (literally "hunter soldier"), a paramilitary unit that fought insurgents along Thailand's northeastern border in the late 1970s and 1980s. Although they are often called "Thai Rangers," the Thahan Phran were less like the elite US Army Rangers and more like a motley force composed of professional soldiers, local volunteers, and ill-disciplined thugs. Frequently, they were accused of using terror tactics and extrajudicial killings against suspected communists.

For several years, Khattiya had spoken out about the Red Shirts' need to learn military tactics to protect themselves. He helped train the Red Shirt guards tasked with defending the demonstrators and their encampments, and appeared to be one of the leaders of the militant Black Shirts. Khattiya's own uniform, he said, was the same one he had worn while fighting the communists as a Thahan Phran. His pro-Thaksin stance and political activity had drawn censure from the RTA leadership when he first started to speak out against the government. The army sought to neutralize him by assigning duties that would keep him away from the street confrontations. When he returned to the Red Shirts, Khattiya became something like a talismanic celebrity. Known popularly by his nickname "Seh Daeng," he signed autographs on the demonstrators' shirts, posed for photos, and gave interviews to local and foreign press. He had written about his military exploits in several books, and his followers devoured these tales of derring-do. Khattiya believed that his presence made the demonstrators feel safe. But not all agreed with his activities at the barricades. Some Red Shirts blamed him for escalating the tension and increasing the threat of more violence.

On April 22, militants in the camp fired five M-79 grenades striking the Sala Daeng BTS station and Silom Road. Their target was a group of pro-government demonstrators who had gathered on Silom. Yellow Shirt activists had started to organize counterdemonstrations at Ratchadamnoen Avenue and Silom Road to express their support for the king. Their secondary message, equally important, was to support the government and denounce Thaksin and his followers. They demanded a crackdown on the Red Shirts. The grenade attack targeting them on Silom Road killed three and wounded eighty. Unidentified assailants carried out other bombings and arson attacks across Thailand in late April. The militancy spurred by the "Men in Black" faction had started to undermine support for the Red Shirt movement, including from those who favored a more democratic political system. Khattiya continued to challenge the surrounding troops with escalating bravado. His outspoken militancy made him a target for the army units targeting the camp. While being interviewed by a *New York Times* reporter, Khattiya said, "The military cannot get in here." A moment later, a sniper's bullet struck him in the head. He lingered for a day in the hospital before dying of the head wound.

The crisis of 2010 came to a bloody end on May 19. Just after 6:00 am, Royal Thai Army troops in armored vehicles smashed through the spiked bamboo barricades at the southern end of the site. Militants inside set fire to their fortifications to shield their positions and cover their escape in clouds of black smoke. Troops charged into the camp, firing their assault rifles as they advanced. "Come out and surrender or we'll kill you," the soldiers called to the demonstrators. Some protestors surrendered, but most fled in panic. Soldiers fired wildly into the camp, hitting not only some surrendering demonstrators but also some journalists and medical workers. According to press accounts, a hardcore unit of Red Shirt guards remained to fire upon the advancing troops. Red Shirt leader Jatuporn Prompan surrendered to the soldiers. He called for a peaceful cessation to protestors' activities, but the chaos and violence continued. Arsonists among the Red Shirts set fire to more than thirty buildings throughout Bangkok. Government offices, supermarkets, and even a grand old cinema went up in flames. The Central World Shopping Plaza, the giant mall at the center of the Ratchaprasong encampment, burned spectacularly.

The security forces and Red Shirt guards battled throughout the day as casualties mounted on both sides. By midday, the Red Shirt resistors had lost most of their encampment. Outnumbered and outgunned, they withdrew to positions farther north up Ratchadamri Road. The troops pressed on, capturing sections of Lumpini Park claimed by Red Shirts. Protestors fled into the grounds of Wat Pathum Wanaram, a leafy Buddhist temple complex wedged between two shopping malls, and tried to hide in the buildings. Army riflemen positioned along the BTS rail track and on Rama I Road fired into the temple grounds, hitting the demonstrators who had taken refuge in the *wat*. The site had been designated a "safe zone," a religious site to be left alone by both sides. Later, the soldiers would say they fired upon

Black Shirts who were shooting at them from the temple. Six died from gunshot wounds there. A day later, on May 28, the government issued an arrest warrant for Thaksin on terrorism charges stemming from the militant-led violence. They issued similar warrants for top leaders of the Red Shirts' United Front for Democracy Against Dictatorship.

For all of the bloodshed, destruction, and anxiety caused by the crisis of 2010, very little changed on Thailand's political landscape. The public largely scorned both factions and their leaders for their roles in the disorder visited upon the capital. The Red Shirts sacrificed the public's sympathy by tolerating or even encouraging the militants among their ranks to use violence against the soldiers. The government lost the people's support when it appeared unable to end the protests quickly or peacefully. Negotiators for both sides seemed beholden to the hardliners of their factions. Attempts at compromise went nowhere as each side repeatedly rejected the other's offers while never moving far from their original positions. The two sides remained intransigent in their allegiances and antipathies. The army steadfastly maintained its right to intervene in politics. And the palace's influence continued to fade even as pro-monarchy forces grew ever more strident. Thai people outside the Yellow Shirt and Red Shirt movements were fed up with the divisions and disruptions of the political battles, but had little power to stop them.

Yingluck Shinawatra, Thailand's First Female Prime Minister
In 2011, the government tried to move forward by holding elections. On July 3, the voters put Abhisit's Democrat-led coalition out of power and made Thai Rak Thai's successor party, Pheu Thai, the winner. Pheu Thai took a majority with 265 seats to the Democrats' 158. Pheu Thai's landslide was evidence that Thaksin's followers had not abandoned him even in his exile. Thaksin made his younger sister, Yingluck Shinawatra, his proxy as head of Pheu Thai. A month later, the 44-year-old Yingluck became Thailand's first female prime minister. Despite Thailand's history of affording women power in business and society, they have rarely achieved national leadership positions. Initially, Yingluck's political opponents dismissed her as a mere puppet for her brother. But Yingluck proved she was more than a stand-in for the exiled Thaksin. She had learned a lot from her

involvement with Thai Rak Thai, and proved adept at politicking and administration. She was a disciplined campaigner who projected both high glamor and the common touch. Her charisma was nearly as resonant as that of her brother. She reassured many of the original Thai Rak Thai supporters by promising to continue policies that helped the rural poor and middle class. Among Pheu Thai's campaign planks was a sizable raise in the national minimum wage and tablet computers for every elementary school student. Yingluck sought to appeal to Thailand's wary populace by pledging to work for national reconciliation. At Yingluck's campaign stops throughout the northeast and north, huge crowds gathered to express their support. During visits to self-designated "Red Shirt villages," people hailed Yingluck as a potential national savior, someone who could heal the rift between Thaksin and the palace. Many hoped she could bring about Thaksin's return.

Yingluck faced much of the same political opposition that had brought down Samak Sundaravej and Somchai Wongsawat as prime ministers a few years earlier. Yellow Shirt groups rallied and demonstrated continually to oppose her. Led by former Democrat MP Suthep Taugsuban, thousands of antigovernment protestors occupied numerous areas around Bangkok. Some of the spots, particularly around Government House, were the same that the Red Shirt protestors (and earlier Yellow Shirts protestors) had claimed in 2009 and 2010. Suthep created what he called a "people's council" to reform the Thai political system. His stated goal was to root out corruption while protecting the monarchy from any move to diminish its official role, and unofficial status, in the kingdom's political affairs. Suthep's use of the word "people's" harkened back to the so-called People's Constitution that had guided Thaksin to power. But the effort did not include a broadening of democratic principles like those guaranteed in the much-admired 1997 constitution. Instead, his movement tried to turn back the clock to a time before a populist-style leader like Thaksin could gain the premiership through rural support in the ballot box.

The impetus for the new round of protests was an amnesty bill proposed by Yingluck's government in early November 2013. The bill offered amnesty to key figures from both sides of the political divide. It would have pardoned Thaksin's convictions for corruption and allowed him to return to Thailand. But it also granted amnesty to Abhisit and Suthep for their roles in protesters' deaths when the Democrats were in power. The controversial bill sparked outrage in both camps. Neither faction wanted to see the object of their hatred absolved for past misdeeds. The bill's unpopularity with both Red Shirts and Yellow Shirts was evidence that the two polarized factions were not ready to reconcile. With Yingluck's strong urging, the House of Representatives passed the bill. But the Senate soundly rejected it, making a compromise version all but impossible. The bill's death did little to dampen the antigovernment protests. The anti-Yingluck fervor only intensified in the early months of 2014.

As with Thaksin's political demise, the courts and the army contributed to Yingluck's downfall. In early May 2014, the Thai Supreme Court found her guilty of abuse of power. Later in the month, the army came forward to seize power. Yingluck fled the country while awaiting the court's sentence. In September 2014, the courts sentenced her to five years in jail for her part in the rice subsidy scheme that had lost enormous amounts of money for the government. Like her brother, she opted to stay abroad rather than face imprisonment in the kingdom.

General Prayuth Chan-ocha seized power on May 22, 2014. Prayuth was the commander in chief of the Royal Thai Army. As a member of the Queen's Guards, he sided with the anti-Thaksin monarchists who made up the Privy Council. Prayuth called his junta the National Council for Peace and Order (NCPO). Almost immediately, Thais of various political stripes gathered in public to protest the latest coup. Prayuth's reaction was extreme. His junta banned gatherings of five or more people. It arrested hundreds of people deemed a threat to military rule. It hauled in pro-democracy activists, academics, journalists, students, and especially Red Shirt politicians. The military held and questioned some detainees without due process in secret military facilities throughout the country. Later, it issued a constitution that gave Prayuth and the junta sweeping powers. The constitution allowed for the warrantless arrest and detention of anyone for up to seven days. Article 44 of the new charter gave Prayuth the authority to override any branch of government to strengthen public unity and maintain peace. It also absolved him legally for any actions he might take in office. When university students challenged the ban on assembly by gathering together over lunch to talk about politics, the junta arrested and charged some of them for eating sandwiches with "political intent." It also went after students who read George Orwell's *1984* in public.

To justify his coup d'état and draconian security measures, Prayut cited the public's continuing uneasiness with political polarization and the violence it caused. He asserted that the ongoing divide between the Yellow Shirts and Red Shirts was affecting the normally easygoing public exchanges between Thais. The general believed that the climate of mistrust was threatening to undermine "Thai-ness." And lest anyone be confused about the definition of Thai-ness, he proclaimed the 12 Core Values of the Thai People. His list included love for the monarchy, Buddhism, and the nation; the preservation of customs and tradition; respect for the elderly; and discipline.

Prayuth pledged to restore social harmony and revive happiness. He hosted a weekly television program called "Returning Happiness to the People." On it, he explained his reasons for the coup and instructed the Thai public on how to move beyond political division to find collective social contentment. The NCPO oversaw programs designed to foster exhibitions of joy in the public sphere. In one early attempt, they set up a petting zoo at the Victory Monument on the site where the factions had battled repeatedly in previous years. The army offered free haircuts, desserts, and music performances. They invited citizens to have their pictures taken with smiling soldiers sporting riot gear and weapons. Prayuth sought to smother public expressions of discontent by generating more smiles in "the Land of Smiles." Some people liked the junta's initiatives. They found them a welcome change from the violent demonstrations of previous years. But for many, the efforts came across as artificial, off-key, and even coercive. They waited for Prayuth to act on his promise to restore "Thai-style democracy." They are still waiting. Six years after he seized power, in 2014, the nation had yet to hold an election.

*****

On October 13, 2016, at 3:52 pm, King Bhumibol died at Siriraj Hospital. Having been Thailand's king for seventy years, he was the only Thai monarch most of his people had ever known. He had so remade the role of the monarchy in his image that many viewed the man and the institution as utterly inseparable. In the days leading up to his death, thousands of his subjects, many dressed in the king's auspicious colors of pink or yellow, gathered outside the hospital to pray, chant, and sing. When his death came, it was a momentary respite from the ongoing political tension as the kingdom paused to mourn and remember him. On both sides of the Red Shirt-Yellow Shirt divide, there was an acknowledgment that his passing would likely have a profound effect on the future of the kingdom. The idea of Bhumibol's kingship had been central in both factions' motivations. It is easy to imagine Yellow and Red leaders hoping that his passing would benefit their cause.

FURTHER READING

No matter what aspect of Thai history interests you, you should be able to find a good book or two on that topic. There are excellent historical studies that focus on religion, warfare, literature, economics, sexuality, law, aviation, music, medicine, art, politics, and more. Here is a list of good books that I like. I use them, as well as many of the other texts listed in the Bibliography, when I teach.

Freeman, Andrew A., *Brown Women and White* (1932; reissued as *A Journalist in Siam*, Bangkok: White Lotus, 2007). Freeman was an American journalist hired by a Siamese prince to run a Bangkok newspaper. He writes about his time in Siam in a series of episodes that could almost stand alone as short stories. Ostensibly based on actual events, the book includes unforgettable tales of tragicomic culture collisions, lost souls, and a kingdom undergoing transformation.

Guelden, Marlane, *Thailand: Into the Spirit World* (Singapore: Times Editions, 1995). This volume is a visually haunting and sometimes unsettling study of the supernatural beliefs that animate the everyday lives of Thai people. Vampires, witches, ghosts, magic fetuses, placenta-eating demons, and other terrifying creatures are the stars of this brilliant exploration. Gueldan's study helps us understand why these phantoms populate the nightmares – and hearts – of so many.

Haberkorn, Tyrell, *Revolution Interrupted: Farmers, Students, Law, and Violence in Northern Thailand* (Madison: University of Wisconsin Press, 2011). While too many histories give the lion's share of their attention to Bangkok, this study explores how national events affect the lives of Thais in the provinces. Haberkorn shows how the massacring of student activists in the capital inspired similarly sinister actions in Chiang Mai and other northern towns.

Handley, Paul M., *The King Never Smiles: A Biography of Thailand's King Bhumibol* (New Haven, Connecticut: Yale University Press, 2006). This volume is really the only book to provide a full and unvarnished view of the extraordinary life of Thailand's longest reigning monarch. Handley's book is a corrective to the countless profiles of Bhumibol that present the king as a flawless virtuoso renaissance man. Bhumibol is all the more fascinating for his human frailties. This big book is a page-turner that will help you understand the importance of the Thai monarchy in politics, history, economics, religion, and, most affectingly, the lives of ordinary Thais.

Kamala Tiyavanich, *Sons of the Buddha: The Early Lives of Three Extraordinary Thai Masters* (Boston: Wisdom Publications, 2007). Long before they were influential monks, the Theravada "masters" of this study were clever boys learning to take care of themselves and their loved ones. Studying at Buddhist temples, the boys learned boxing, medicine, languages, logic, and, of course, the Dharma. Kamala's book will introduce you to traditional Thai culture and Buddhism through unforgettable anecdotes and youthful adventures. And you will learn how to take better care of yourself.

Kampoon Boontawee (trans. Susan Fulop Kepner), *A Child of the Northeast* (1976; reissued Bangkok: Editions Duang Kamol, 1994). Written in the 1960s about a childhood in the 1930s, Kampoon's semiautobiographical novel describes the hardscrabble lives of Isan farmers. This novel is full of warmth and good humor amidst the sometimes-tragic circumstances of rural life.

Nidhi Eoseewong, *Pen & Sail: Literature and History in Early Bangkok* (Chiang Mai: Silkworm Books, 2006). This is a superb introduction to Thai literature, commercial systems, and Buddhism by one of the giants of Thai historical studies. We are fortunate to have this superb translation, which conveys the beauty of the Thai poetry and literature it explores.

Pasuk Phongpaichit and Chris Baker, *Thailand: Economy and Politics* (Kuala Lumpur: Oxford University Press, 1995). Read any book by Pasuk and/or Baker, and you will get a penetrating view into Thailand's history, but this is a good one to start with. Its bare bones title belies the fascinatingly intricate history contained within. In clear and accessible language, the historians show how national (or kingdom-wide) policies transformed the lives of farmers, laborers, and soldiers in the modern era.

Reynolds, Craig J., *Seditious Histories: Contesting Thai and Southeast Asian Pasts* (NUS Press and University of Washington Press, 2006). In this collection of scholarly articles, Reynolds analyzes – and sometimes upends – longstanding tropes about Thailand's past. Few historians have changed the field of Thai studies as much as Reynolds has, and these works demonstrate why he has been so influential.

Reynolds, E. Bruce, *Thailand's Secret War: OSS, SOE, and the Free Thai Underground During World War II* (New York: Cambridge University Press, 2005). The author interviewed many of the surviving Free Thai agents to supplement his thorough archival research. The resulting book offers unforgettable wartime tales of intrigue, double-crossings, bravery, cravenness, and luck.

Thak Chaloemtiarana, *Thailand: The Politics of Despotic Paternalism* (Ithaca: Cornell University Press, 2007). This blend of history and political science is an engaging and insightful study of Field Marshal Sarit's era by a Thai-American scholar of great depth. Although the book's principal figure is a murderous and dissolute military strongman, Thak's monograph helps readers understand why such an outwardly repulsive figure could become so loved by Thais in the late 1950s and early 1960s.

Wyatt, David K., *Siam in Mind* (Chiang Mai: Silkworm Books, 2002). This short book was one of the last publications by a remarkable historian who helped several generations of graduate students to become Thai studies scholars. Its 24 short chapters convey the impressive breadth of Professor Wyatt's interests. Astronomy, temple murals, elephant warfare, a garden of wooden phalluses, a king's attempt at rewriting Gilbert & Sullivan, and other unusual topics are delightfully explored in their own short chapters. Any of these varied topics could be the heart of a master's thesis, dissertation, or monograph. Whenever I pick the book up, I get the feeling that Professor Wyatt wrote these mini-explorations specifically to inspire would-be historians to pursue their intellectual passions in Thailand. Rather than representing the end of a storied career, I hope it propels some of its readers into starting theirs.

BIBLIOGRAPHY

Anderson, Benedict R. O'G., and Ruchira Mendiones, eds. and trans. *In the Mirror: Literature and Politics in Siam in the American Era*. Bangkok: Editions Duang Kamol, 1985.

Apichat Satitniramai. "Yellow vs. Red and the Rise of a New Middle Cass in Thailand." In *Citizenship and Democratization in Southeast Asia* by Ward Berenschot, Henk Schulte Nordholt, and Laurens Bakker. Leiden: Brill, 2017.

Augustin, Andreas and Andrew Williamson. *The Oriental Bangkok*. London: The Most Famous Hotels in the World Ltd., 1997.

Baker, Chris and Pasuk Phongpaichit. *A History of Thailand*. New York: Cambridge University Press, 2005.

Barmé, Scot. *Luang Wichit Wathakan and the Creation of Thai Identity*. Singapore: Institute of Southeast Asian Studies, 1993.

Batson, Benjamin A. *The End of the Absolute Monarchy in Siam*. Singapore: Oxford University Press, 1984.

Blackburn, Robert M. *Mercenaries and Lyndon Johnson's "More Flags": The Hiring of Korean, Filipino, and Thai Soldiers in the Vietnam War*. Jefferson, North Carolina: McFarland & Company Inc., 1994.

Bowie, Katherine A. *Rituals of National Loyalty: An Anthropology of the State and Village Scout Movement in Thailand*. New York: Columbia University Press, 1997.

Brailey, Nigel J. *Thailand and the Fall of Singapore: A Frustrated Asian Revolution*. Boulder, Colorado: Westview Press, 1986.

Carter, Paul. *CIA Secret Warriors: Thai Forward Air Guides in the US War in Laos*. Bangkok: Varanya Publishing, 2019.

Castle, Timothy N. *At War in the Shadow of Vietnam: U.S. Aid to the Royal Lao Government, 1945–1975*. New York: Columbia University Press, 1993.

Chai-Anan Samudavanija. *The Thai Young Turks*. Singapore: Institute of Southeast Asian Studies, 1982.

Chambers, Paul. "Evolving Toward What? Parties, Factions, and Coalition Behavior in Thailand Today." *Journal of East Asian Studies* 5, no. 3. (2005): 495–520.

———. "Thailand on the Brink: Resurgent Military, Eroded Democracy." *Asian Survey* 50, no. 5 (2010): 835–58.

———. *Unruly Boots: Military Power and Security Sector Reform Efforts in Thailand*. Frankfurt: Peace Research Institute Frankfurt, 2013.

Cohen, Erik. "Contesting Discourses of Blood in the 'Red Shirts' Protests in Bangkok." *Journal of Southeast Asian Studies* 43, no. 2 (2012): 216–33.

Counihan, Carole, and Penny Van Esterik. *Food and Culture: A Reader*. New York: Routledge, 1997.

Cushman, J. W. "Siamese State Trade and the Chinese Go-between, 1797–1855." *Journal of Southeast Asian Studies* 12, no. 1 (1981): 46–61.

Ferrara, Federico. "The Legend of King Prajadhipok: Tall Tales and Stubborn Facts on the Seventh Reign in Siam." *Journal of Southeast Asian Studies* 43, no. 1 (2012): 4–31.

Fineman, Daniel. *A Special Relationship: The United States and Military Government in Thailand, 1947–1958*. Honolulu: University of Hawai'i Press, 1997.

Ford, Eugene. *Cold War Monks: Buddhism and America's Secret Strategy in Southeast Asia*. New Haven: Yale University Press, 2017.

Freeman, Andrew A. *Brown Women and White*. New York, New York: John Day Company, 1932.

Gregory, Sandra, with Michael Tierney. *Forget You Had a Daughter: Doing Time in the 'Bangkok Hilton.'* London: Vision, 2002.

Gwyer, W. L. "The Bridge That Never Was: But the Death Toll from Building Japan's Military Railroad Was All Too Real." *Railroad History* 191 (2004): 107–11.

Haberkorn, Tyrell. *Revolution Interrupted: Farmers, Students, Law, and Violence in Northern Thailand*. Madison, Wisconsin: University of Wisconsin Press, 2011.

Handley, Paul M. *The King Never Smiles: A Biography of Thailand's King Bhumibol*. New Haven: Yale University Press, 2006.

Harness, Bruce. "The Secret of 'The Secret Sharer' Bared." *College English* 27. no. 1 (1965): 55–61.

Haseman, John B. *The Thai Resistance Movement During World War II*. Chiang Mai: Silkworm Books, 2002.

Hell, Stefan. *Siam and World War I: An International History*. Bangkok: River Books, 2017.

Hodges, Ian. "Western Science in Siam: A Tale of Two Kings." *Osiris* 13 (1998): 80–95.

Hunter, Eileen, and Narisa Chakrabongse. *Katya & the Prince of Siam*. Bangkok: River Books, 1994.

Ivarsson, Soren, and Lotte Isager, eds. *Saying the Unsayable: Monarchy and Democracy in Thailand*. Copenhagen: NIAS Press, 2010.

Jerryson, Michael K. *Buddhist Fury: Religion and Violence in Southern Thailand*. New York, New York: Oxford University Press, 2011.

Jory, Patrick. *Thailand's Theory of the Monarchy: The Vessantara Jataka and the Idea of the Perfect Man*. Albany, New York: State University of New York Press, 2016.

Kamala Tiyavanich. *Sons of the Buddha: The Early Lives of Three Extraordinary Buddhist Masters*. Boston: Wisdom Publications, 2007.

Kampoon Boontawee. *A Child of the Northeast*. Translated by Susan Fulop Kepner. Bangkok: Editions Duang Kamol, 1988.

Kasian Tejapira. *Commodifying Marxism: The Formation of Modern Thai Radical Culture* Kyoto: Kyoto University Press, 2001.

Keyes, Charles F. "Buddhist Politics and Their Revolutionary Origins in Thailand." *International Political Science Review* 10, no. 2 (1989): 121–42.

———. *Thailand: Buddhist Kingdom as Modern Nation-State*. Boulder, Colorado: Westview Press, 1987.

Kruger, Rayne. *The Devil's Discus*. London: Cassell, 1964.

Kuhonta, Erik Martinez, and Alex B. Mutebi. "Thaksin Triumphant: The Implications of One-Party Dominance in Thailand." *Asian Affairs: An American Review* 33, no. 1 (2006): 39–51.

Landon, Margaret. *Anna and the King of Siam*. New York: The John Dow Co., 1944.

Lim, Samson. *Siam's New Detectives: Visualizing Crime and Conspiracy in Modern Thailand*. Honolulu: University of Hawai'i Press, 2016.

Loos, Tamara. *Bones Around My Neck: The Life and Exile of a Prince Provocateur*. Ithaca: Cornell University Press, 2016.

———. "Sex and the Inner City: Fidelity between Sex and Politics in Siam." *The Journal of Asian Studies* 64, no. 4 (2005): 881–909.

———. *Subject Siam: Family, Law, and Colonial Modernity in Thailand*. Ithaca, New York: Cornell University Press, 2006.

Marshall, Andrew MacGregor. *A Kingdom in Crisis: Thailand's Struggle for Democracy in the Twenty-First Century*. London: Zed Books, 2015.

May, Jacques M. *Siam Doctor*. New York: Doubleday and Company, 1949.

Mayoury Ngaosyvathn and Pheuiphanh Ngaosyvathn. *Paths to Conflagration: Fifty Years of Diplomacy and Warfare in Laos, Thailand, and Vietnam, 1778–1828*. Ithaca, New York: Southeast Asia Program Publications, 1998.

McDaniel, Justin. *The Lovelorn Ghost and The Magical Monk Practicing Buddhism in Modern Thailand*. New York: Columbia University Press, 2011.

Moffat, Abbot Low. *Mongkut the King of Siam*. Ithaca: Cornell University Press, 1961.

Morell, David, and Chai-anan Samudavanija. *Political Conflict in Thailand: Reform, Reaction, Revolution*. Cambridge, Massachusetts: Oelgeschlager, Gunn & Hain, 1981.

Morgan, Susan. *Bombay Anna: The Real Story and Remarkable Adventures of the King and I Governess*. Berkeley: University of California Press, 2008.

Neher, Clark. "Thailand in 1987: Semi-Successful Semi-Democracy." *Asian Survey* 28, no. 2 (1988): 192–201.

Nidhi Eoseewong. *Pen and Sail. Literature and History in Early Bangkok*. Translated by Chris Baker. Chiang Mai: Silkworm Books, 2005.

Nikom Rayawa. *High Banks, Heavy Logs*. New York: Penguin Books, 1991.

Padoongpatt, Mark. *Flavors of Empire: Food and the Making of Thai America*. Oakland, California: University of California Press, 2017.

Pasuk Phongpaichit and Chris Baker. *Thailand Economy and Politics*. Kuala Lumpur: Oxford University Press, 1995.

———. *Thaksin*. 2nd ed. Chiang Mai: Silkworm Books, 2009.

Pasuk Phongpaichit and Sungsidh Piriyarangsan. *Corruption and Democracy in Thailand*. Chiang Mai: Silkworm Books, 1996.

Peleggi, Maurizio. *Lords of Things: The Fashioning of the Siamese Monarchy's Modern Image*. Honolulu: University of Hawai'i Press, 2002.

———, ed. *A Sarong for Clio: Essays on the Intellectual and Cultural History of Thailand*. Ithaca, New York: Cornell Southeast Asia Program Publications, 2015.

Prasit Lulitanond. *A Postman's Life*. Bangkok: Post Books, 1999.

Ramsay, Ansil. "Modernization and Rebellions in Northern Siam." *Journal of Asian Studies* 38, no. 2 (1979): 283–97.

Reynolds, Craig J. "Buddhist Cosmography in Thai History, with Special Reference to Nineteenth-Century Culture Change." *The Journal of Asian Studies* 35, no. 2 (1976): 203–20.

———, ed. *National Identity and Its Defenders: Thailand Today*. Chiang Mai: Silkworm Books, 2002.

———. *Seditious Histories: Contesting Thai and Southeast Asian Pasts*. Seattle: University of Washington Press, 2006.

———. *Thai Radical Discourse: The Real Face of Thai Feudalism Today*. Ithaca, New York: Southeast Asia Program Publications, 1987.

Reynolds, E. Bruce. *Thailand and Japan's Southern Advance, 1940–1945*. New York: St. Martin's Press, 1994.

———. *Thailand's Secret War: OSS, SOE, and the Free Thai Underground During World War II*. Cambridge: Cambridge University Press, 2005.

Rhum, Michael R. "'Modernity' and 'Tradition' in 'Thailand.'" *Modern Asian Studies* 30, no. 2 (1996): 325–55.

Richter, Linda K. *The Politics of Tourism in Asia*. Honolulu: University of Hawaii Press, 1989.

Roberts, Stephen S. "The Thai Navy." *Warship International* 23. no. 3 (1986): 217–65.

Ruth, Richard A. *In Buddha's Company: Thai Soldiers in the Vietnam War*. Honolulu: University of Hawai'i Press, 2011.

Sablon du Corail, Amable. "The French Army and Siam, 1893–1914." *Journal of the Siam Society* 99 (2011): 243–68.

Sherry, Norman. "Conrad and the Bangkok Times." *Nineteenth-Century Fiction* 20, no. 3. (1965): 255–66.

————. *The Life of Graham Greene, Volume III: 1955–1991*. New York: Viking, 2004.

Sirin Phathanothai, with James Peck. *The Dragon's Pearl*. New York: Simon & Schuster, 1994.

Smyth, David, and Manas Chitakasem, trans. *The Sergeant's Garland and Other Stories*. Kuala Lumpur: Oxford University Press, 1998.

Stengs, Irene. "A Kingly Cult: Thailand's Guiding Lights in a Dark Era." *Etnofoor* 12, no. 2, (1999): 41–75.

————. *Worshipping the Great Modernizer: King Chulalongkorn, Patron Saint of the Thai Middle Class*. Singapore: NUS Press, 2009.

Stowe, Judith. *Siam Becomes Thailand*. Honolulu: University of Hawai'i Press, 1991.

Strate, Shane. *The Lost Territories: Thailand's History of National Humiliation*. Honolulu: University of Hawai'i Press, 2015.

————. "An Uncivil State of Affairs: Fascism and Anti-Catholicism in Thailand, 1940–1944." *Journal of Southeast Asian Studies* 42, no. 1 (2011): 59–87.

Streckfuss, David. "An 'Ethnic' Reading of 'Thai' History in the Twilight of the Century-old Official 'Thai' National Model." *South East Asia Research* 20. no. 3 (2012): 305–27.

Streicher, Ruth. *Uneasy Military Encounters: The Imperial Politics of Counterinsurgency in Southern Thailand*. Ithaca, New York: Southeast Asia Program Publication, 2020.

Stuart-Fox, Martin. "The French in Laos, 1887–1945." *Modern Asian Studies* 29, no. 1 (1995): 111–39.

Swan, William L. "Thai-Japanese Relations at the Start of the Pacific War: New Insight into a Controversial Period." *Journal of Southeast Asian Studies* 18, no. 2 (1987): 270–90.

Swearer, Donald K. *The Buddhist World of Southeast Asia*. 2nd ed. Albany: State University of New York Press, 2010.

Tagliacozzo, Eric. "Ambiguous Commodities, Unstable Frontiers: The Case of Burma, Siam, and Imperial Britain, 1800–1900." *Comparative Studies in Society and History* 46, no. 2 (2004): 354–77.

Tausig, Ben. *Bangkok is Ringing: Sound, Protest, and Constraint*. New York, New York: Oxford University Press, 2019.

Terwiel, B. J. "Tattooing in Thailand." *The Journal of the Royal Asiatic Society of Great Britain and Ireland* no. 2 (1979): 156–66.

————. *Thailand's Political History: From the 13th Century to Recent Times*. Bangkok: River Books, 2005.

Thak Chaloemtiarana. "Making a New Space in the Thai Literary Canon." *Journal of Southeast Asian Studies* 40, no. 1 (2009): 87–110.

————. *Thailand: The Politics of Despotic Paternalism*. Ithaca, New York: Southeast Asia Program Publications, 2007.

Thamsook Numnonda. "Phibunsongram's Thai Nation-Building Programme During the Japanese Presence, 1941–1945." *Journal of Southeast Asian Studies* 9, no. 2 (1978): 234–47.

Thongchai Winichakul. *Siam Mapped: A History of the Geo-Body of a Nation.* Honolulu: University of Hawai'i Press, 1994.

Van Esterik, Penny. "From Marco Polo to McDonald's: Thai Cuisine in Transition." *Food and Foodways* 5, no. 2 (1992): 177–93.

Vella, Walter F. *Chaiyo! King Vajiravudh and the Development of Thai Nationalism.* Honolulu: University of Hawaii Press, 1978.

Vickery, Michael. "Thai Regional Elites and the Reforms of King Chulalongkorn." *The Journal of Asian Studies* 29, no. 4 (1970): 863–81.

Warren, William. *Jim Thompson: The Unsolved Mystery.* Singapore: Archipelago Press, 1998.

Wilson, Constance. "The Holy Man in the History of Thailand and Laos." *Journal of Southeast Asian Studies* 28, no. 2 (1997): 345–64.

Wyatt, David K. *The Politics of Reform in Thailand: Education and the Reign of Chulalongkorn.* New Haven: Yale University Press, 1969.

———. *Reading Thai Murals.* Chiang Mai: Silkworm Books, 2004.

———. *Siam in Mind.* Chiang Mai: Silkworm Books, 2002.

———. *Thailand: A Short History.* New Haven: Yale University Press, 1982.

Yuangrat Wedel. "The Communist Party of Thailand and Thai Radical Thought. Southeast Asian Affairs." Singapore: ISEAS – Yusof Ishak Institute (1981): 325–39.

Young, Edward M. *Aerial Nationalism: A History of Aviation in Thailand.* Washington, Smithsonian Institution Press, 1995.

News Outlets Used

Bangkok Post
BBC.com
Thai Rath
The Guardian
The Nation (Thailand)
The New York Times
The Washington Post

INDEX